REIMAGINING GLOBALIZATION AND EDUCATION

This book brings together leading scholars in Global Studies in Education to reflect on how various developments of historic significance have unsettled the neoliberal imaginary of globalization. The developments include: greater recognition of inequalities and the changing nature of work and communication; the emergence of new technologies of governance; a greater awareness of geopolitical shifts; the revival of nationalism, populism and anti-globalization sentiments; and the recognition of risks surrounding pandemics and climate change. Drawing from a range of disciplinary perspectives, the chapters in this collection examine how these developments demand new ways of thinking about globalization and its implications for education policy and practice—beyond the neoliberal imaginary.

The significance of this book lies in the robust conversations it is expected to stimulate about the ways in which globalization and education might now be reimagined in the light of the growing recognition of the contradictions of neoliberalism, as well as a range of historical transformations that have taken place over the past decade.

Fazal Rizvi is an Emeritus Professor at the Universities of Melbourne in Australia and Illinois at Urbana-Champaign in the United States.

Bob Lingard is a Professorial Fellow in the Institute for Learning Sciences and Teacher Education at Australian Catholic University and Emeritus Professor at The University of Queensland.

Risto Rinne is an Emeritus Professor at the University of Turku and was, until 2020, the Foundation Director of the Centre for Lifelong Learning and Education.

REIMAGINING GLOBALIZATION AND EDUCATION

Edited by Fazal Rizvi, Bob Lingard, and Risto Rinne

Routledge
Taylor & Francis Group

NEW YORK AND LONDON

First published 2022
by Routledge
605 Third Avenue, New York, NY 10158

and by Routledge
4 Park Square, Milton Park, Abingdon, Oxon, OX14 4RN

Routledge is an imprint of the Taylor & Francis Group, an informa business

Library of Congress Cataloging-in-Publication Data
A catalog record for this title has been requested

ISBN: 978-1-032-07530-3 (hbk)
ISBN: 978-1-032-07529-7 (pbk)
ISBN: 978-1-003-20752-8 (ebk)

DOI: 10.4324/9781003207528

Typeset in Bembo
by SPi Technologies India Pvt Ltd (Straive)

CONTENTS

ACKNOWLEDGEMENTS

This book has emerged out of discussions between Bob Lingard and Fazal Rizvi about the best way of updating their 2010 book, *Globalizing Education Policy*. These discussions were further developed with Risto Rinne during Fazal's visiting professorship at the Centre for Lifelong Learning and Education (CELE) at the University of Turku, Finland. We would like to thank staff and students at CELE and particularly the department of education and its director, Professor Tero Järvinen, for his intellectual and financial support. Additionally, we would like to acknowledge similar support from Professor Claire Wyatt-Smith and the Institute for Learning Sciences and Teacher Education at Australian Catholic University. We are grateful to Matthew Friberg and Jessica Cooke in the New York Office of Routledge for their encouragement and support for this book from its proposal through to its production stages. We would also like to thank Diana Langmead for her wonderful assistance with the editing of the chapters in this collection. On a personal level, Fazal would like to thank his wife, Pat, for her continuing patience and support. Bob offers his thanks to his wife, Carolynn, for all of her support. Risto would like to give a hug to his supporting wife, Pirjo.

CONTRIBUTORS

Cash Ahenakew is a Canada Research Chair in Indigenous Peoples' Well-Being and an Associate Professor in the Department of Education at the University of British Columbia. He is Cree and a member of Ahtahkakoop Cree Nation. His research is based in a commitment to the development of Indigenous theories and methodologies. It addresses complexities at the interface between Indigenous and non-Indigenous knowledges, education, pedagogy, methodology, and ceremony.

Vanessa de Oliveira Andreotti is a Canada Research Chair in Race, Inequalities and Global Change and Professor in the Department of Educational Studies at the University of British Columbia. Her research focuses on analyses of historical and systemic patterns of reproduction of knowledge and inequalities and how these mobilize global imaginaries that limit or enable different possibilities for (co)existence and global change.

Debbie Epstein is Emerita Professor the University of Roehampton and Visiting Professor at Anglia Ruskin University. She has published widely on gender, sexualities and cultural formations. Her most recent co-authored book is *Class Choreographies: elite schools and globalization* (2017). She has published a large number of articles, most recently, "The Covid Conjuncture: rearticulating the school/home/work nexus" (2021), with Jane Kenway, in *International Studies in the Sociology of Education*.

Clara Fontdevila holds a PhD in Sociology from Universitat Autònoma de Barcelona and is currently a Research Associate at the University of Glasgow. Much of her research has involved collaboration with various educational and research organizations, including Education International, Open Society

Foundation and UNESCO. Her research interests are market policies in education, the comparative analysis of education reforms, and education and international development.

Kalervo N. Gulson is a Professor in the School of Education and Social Work, University of Sydney, Australia. His current research program investigates the links between Artificial Intelligence and education policy and governance. His most recent book with Sam Sellar and Taylor Webb is *Algorithms of Education* (University of Minnesota Press, 2022).

Jessica Holloway is a Senior Research Fellow and Australian Research Council DECRA Fellow within the Institute for Learning Sciences and Teacher Education (ILSTE) and the Research Centre for Digital Data and Assessment in Education at Australian Catholic University. Her research draws on political theory and policy sociology to examine how metrics, data and digital tools produce new conditions, practices and subjectivities of teachers and schools. She is an author of *Metrics, Standards and Alignment in Teacher Policy: Critiquing Fundamentalism and Imagining Pluralism* (Springer Nature, 2021).

Dallas Hunt is an Assistant Professor of Indigenous Literature at the University of British Columbia. He is Cree and a member of Wapsewsipi (Swan River First Nation) in Treaty 8 territory in Northern Alberta, Canada. His research interests include Indigenous literatures, Indigenous theory and politics, speculative fiction, settler colonial studies, and environmental justice.

Tero Järvinen is Professor of Learning and Education at the Department of Education/Centre for Lifelong Learning and Education (CELE) in the University of Turku, Finland. His main research interests are related to comparative studies on educational and school-to-work transitions of young people, as well as education systems and policies governing these transitions.

Arto Jauhiainen is a Professor of Education at the Department of Education, University of Turku, and in the Centre for Research on Lifelong Learning and Education (CELE). His research interests cover sociology and policy of education, especially in relation to higher education, doctoral education, and academic governance. He acts as a leader of CELE's Research Group for University and Higher Education.

Suvi Jokila is a postdoctoral researcher in the Centre for Research on Lifelong Learning (CELE), University of Turku, and currently works with the Privatisation and Access to Higher Education (PAHE) research project. Her research interests include international student mobility policies and practices, access to higher education and the processes of privatization. She is currently leading a research project on 'International Students in Times of Crisis', examining international students' experiences during the pandemic in Finland.

Johanna Kallo is an Academy Research Fellow in the Department of Education at the University of Turku. Her current research project funded by the Academy of Finland explores the construction of higher education policy futures by focusing on the varied expressions of predictive expertise and the way they spread across a number of institutional loci at local, national and transnational scales. She is interested in the construction of shared beliefs and the arrangements of knowledge creation within organizations.

Jane Kenway is an Emeritus Professor (Monash University) and Professorial Fellow (Melbourne University), Australia. Prior to this she was a Professorial Fellow with the Australian Research Council and Professor of Global Education Studies in the Education Faculty at Monash University. Her research expertise is in educational sociology. Broadly, she studies education, and education policy, in the context of wider social and cultural change, focusing particularly on power, politics and inequality.

Hugh Lauder is Professor of Education and Political Economy at the University of Bath, UK. He is editor of the *Journal of Education and Work*. His latest book is, *The Death of Human Capital? Its Failed Promise and How to Renew It in an Age of Disruption* (Oxford University Press, 2020; co-edited with Philip Brown, Hugh Lauder and Sin Yi Cheung).

Steven Lewis is a Senior Research Fellow and an ARC DECRA Fellow at the Institute for Learning Sciences and Teacher Education at Australian Catholic University. His research investigates how education policymaking and governance, and topological time space-making, are being reshaped by new forms of digital data, infrastructures and platforms. His most recent monograph is *PISA, Policy and the OECD: Respatialising Global Educational Governance Through PISA for Schools*, which was published by Springer in 2020.

Bob Lingard is a Professorial Fellow at the Institute for Learning Sciences and Teacher Education (ILSTE) at Australian Catholic University and Emeritus Professor at the University of Queensland, as well as Visiting Professor at the Education University of Hong Kong. His research is situated within the fields of sociology of education and policy sociology in education. His most recent books include *Globalisation and Education* (Routledge, 2021) and *Digital Disruption in Education* (Routledge, 2021).

Simon Marginson is Professor of Higher Education at the University of Oxford, UK, and the director of the ESRC/OFSRE Centre for Global Higher Education. He works primarily on international and global aspects of higher education and is also interested in the public and common aspects of the sector. His most recent book is *Changing Higher Education in East Asia* (2022, with Xin Xu).

Marcia McKenzie is a Professor in the Melbourne Graduate School of Education at the University of Melbourne, Australia, and Professor on leave from the

University of Saskatchewan, Canada. She is a member of the Royal Society of Canada's College of New Scholars, Artists, and Scientists; and Director of the SSHRC-funded Monitoring and Evaluating Climate Communication and Education Project (www.mecce.ca), and Sustainability and Education Policy Network (www.sepn.ca).

Michael A. Peters is Distinguished Professor of Education at Beijing Normal University, China, Emeritus Professor at the University of Illinois at Urbana-Champaign, Senior Research Fellow at the University of Auckland and Research Associate in the Philosophy Programme at the University of Waikato. He is the Editor-in-Chief of *The Beijing International Review of Education* and Editor-in-Chief of *Educational Philosophy and Theory*.

Marja Peura is a doctoral candidate at the Department of Education, University of Turku, Finland, and in the Centre for Research on Lifelong Learning and Education (CELE). Her research examines the experiences of internationally mobile doctoral students from life-course and identity perspectives.

Risto Rinne is Emeritus Professor of Education in the Centre for Lifelong Learning and Education at the University of Turku, Finland, a member of the Finnish Academy of Science and Letters and has published extensively in sociology of education, comparative education, politics and history of education. His most recent books include: *The Nordic Historical Tunes of Social Democratic Educational Politics Regime Colliding the Mainstream of Global Neo-Liberal Regime and Governance* (Springer 2021) and *The Future of Glocal Education Politics* (Springer 2020).

Fazal Rizvi is an Emeritus Professor at the Universities of Melbourne, Australia, and Illinois at Urbana-Champaign, USA, as well as a Visiting Professor at the University of Turku in Finland. He has written extensively on globalization and education policy, the politics of educational reforms, postcolonialism, Asia–Australia relations, issues of culture and identity in transnational contexts and, more recently, on the global rise of populism. He is an editor-in-chief of the 4th edition of the *International Encyclopedia of Education* (Elsevier 2022).

Sharon Stein is an Assistant Professor in the Department of Educational Studies at the University of British Columbia. Her scholarship addresses the role of higher education in society, especially as this relates to decolonization, internationalization, and climate change. In her work, she emphasizes the educational challenges of addressing the interrelated ecological, cognitive, affective, relational, and economic dimensions of justice, responsibility, and change.

Antoni Verger is Professor of Sociology at the Universitat Autònoma de Barcelona and Research Fellow at the Catalan Institution for Research and Advanced Studies (ICREA). With a cross-disciplinary training in sociology and education studies, his research examines the relationship between globalization, governance institutions and education policy.

Adrián Zancajo is a Lecturer in Education at the Manchester Institute of Education (University of Manchester), UK. His research interests focus on education privatization, education markets and inequalities. He is currently conducting a research project on the governance and regulation of education markets.

1

REIMAGINING GLOBALIZATION AND EDUCATION: AN INTRODUCTION

Fazal Rizvi, Bob Lingard, and Risto Rinne

The imaginary of a globally connected world is not new. Most of the world's major religious traditions have long imagined the world as a whole, along with a concept of universal humanity. Incipient global consciousness was evident in the eighteenth-century Enlightenment thinking. In the nineteenth century, industrial developments enabled capital to go in search of new markets tied to colonial exploits around the world. Within the context of complex articulations between capitalism, colonialism and industrialization, global integration of the world became a distinct possibility. This led early sociologists, such as Saint-Simon, Comte and Marx, to envisage an increasingly interconnected world in which national identities would no longer be so important. In the twentieth century, Weber's account of the processes of rationalization referred to the global spread of systems of rational action and organization. After the Second World War, a range of international organizations emerged to coordinate interactions across national borders; for example, relating to trade and travel. In the 1970s, World Systems Theory understood capitalism as a single, interconnected, global system in which events on the periphery were structured around the core (Wallerstein, 1974).

From the 1980s, the term 'globalization' became widely used to describe the rapidly expanding scope, speed and intensity of global interconnectivities. Driven largely by the revolutionary developments in technology, globalization pointed to the possibilities of capital, people and ideas moving across national borders to an unprecedented extent. People were now able to develop complex social and commercial networks across vast distances, within and beyond national and cultural boundaries. Advances in communication and transport technologies transformed the nature of capitalism with the emergence of transnational modes of production and distribution of goods and services, along with new methods in the coordination of economic exchange. International organizations acquired

DOI: 10.4324/9781003207528-1

greater significance, not only in the governance of economic activity but also in the development of public policy and management transformed by a changing perspective on the role and responsibilities of the state. These changes were based on, and promoted, a particular ideological understanding of the nature and scope of global interconnectivity that favored the interests of global capitalism.

By the end of the twentieth century, this understanding became globally hegemonic. It transformed the meaning of the traditional concept of liberalism and rearticulated it into a register. As a political ideology, the traditional notion of liberalism emphasized the freedom of individuals regarding religion, association and thought. It represented a philosophy that treated individuals as the bearers of certain rights, recognized within a system of sovereign law. Neoliberalism, in contrast, is best understood as an ideological construct that sought to reinvent liberalism within the late twentieth century, capitalist context, and emphasized the need to rethink the idea of freedom in economic terms. It looked to the state to remake society in market terms, shaping the ways in which economic freedom should be defined and instantiated. It abandoned the distinction between political and economic realms of life and, instead, highlighted competition as the most important feature of capitalism.

Intellectually, the conceptualization of neoliberalism gained momentum, initially in the 1960s, through the work of economic theorists, such as Hayek and Friedman, as well as a growing number of politically-motivated think tanks, such as the American Enterprise Foundation. These intellectuals suggested that social democracy and the ideas associated with Keynesian economics were far too inefficient and no longer appropriate for a rapidly globalizing economy since they prevented a culture of enterprise and entrepreneurialism from flourishing by subduing economic freedom. They highlighted the importance of competition as the major driver of social mobility and progress, as well as national development. Since the 1970s, the highly ideological notions of neoliberalism succeeded in getting a firm grip on governments and multilateral institutions and have been widely sanctioned and implemented by aid agencies, both national and global, as conditions of loans and grants associated with structural adjustment schemes.

During the 1980s, the neoliberal policies of Margaret Thatcher in the United Kingdom (UK) and Ronald Reagan in the United States (US) sought to apply the core ideas of neoliberalism to almost all spheres of life. Preaching the gospel of small government, they privatized many public services and encouraged public institutions to embrace the operational principles of corporate governance. Such principles were embedded within the new public management theories incorporating assumptions of rational choice theory and audit culture. These ideas were furthered consolidated by the 'Third Way' (Giddens, 1998) politics of Bill Clinton in the US and Tony Blair in the UK. They had already begun to be embraced by countries around the world, including many large socialist states, such as China and Vietnam, as well as economically troubled states, like India and Argentina, which had previously resisted the lure of neoliberalism.

By the turn of the century, neoliberal sentiments had become globally hege-monic, acquiring the status of what Michael Apple (2014) refers to as 'a new common sense'. Using Foucauldian theoretical resources, Wendy Brown (2015, p. 36) argues that, within this neoliberal rationality, human capital has become "both our 'is' and our 'ought' – what we are said to be, what we should be, and what rationality makes us into through its norms and construction of environ-ment". This rationality has become so influential that, as Harvard philosopher Michael Sandel (2012) shows, almost everything is now regarded as an object or activity that could be 'commodified', acquiring exchange value. Education has not been exempted from this logic of neoliberalism. Systems around the world have applied the assumptions of neoliberalism to reframe the purposes of educa-tion, linking them to the requirements of the globalizing knowledge economy, as well as the governance of education. This occurs through attempts to corporatize and privatize the provision of education within a regulatory framework through which the states can steer institutional practices from a distance, often toward more competition.

In 2010, drawing on the work of Charles Taylor and Arjun Appadurai, Rizvi and Lingard (2010) published a book, *Globalizing Education Policy*, that portrayed neoliberalism as a social imaginary. They argued that, in terms of spatio-temporal specificities, the notion of global interconnectivity was now widely understood in neoliberal terms, as a way both of *describing* the world and of *prescribing* how it ought to be. Through a range of examples, they showed how the neoliberal social imaginary of globalization was now used around the world to rearticulate the imperatives of educational reform. Subsequently, Pasi Sahlberg (2011) referred to these imperatives as constituting a 'Global Educational Reform Movement' (GERM). GERM highlighted the operational principles of competition as a tool of producing better outcomes for students; school autonomy; freedom of parents to choose; and the necessity of information systems to enable comparisons of the patterns of achievement across students, schools and systems of education. Each of these ideas of reform advocated educational policies and practices with poten-tial to increase economic competitiveness among individuals and nations alike.

Ten years after the publication of *Globalizing Education Policy*, the contradic-tions of the neoliberal imaginary of globalization have now become evident, as have its associated educational prescriptions. GERM has failed to produce the outcomes it promised. While the number of students attending school has increased markedly, globally, the quality of educational performance remains uneven. Inequalities of educational opportunities have increased, as educational outcomes are now increasingly linked to the ability to pay. A rapidly growing, privatized education sector has been able to make massive profits while the much-needed resources for public institutions have failed to keep with up with demand. International organizations have become more influential than ever before. These organizations oversee comparative programs of student assessment within the terms of which national systems of education conceptualize their efforts to reform curriculum pedagogy and assessment, and, more importantly, techniques of governance.

As the promise of some of these reforms in education remain undelivered, a number of historically significant developments have taken place over the past decade that have also unsettled the neoliberal imaginary of globalization. These developments include: the greater recognition of inequalities within and across nations; innovations in mobile technologies and shifts in communicative cultures; growing awareness of environmental issues and climate change; the rise of Asia and the changing geopolitics of the world; 'datafication' and the consolidation of audit cultures and new modes of governance; developments in artificial intelligence and biotechnology; and the revival of nationalism, populism and anti-globalization sentiments. The recent pandemic associated with COVID-19 has also resulted in new ways of thinking about the state and its role not only in the management of risks but also in coordination of social institutions such as education.

These developments have created conditions whereby the emerging forms of global interconnectivity can no longer rely on the assumptions of the neoliberal imaginary of globalization. Such an imaginary had re-cast the purposes and governance of education in human capital terms, while promoting individual self-interests in an increasingly competitive society. Contemporary conditions have intensified demands for cooperation and collaboration. A new way of interpreting global interconnectivity and interdependence, beyond globalization's economic possibilities, is required; with the potential for a normativity that is underpinned by the moral and intercultural concerns of education. The neoliberal imaginary has hollowed out public spaces within which education takes place and also helps create. The need to work for the recreation of these spaces, within and across national borders, toward common goods is now greater than ever before. New versions of public spaces are required as a way of ensuring the world does not continue to slide into ever-increasing levels of inequalities, distrust and social conflict.

The essays contained in this book take up the educational challenges to which the emerging historical conditions have given rise. Using the arguments that were presented in 2010 in *Globalizing Education Policy* as a point of reference, these essays consider how the cultural and political authority of the neoliberal imaginary of globalization can no longer be taken for granted: the idea of globalization itself needs to be reimagined, along with its implications for thinking about educational policy and practice. Each essay in this collection takes up a particular issue or a particular instance of historical transformation and considers how an analysis of this transformation demands new ways of thinking about globalization and its implications for education policy, beyond the neoliberal imaginary. The main aim of this book is thus to promote wide-ranging debates about the shifting conditions under which education now takes place, and the ways in which its purposes and governance may now be reimagined.

The chapters

The chapters in this collection variously describe some of the most critical transformations that have taken place over the past decade, how they have demanded new ways of imagining global interconnectedness and the new educational challenges emergent therefrom. In Chapter 2, Simon Marginson provides a granular account of the changing practices of what he calls 'communicative globalization', facilitated by the advent of the Internet, resulting in major shifts in the nature of global capitalism and the ways in which knowledge is now created and utilized. He shows how these shifts have transformed the policy terrain of higher education policies around the world. His discussion focuses on three aspects to this transformation; namely, neoliberal models of national regulation of higher education and internationalization, the Anglo-American hegemony in the organization of knowledge in a one-world science system, and related global practices that embody White Supremacy.

Jane Kenway and Debbie Epstein also address the crises facing systems of higher education. In Chapter 3, they argue that the crises in universities are not simply related to changing manifestations of globalization. Instead, they insist on the need to understand crises in broader historical, spatial and comparative terms. They use Stuart Hall's notion of 'conjunctural analysis' to understand how universities managed what they call a deluge of crises before the COVID-19 pandemic hit them, and how these crises have now been compounded and extended.

In Chapter 4, Johanna Kallo also addresses the ways in which national systems of education have addressed the challenges relating to the COVID-19 crisis, and how they have utilized the knowledge resources provided by Intergovernmental Organizations (IGOs). She notes that, while IGOs have been central in the post-Cold War period in circulating global education policy discourses, their claims to epistemic authority have never been static. In recent decades, much of the epistemic authority of IGOs, such as the Organisation for Economic Cooperation and Development (OECD), has been derived from the assumptions of the neoliberal imaginary of globalization. This authority, she shows, was unsettled by the global financial crisis of 2007 and may be further diminished by the global COVID pandemic, the management of which has required nation states to reassert some of the authority they had lost with the knowledge claims of the IGOs. She explores how IGOs might now rethink and reposition their authority, retaining some of assumptions of the neoliberal imaginary while abandoning others.

In recent decades, the claims to technical expertise that the IGOs make have enabled them to provide technocratic information helpful to the national systems of education interested in comparative performance and in identifying policy solutions to complex problems of educational governance. Recent developments in computational technologies have expand their role in policy processes. Chapters 5 and 6 examine how recent developments in datafication and digitalization and in Artificial Intelligence (AI) are giving rise to various new policy concerns in education. In their chapter, Steven Lewis, Jessica Holloway and Bob Lingard argue that these developments are altering the ways in which policies are now developed and analyzed. Kalervo Gulson demonstrates, in his chapter, how the growing usage of AI by educational systems is concerned with what he calls anticipatory governance, an attempt to control the future, as a complement to existing approaches to policy production. He shows how attempts to regulate this usage are, at best, partial and thus constitute a new policy problem for education systems.

In Chapter 7, Hugh Lauder also explores the connections between education and labor markets, both national and global. He shows how claims to meritocracy were always difficult to maintain but have now become even more unsustainable because of dysfunctional labor markets. The discourses of human capital theory and the knowledge economy, circulated by the OECD as necessary frames for education policy can no longer be justified. What is required, he argues, is not only a universal basic wage but a new form of liberal education aimed at producing citizens able to critically think about issues such as the climate emergency and threats to democracy.

Issues of regulation are central to Adrián Zancajo, Toni Verger and Clara Fontdevila's analysis in Chapter 8 of the swelling spaces of educational privatization. They interrogate the growing expansion of educational markets through public–private partnerships in education, along with the so-called government-funded, autonomous, free schools and, in developing nations, low-fee, for-profit schools. They argue that, since the research evidence globally is strong in its conclusion that privatization of education in its various forms exacerbates inequalities, there is a need for regulatory frames that recognize the context-sensitive nature of privatization in different national systems.

In Chapter 9, Tero Järvinen documents the growth in inequalities within and across nations but argues that the nature of these inequalities cannot be adequately understood without appreciating their impact on the identity formation of young people. He insists that redistributive education policies need to deal with questions of social inequalities and identity in tandem, recognizing, at the same time, how they are locally experienced within the context of shifting global transformations.

In Chapter 10, Suvi Jokila, Arto Jauhiainen, and Marja Peura pick up the theme of the global mobility, focusing on the mobility of researchers and students. They look at how this has been disrupted by the experiences of COVID-19. They ponder what forms of academic mobility might look like in the context of global challenges associated not only with the pandemic but with the rise of ethno-nationalism as well as the climate emergency and resultant energy crisis. The chapter emphasizes the need to examine issues of academic mobility in the broadest framework of the complex relationships across national interests, policies and governing structures and matters of inequality.

Marcia McKenzie, in Chapter 11, analyses, more specifically, the current climate emergency and considers its implications for education. She documents the complexities and conflicts in relation to affective biopolitics, arguing that the contemporary structure of feeling is now applicable within national contexts at the same time as being networked globally. Given the anxiety felt by young people around the globe in relation to the climate emergency, she shows how the traditional tools of digital and algorithmic governance, corporate politics and global agreements such as the Kyoto and Paris Agreements are not sufficient: new approaches for addressing climate change are needed in this era of post-truth politics where affect has as much impact as facts and evidence.

In Chapter 12, Risto Rinne considers the bearing of neoliberal globalization and subsequent developments on schooling policies of the five Nordic nations usually characterized as having social-democratic welfare states. He demonstrates that, while Norway, Finland and Iceland have taken up some of the discourses of market reforms in schooling, by and large they have retained many of the features of their social-democratic comprehensive schooling systems. In contrast, national path-dependent factors and changing politics have seen the schooling systems in Sweden, in particular, and Denmark moving in the direction of neoliberal market reforms along with the rise of new nationalisms. It remains to be seen if these trends persist in the light of growing recognition of the contradictions of the neo-liberal social imaginary. This imaginary of globalization is already beginning to be ruptured and discredited in many parts of the world. The economic and political rise of China in the so-called Asian century, Michael Peters argues in Chapter 13, is already pointing to a different understanding of globalization. He draws out the implications for education of this changing geopolitics, including a range of new Asian Banks and China's Belt and Road Initiative with its determination to project its power globally through educational aid and public diplomacy.

In many parts of the world, the contradictions of neoliberal globalization are widely recognized, as indeed is its embeddedness within the traditions of global modernity. This has led to decolonization movements in education, not only in countries of the Global South but also in the so-called settler colonies where Indigenous peoples are determined to have their political voices heard. Yet the notion of decolonization lacks clarity and direction. In Chapter 14, Sharon Stein, Vanessa Andreotti, Cash Ahenakew, and Dallas Hunt document decolonial critiques of the colonial present and their different manifestations in varying geopolitical contexts. They then consider how these apply in various kinds of decolonizing education projects within the context of the shifting expressions of globalization. They put forward four possible approaches: working to change the system from within; replacing the current system with a pre-determined alternative; hacking the current system to allow for multiple alternatives; and/or ushering in something new and not, as yet, defined.

In the concluding chapter, Fazal Rizvi suggests that, across the 1990s, political opposition to neoliberal globalization came largely from activists and scholars on the broad left, who viewed it as a manipulative and pernicious manifestation of capitalism. In contrast, he shows how the opposition to neoliberal globaliza-tion across the past decade has come largely from the populist, nationalist right.

Central to Rizvi's argument is acknowledgment of political transference whereby the earlier critiques proffered by the left have been co-opted by the populist, nationalist right in the context of growing economic inequality. The populist right's critique of globalization has accompanied a reassertion of ethno-nationalism. This gives priority to the dominant ethnic group within the nation and sees the 'problems' associated with globalization linked to challenges to nationalism and the mobility of migrants and refugees, rather than the structure of global capitalism. It does not challenge the assumptions of neoliberal rationality. Rizvi insists that a way forward requires us to rethink a new governing rationality as a frame for reimagining education.

Educational futures

Collectively, the chapters in this collection demonstrate how many of the global transformations that have taken place over the past decade were already incipient around the turn of the century. However, they have now acquired new forms, greater intensity and wider global significance. Most of the regions of the world have been affected, as well as most of our social practices and institutions, including education. At the same time, our politics, both within and across nation states, has become fractured. The emergence of new social media and the new technologies of control and surveillances have normalized social conflict, accompanied by a loss of trust in the institutions that could have once been relied upon to resolve disputes. Intergovernmental organizations, for example, appear to have lost much of their moral authority, even if they are now able to produce more comparative knowledge than ever before. The sense we have of our social identities is now increasingly aligned to ideological disagreements which have been cynically exploited by nationalist leaders and populist parties around the world.

These changes have given rise to a new set of challenges for educational policy and practice. The tools we employed some ten years ago to address these challenges were couched mostly in terms of a particular view of globalization and its imperatives for education. It was argued that globalization had created new opportunities to solve many of the intractable problems of illiteracy, inequality and social conflict, through the deployment of the governing rationality of markets. In this way, globalization was viewed through the ideological prism of a neoliberal social imaginary. The chapters in this collection show how this imaginary is no longer analytically and politically sustainable. Its contradictions have become all too evident, especially after the global financial crisis of 2007–2008. Not only have policies expressed in neoliberal terms resulted in growing levels of economic and social inequalities, they have also hollowed out the civic space committed to public goods. This neoliberal social imaginary has failed to deliver the economic and social benefits it promised.

Since the publication of *Globalizing Education Policy*, there has been much critical, scholarly analysis of the shortcomings and depredations of neoliberalism, as well as what we might see as its existential crisis. Yet, as many of the chapters in the collection have shown, various aspects of neoliberal rationality persist in our educational thinking. We continue to promise students, for example, a world of stable employment, opportunities and the fiction of meritocracy, even when the conditions of work have become ever more uncertain and precarious. The neoliberal assumptions implicit in the so-called Global Educational Reform Movement continue to inform proposals for reforming educational institutions through privatization, corporatization and audit cultures. Several chapters in this collection have demonstrated how new technologies associated with recent innovations in digitization, datafication and artificial intelligence have been bolted onto the old administrative tools based on neoliberalist assumptions. Despite the COVID-19 pandemic, the valorization of academic mobility appears undiminished in imagining the new possibilities of educational internationalization. Systems of higher education appear besieged by multiple crises, not only financial but, also, cultural.

More generally, the global order has been transformed over the past decade or so. The assumptions of a world framed around Anglo-American values preferences can no longer be taken for granted. The discourses, practices and institutions that were built on the premises of colonial modernity are now challenged by the rise of Asia, generally, and China in particular. The Rest has become highly critical of the house that the West built, as indeed have Indigenous communities whose political demands of restitution and social justice can no longer be ignored. The fiction of a globally integrated world based on European and Anglo-American interests has been challenged. The challenges come from other economically rising powers, not just China, who demand a multipolar world in which geopolitical power is more evenly distributed, especially within the context of the environmental crisis that is likely to affect poorer countries more severely. The calls for the decolonization of education have become ubiquitous and can no longer be marginalized at the same time as being strongly contested.

What these chapters have thus demonstrated is that, while there is no turning back from the facts of global interconnectivity and interdependence, the notion of globalization needs to be reimagined. It needs to be reimagined beyond the neoliberal precepts and the assumptions of colonial modernity upon which it was elaborated during the 1990s and became hegemonic in the 2000s. It was this neoliberal imaginary of globalization and its uses in reframing the purposes and governance of education that Rizvi and Lingard critiqued in 2010 in *Globalizing Education Policy*. What the chapters by world leading scholars in this collection have shown is that Rizvi and Lingard's earlier critique is now superseded by major transformations that have altered the geopolitics of education, spurring demand for new ways of thinking about globalization and its implications for education policy and practice.

In recent years, the probabilities and possibilities of educational futures have been widely debated, bringing the challenges of reimagination to the center of educational policy processes. All education policy is, in a sense, about an imagined better future. This book does not claim to provide a set of definitive solutions to these challenges but, hopefully, provides some conceptual and political tools for students and scholars alike to use to understand the nature of the transformations reconfiguring the educational landscape. It suggests that the traditional modes of analysis are no longer sufficient and new ways must be found to address our current dilemmas about how best to think about our global interconnectivity, imagine its possibilities and develop morally and culturally robust educational futures.

This challenge is in line with recent initiatives of various international organizations, including UNESCO (2021), which has recently published its blueprint in *Reimagining our Futures Together: A New Contract*. The OECD (2021) too has articulated its vision of the future of education in its report *Future of Education and Skills 2030*. These organizations present contrasting understandings of the challenges facing the world and, not unexpectedly, the solutions differ greatly. This book presents yet another account of the shifting nature of the global forces affecting educational policy and practice, and how we might engage critically with these forces, both intellectually and politically. The book also contributes to the necessary debates about how to research education in these changing circumstances and how to imagine better education futures. In this way, the significance of this book lies not only in its academic contribution but, also, in its pedagogic potential.

References

Apple, M. (2014). *Official Knowledge: Democratic Education in a Conservative Age*, Routledge.

Brown, W. (2015). *Undoing Demos: Neoliberalism's Stealth Revolution*, Zone Books.

Giddens, A. (1998). *The Third Way: The Renewal of Social Democracy*, Polity Press.

OECD (2021). *Future of Education and Skills 2030*, OECD.

Rizvi, F. & B. Lingard (2010). *Globalizing Education Policies*, Routledge.

UNESCO (2021). *Reimagining our Futures Together: A New Contract*, UNESCO.

Sahlberg, P. (2011). *Finnish Lessons: What Can the World Learn from Educational Change in Finland*, Teachers College Press.

Sandel, M. (2012). *What Money Cannot Buy: Moral Limits of Markets*, Penguin.

Wallerstein, I. (1974). *The Modern World-System*, Academic Press.

2

GLOBALIZATION IN HIGHER EDUCATION

The good, the bad and the ugly

Simon Marginson

Introduction

The advent of communicative globalization in the 1990s was a great change in human relationality, akin to the invention and generalization of printing in late medieval Europe and the diffusion of transport driven by fossil fuels in the nineteenth century. The 'network society' (Castells, 2000) would have constituted a fundamental change in any era. In any era, its meanings would be colored by the historical context. So it was in the 1990s and after.

David Held and colleagues (1999) define globalization as processes of convergence and integration on a planetary scale. The proportion of the world's population connected through the Internet grew from 0.05 per cent in 1990, mostly in the early adopting United States' (US) universities, to 6.53 per cent in 2000 and 15.67 per cent in 2005 (World Bank, 2021). The rollout of the communications network coincided with the dissolution of the Soviet Union in 1991 and spread of capitalist market relations to the former Soviet bloc, along with the worldwide spread of neoliberal deregulation policies in trade, finance and public sectors worldwide, facilitated by the templates of the World Trade Organization (Rodrik, 2018). Taken together, geopolitics, the high capitalist neoliberal ascendancy, communications, financial flows, the offshoring of production, trade liberalization, worldwide consumption and iconic brands suggested an outcome that was combined, singular and hegemonic. An Anglo-American-dominated economic, cultural and technological globalization seemed to be on the brink of remaking the whole world as an Americanized world order. In *Empire* (2000), Michael Hardt and Antonio Negri described a networked power that was centered on the United States (US), that combined political economy, cultural practices and universalizing ideological forms, and that was expanding outwards without limit across the whole global space.

DOI: 10.4324/9781003207528-2

In the explosion of commentary, analysis and theorization that followed the advent of communicative globalization, there was again much agreement initially. In their respective readings of the world situation, advocates of global markets often coincided with globalist sociologists and critically minded social-cultural theorists energized by the new potentials for stateless, cosmopolitan, and, in some cases, postcolonial community. All believed that the nation state was being fundamentally destabilized by global forces. In this, they each saw possibilities for their own utopia while ignoring the utopias of others. Hence, Anglo-European ('Western') advocates of deregulated world markets ignored the potential for the destabilization of old certainties in a world of open communications and cultural differences, including the rise of China and other non-Anglo-European powers. Neither the high capitalists nor the globalist sociologists grasped that the expanding Anglo-European hegemony, that seeming to carry all before it, might run into limits. The social and cultural theorists who celebrated the liberating possibilities of global community underestimated the potential closures in the neoliberal version of the communicative global project.

Higher education and knowledge, which are continually impacted by relations beyond national borders, provide one case study of the thirty-year evolution of communicative globalization. Starting from a continuing interest in relations of power in higher education, this chapter reviews the evolution of higher education, research and associated activities in the post-1990 period. It has been prepared from an emancipatory and cosmopolitan viewpoint, spatially framed by 'thinking through the world' in the manner first developed in China's Zhou dynasty concept of *tianxia* (Tingyang, 2018) and reprised in today's ecological imaginary. This perspective is mindful of the potentials in global convergence and integration for a new unity-in-diversity, *heer butong* in the Sinic sense. This is the 'good' globalization in the chapter title. However, the chapter is largely focused on the limitations inherent in the present global hegemony, which constitute the 'bad' and 'ugly' aspects.

The next section of the chapter reviews the early discussion of and expectations of communicative globalization, in general and in relation to higher education, in the light of later developments. It leads to a section that focuses on current problems of global relations in higher education, in relation to three overlapping areas: neoliberal political economy, the monoculture in language and knowledge, and White Supremacy. The conclusion follows.

Dynamics of communicative globalization

The 1990s: death of the nation state?

In the face of the 1990s' global tide, many business analysts and social theorists forecast the decline or even the vanishing of the nation state as a fundamental social form. Two decades later, this seems remarkable. It is easy to forget how widely this position was held. This points not only to the divergence between prognosis and reality but also to the constantly changing, emergent character of reality itself, including its interpretation (Sayer, 2000).

Orthodox business literature hailed the weakening of barriers to mobile capital while, at the same time, believing that the world had been made safe for Euro-American business by the imperial 'submerged state' (Mettler, 2011), the US polity. The US state was expected to protect the essential freedom to trade through its ascendancy over other political powers, underpinned by political authority and military ascendancy. Meanwhile, the decline of non-American nation states was both a norm to be achieved and a fact already apparent.

Social theorists and sociologists had other goals. They celebrated the more porous political and cultural borders and an emerging cosmopolitan super-space. Some were sanguine about an Anglo-American world, others were trenchant critics, but all agreed with the neoliberal analysts and multinational corporations who argued that the nation state was in trouble. In *Globalization* (1995), Malcolm Waters acknowledged that while, so far, the impact of globalization had been more cultural than political, it seemed to be irresistible – though he hesitated at the end of his book, stating that "if states survive globalization then it cannot be counted the force that it currently appears to be" (p. 122). Arjun Appadurai (1996) was more certain: "I have come to be convinced that the nation-state, as a complex modern political form, is on its last legs" (p. 19). And good riddance: the nation state system "seems plagued by endemic disease" (p. 20). Ulrich Beck (2005) declared that the "national era" was passing and the "cosmopolitan era" had begun (p. 2). Saskia Sassen (2002) talked about the "partial unbundling or at least weakening of the nation as a spatial unit." She found that the architecture of cross-border flows, in which global cities were centrally placed nodes in a network, "increasingly diverges from that of the interstate system" (p. 1).

In *Globalization and Organization* (2006), sociologists Gili Drori, John Meyer and Hokyu Hwang saw something similar, though their focus was at a more disaggregated level than that of cities. They believed that the locus of activity had moved above the state to the level of world society where common templates "construct the world as an integrated collectivity," and also downwards below the state to the real players, the "autonomous organisations" (19). This argument resonated with the global/local dual (glolocal) often referenced in public commentary. Marie-Laure Djelic and Kerstin Sahlin-Andersson (2006) agreed with the Stanford institutionalists that 'world society', permeated by common 'rational, organized and universalist' institutional frames, was the reference point. Though there was no global state, "the alternative to state power is not anarchy and chaos" because "the cultural and institutional web characteristic of world society can be, at least in part, a functional equivalent to a centralized, state-like global power" (14). This vision was not far from that of Hardt and Negri (2000), though the networked world imagined by Djelic and Sahlin-Andersson was more benign and the normative Anglo-American center less obvious.

In retrospect, the degree of agreement is very striking. So is the degree of error. What distinguished all of these arguments was the either/or logic of relations between the global and national scales – the assumption that globalization necessarily meant a reduction in the role or potency of the nation and this had enabled new relations of power to form. Globalist advocates of free market capitalism imagined a flat world of meritocratic commerce, while social theorists and sociologists saw the cosmopolitan super-space. Some, like the Stanford institutional theorists, seemed to see both. Yet, historically, the evolving nation state had always been joined at the hip to global developments. The rise of the modern state in the nineteenth century was stimulated by global convergence, comparison and competition between Britain, Prussia, France and, later, the US, Japan and others (Bayly, 2004). There was more continuity here than first it seemed. Notwithstanding the anti-statist and submerged state ideology in the politics of deregulation, and the post-national cosmopolitan dream, the accelerated globalization of the 1990s meant not the withering of the nation state but a change in its conditions of operation and a partial transformation of its activities, while all units of the world order became more engaged and interdependent.

As the 1990s passed into the 2000s and beyond, the high capitalists, the sociologists and the social theorists found themselves aligned in more familiar ways, diverging between the capitalist and post-capitalist potentials of globalization. Each group found itself alternately rejecting global convergence and struggling to convert it to the preferred forms they had imagined. Each also found that, in one respect, it had profoundly misread the new era.

Relations of power had not been opened up or transformed as much as imagined. Despite the intersubjective realm created by the new medium of synchronous community, traditional hierarchies remained potent, sustained by the reproductive structures of national and neo-imperial power. This applied in higher education as it did elsewhere.

Globalization in higher education

Not everyone in the 1990s saw the nation state as finished or even diminished. In their detailed review of globalization across multiple fields, David Held and colleagues (1999) kept the question open. Universities provided one test of the 1990s' arguments about decline in the role of the state. The higher education sector had been state-built across the world after World War II and was also implicated in global communications and cross-border flows, especially in science, and policy models of the university (Kerr, 2001). As communicative globalization took hold in higher education, it became apparent that, while the universities and individual scientists had substantial room to move in the new global space, the nation state remained potent. Whereas in science it was rivalled by the emerging global science system (Wagner et al., 2015), it lost no real ground in the higher education sector.

In higher education studies, the 'glonacal' paper by Simon Marginson and Gary Rhoades (2002) responded to claims that a global/local dialectic was displacing the role of the nation state. The authors argued that while the global scale had become more significant, growing global integration and activity did not necessarily constitute a decline in the role of national government. Higher education was irreducibly global, national and local at the same time and agency was exercised in each scale. The scales were not mutually exclusive. Relations between scales were an open question. It was essential to understand the potential of simultaneous actions in different scales, and the strategic intersections between scales.

In higher education, the 1990s launched a long wave of globalization in student and academic mobility, research collaboration, offshore campuses, the diffusion of common systemic and institutional templates, global rankings and evolving policies on fostering cross-border passage, international collaboration in science, and global university missions. The growing neoliberal ascendancy in government (Olssen & Peters, 2005) meant that much of this was interpreted in terms of the global market imaginary. Discourses of neoliberal globalization were blended with discourses about marketization. Neoliberalism provided a control system for nationally containing and managing globalization in higher education. For example, the global student market in UK, Australia and New Zealand was platformed and regulated by the Anglophone states and often over-determined by national security criteria, for example in relation to policy on student visas. The expanding numbers of incoming students, and potential migrant graduates, were managed by state authorities.

The times, in higher education, were patterned by the conjunctural association of global convergence and integration, within an Anglo-American-led global cultural imaginary, with governmental neoliberalism. The 1990s in higher education were associated with continuous corporate and quasi-market reform. This reform wave began in the 1980s in the ideological heartland of neoliberalism, which again was the Anglo-American countries, and spread across the world in neo-imperial fashion into the 2000s and beyond. These marketization reforms, nuanced by country with varying mixes of changes in governance and economics, were always orchestrated by national governments. Marketization enabled states to devolve part of the responsibility for funding and outcomes downwards. They used more competitive systems (Marginson & Considine, 2000) to determine the nature, outcomes and cost of higher education, less through direct administrative fiat and more through programmed self-regulation, 'governmentality' in Foucault's sense (Burchell et al., 1991), and 'responsibilization' (Rose, 1999), the devolution of responsibility for outcomes defined from above. Policy emphasized the abstract imperatives of the 'global knowledge economy' and 'innovation' which, in the manner of Gramscian hegemony, ideologically sutured the university sector to state-led capitalism (Mayo, 2015; Morton, 2007).

It should be emphasized that much of the global and international development in higher education and science did not originate from neoliberal marketization per se. In the first instance at least, it was triggered by the new communicative potentials. While the Anglophone systems of UK, Australia and New Zealand commercialized international education, this approach was not taken in most national systems. Nor was there a strong, empirically verifiable relationship between the development of global science and innovation in national industry (Marginson, 2021a). Arguably, across the world, the fecund globalization in universities and science derived primarily from the informational and cultural aspects of globalization, in association with the cheapening of travel, rather than from economic globalization and neoliberal markets. As with globalization in general, for a time, all the drivers in higher education seemed to coincide, albeit on Anglo-American terms.

Global capitalism was not the primary driver of globalization in higher education. Yet capitalism modified it, especially by articulating, through the framework of neoliberal relations, those global relations that entered the national and local scales. This was more the case in the education function of higher education than in the research function.

In most countries, basic science was (and is) largely housed in nationally-nested universities (Baker et al., 2019). Arguably, however, in the global system of science that first evolved in the 1990s, autonomous global networking in science often became primary in the formation of knowledge (Marginson, 2021a, 2021b). The national and global scales are more equally weighted in science than in education. Global influences have the most sway in those parts of higher education where global science is central, such as the normative power of global rankings and in the role of research in mediating university prestige.

However, while global knowledge is less strictly nation-bound than are universities, this does not mean that knowledge has evolved to become more cosmopolitan. The potential is there. But the global knowledge system that evolved in the 1990s and after has proven to be notably monocultural in character, dominated by scientists from a handful of countries, despite the continuing worldwide dispersal of the capacity to produce knowledge. Knowledge is more closely structured by a neo-imperial hegemony than is education. This was achieved not through the operations of neoliberal markets or business models of higher education but in the autonomous collegial relations within professional science.

After 1990, both the quasi-market in international student mobility and professional scientific networking evolved so as to sustain Anglo-American power in higher education, especially in research universities, though in different ways. Geopolitics is ubiquitous.

Two decades later: the nation state continues

Two decades after the highpoint of Anglo-American globalization, it is instructive to compare the 1990s/2000s forecasts to the outcomes, in general and in higher education and science.

There has been no fundamental destabilization of the nation-state form, nor has there been the increasing replacement of diverse national states by a neo-imperial super-state, as Francis Fukuyama's *End of History* (1992) imagined. The contrary is the case. Supported by a modernization of government partly stimulated by global economic and political-cultural integration, in East Asia and parts of Southeast Asia, South Asia, Africa, the Middle East and Latin America, nation-building has proceeded at a faster pace than in the years prior to 1990. The uplift of states has not happened everywhere. However, it has been sufficiently broad and grounded to lay to rest the claims of world system theorists (e.g. Wallerstein, 1974) that the 'periphery' is trapped in permanent dependency in a Euro-American world and cannot lift itself (Marginson & Xu, 2021; Smith, 1979) the globalist assumptions that modernization is secured by global networks, markets or 'world society' operating independently of states; and the full Americanization variously imagined by Fukuyama and Hardt/Negri. Key events and evolutions, such as the geopolitics after 9/11 in 2001, the stabilization of economies after the 2008–2010 shock, and the governance of the 2020–2021 pandemic in different parts of the world, have asserted the centrality of nation states.

This does not mean that globalization has unilaterally reversed. In some respects, it has continued to roll out. The outcome has been mixed and complex, varying by social sector, demonstrating that spatial transformations are not necessarily universalizing. Arguably, the simultaneity of sectoral tendencies in the 1990s, which for a time provided a unifying framework for the emerging global spatiality, was unusual: episodic rather than permanent.

First, the global communicative network has continued to expand outwards. By 2018, 50.76 per cent of the world's population accessed the Internet in some form (World Bank, 2021). Second, and associated with this, the process of cultural convergence has continued unabated, though this does not mean that a single unified world culture has formed.

In fact, third, the old North–South polarity, grounded in a Euro-American-centric world in which Anglo-American globalization has been the structuring force, is giving way to a more multipolar world order, at least in terms of political economy. China now has the largest Purchasing Power Parity economy, India, Brazil and Indonesia are rising and China–India trade will eventually exceed all others (Pieterse, 2018). There is a new East–South polarity between East Asia and Africa, Southeast Asia and Central Asia. In the emerging world order, there are several civilizational blocs in which agents see the world in distinctive ways. Each bloc is too large and robust to be reduced wholly to domination by another. These include the US, still the strongest, Western Europe, China, Japan and Russia; and emerging India, Brazil and Latin America, and perhaps Indonesia. This combination of global convergence and bristling difference is new. "Due to the onset of global interdependence," the present period is "the first time that such a diverse set of orders intensely and continuously interact with each other" (Macaes, 2018, p. 2).

Fourth, in contrast with the continuing spread of global communications, there has been a slowing and possibly a reversal in the 1990s' formation of world economic markets. In the decade after the 2008 recession, multinational profits declined by 25 per cent, partly because of competition from modernized local firms; the share of exports accounted for by cross-border supply chains stopped growing, and foreign direct investment declined sharply (*The Economist*, 2019). There were few efficiency gains from the further lowering of trade barriers, the number of losers generated by trade liberalization, like American workers displaced by offshoring, grew (Rodrik, 2018, pp. 5–7, 27), and after 2015, in association with fractious geopolitics between the major blocs, competitive protectionism returned.

Higher education continues to globalize

Fifth, however, the global trajectory of higher education, and more so that of codified scientific knowledge, have experienced a globalization trajectory more closely resembling that of global communications than that of global economics. When economic globalization faltered after 2008, the globalization of higher education and science continued unabated.

There are low barriers to the mobility of ideas and data and, prior to the pandemic, to short-term academic travel. Longer-term opportunities to work and study in other countries are more uneven by country and subject to periodic tensions, such as the bans imposed by the US in 2017–2021 affecting travel from selected middle Eastern countries (Chinchilla-Rodriguez et al., 2018). In 2018, the US also began to 'decouple' its scientific connections with China (Sharma, 2020), inhibiting the mobility of students and researchers (Lee & Haupt, 2020). Nevertheless, until the 2020 Covid-19 pandemic, global student mobility rose rapidly, from 1.95 million in 1998 to 5.57 million in 2018, growth of 5.39 per cent per annum (UNESCO, 2021), compared to the annual growth of 3.58 per cent in world GDP PPP (World Bank, 2021). Further, scientists can collaborate without working in the same place. Between 2000 and 2018, papers in Scopus increased by 4.94 per annum and the proportion of papers with authors from two or more countries rose from 13.6 to 22.5 per cent (NSB, 2020).

The continuing globalization of science and higher education, while the political economy became more nation-bound, suggests that the dynamics of global integration and convergence in universities and science are more communicative-cultural than economic, laying to rest the lingering idea that the economy drives everything else. In relation to knowledge, structured by a communicative network that is global in form, relations of power are likely to be increasingly – not decreasingly, as in the economy – structured on the global scale, though the nation continues to resource both science and higher education institutions. The global factor is more directly important in science and knowledge than in the educational functions of higher education institutions (despite the fact that not all knowledge is included in the global system, as will be discussed). In education, global factors are most apparent in relation to cross-border student mobility but this takes in less than 3 per cent of tertiary students. However, globalization indirectly influences the educational function on a much wider basis because the content of all courses in higher education is affected by the evolution of knowledge, where, as noted, the global factor is large.

At the same time that global integration has proceeded in science, the multi-polarity evident in the global political economy has shown itself. China is now the largest annual producer of science papers in Scopus and India is the third-largest producer. Global science output from Korea, Brazil, Iran, Russia, Indonesia, Malaysia is expanding rapidly; and of the 25 fastest-growing national science systems, half are in countries with average incomes below world level (NSB, 2020; World Bank, 2021). Some of these are low-income countries, such as India and Pakistan (Marginson, 2021b). The US is the leading national system in high citation science and is much the strongest in medicine and life sciences. However, in the physical sciences, engineering and, especially, mathematics and computing, the top universities in China and Singapore are now at the level of the top US institutions. Tsinghua University in Beijing has passed MIT to become world number one in the volume of high citation papers in physical sciences STEM (Leiden University, 2021). In short, China, South Korea, Singapore and others now excel at Anglo-European science. Their own idea of science is less apparent.

Here is a paradox. The national-cultural diversification of material power in research has not been matched by a corresponding diversification in the content of knowledge. In the emergent global knowledge system, the question of cultural content has vital implications for relations of power in both knowledge and higher education. Despite the multipolarity of capacity in knowledge production, the continuing momentum of neo-imperial globalization has sustained the dominance of Anglo-American universities and science. The Anglo-American hegemony in knowledge and models of the university has outlasted Anglo-American dominance in the sphere of political economy. The rest of the world, outside Anglo-America, remains educationally and epistemically subordinate.

Global hegemony in higher education

In his analysis of relations of power, Antonio Gramsci (1971) foregrounds hegemony. This is the complex of processes whereby state-led political orders are constructed and sustained on the basis of consent. "The ruling class not only justifies and maintains its dominance, but manages to win the active consent of those over whom it rules" (Gramsci, 1971, p. 178). Gramsci repeatedly emphasizes the importance, and the autonomy, of cultural factors in the exercise of power, including knowledge, language and ideology, and the associated institutions and agendas. He focuses on the junction between economic relations, cultural tropes and subjective affect. Through the painstaking work of hegemony, the worldview of the core socio-economic group, its chosen narratives and other devices, are internalized in social sectors and the mentality of their agents and "transformed into an intersubjectively constituted reality" (Cox, 1994, p. 366) sustained by normalization and universalization. Science is an especially potent form of universalization (Gramsci, 1971, p. 446).

Gramsci also takes these ideas into discussion of "combinations of states in hegemonic systems" (Gramsci, 1971, p. 176) and the "colonial subjection of the whole world to Anglo-Saxon capitalism" (Gramsci, 1977, pp. 79–82, 89–93). The outward expansion of the capitalist mode of production from strong Euro-American centers has provided conditions of possibility for neo-imperial hegemony on a world scale (Morton, 2007, pp. 98–99) and the spread of universal ideas that buttress capitalist accumulation and geopolitical control.

This suggests that, in political terms, there is much at stake in higher education and in the contents of knowledge. It also provides clues about the way that power is exercised in higher education, research and science themselves: through the fostering of consent, voluntary behaviors, the calibration of legitimate knowledge, and dominant institutions. Gramscian hegemony is readily observed. In *Power: A Radical View* (2005), Steven Lukes discusses "the mobilization of bias" (pp. 20–21) and the importance of control over processes and agendas (pp. 25–29). Imanol Ordorika (2003) refers to "shaping and incorporating perceptions, cognitions and preferences into a dominant ideology" (p. 27) in higher education in Mexico.

The Gramscian theorization explains how dominant forms and ideas are bedded down in knowledge and the global higher education of rankings without the necessity for an interventionist state. The idea of hegemony also helps to explain how practitioners of higher education and science outside Euro-America "consent to the terms of the game as if they were their own," thereby investing in their own subordination (Fonseca, 2016, p. 81). It also opens the possibility of counter-hegemonic practices of knowledge and higher education.

The globalization of higher education since 1990 has not created a shared space based on respect for the other and mutual learning. It is a hegemonic globalization grounded in the European (Hellenic-Judeo-Christian) cultural heritage, the heritage of the Euro-American neo-imperial project, which embodies particular social castes and economic interests and is racialized in character. Given its roots, it can be called a Euro-American globalization, though in linguistic and cultural terms it has suppressed non-Anglo-American Europe.

There are three different, overlapping critiques of the ways that Euro-American globalization fosters global hierarchy, closure and inequality in higher education. Each critique contains important truths though, arguably, none on its own is sufficient. The first focuses on the way that globalization in higher education is manifest in the business model of international education and the spread of neoliberal models and templates through policy isomorphism. The second critique concerns linguistic-cultural hegemony in the worldwide organization of knowledge. The third critique is about the way that practices of global mobility and cultural hierarchy and monoculture embody global White Supremacy.

Neoliberal globalization

The first and most prominent critique of Euro-American – primarily Anglo-American – globalization in higher education and knowledge focuses on the neoliberal baggage carried by communicative globalization (Olssen & Peters,

2005; Rizvi & Lingard, 2009). This critique is well published and widely understood and will not be rehearsed in full here.

As discussed above, the post-1990 roll-out of global communications coincided with the spread of state-led strategies of corporate devolution and quasi-market reform. The association was conjunctural, not causal. Neoliberal policies did not drive global convergence, though they influenced its forms and contents; nor did global synchrony create neoliberalism, though it probably quickened its spread. There is always more to globalization than world markets. Nevertheless, neoliberal discourse that equated social relations with economic markets has colonized globalization successfully as an adjunct of global capitalism. As Michel Foucault (1972) puts it, discourses are "practices that systematically form the objects of which they speak" (p. 49). This is apparent, above all, in the commercial model of international education led by the UK, Australia and New Zealand.

A long series of studies has demonstrated that relations of market competition in higher education latch onto and exacerbate vertical hierarchies between persons, groups, institutions and national systems; create social closure where access is mediated by the scarcity of high-value educational opportunities and/or sharply unequal capacity to pay; and strengthen the effects of higher education in reproducing and worsening inequalities between social groups and between different kinds of higher education (e.g. of many overviews see Marginson, 2018; Cantwell & Marginson, 2018). Over time, competition increasingly rewards those people, groups, universities and countries with prior advantages, so that they move further ahead of others (for an empirical illustration of the longitudinal tendency to cumulative advantage in higher education, see Davies & Zarifa, 2012).

The neoliberal market imaginary does have one positive feature. In mass educational provision, the tendencies to market expansion and monopoly inherent in capitalist forms carry a prima facie bias toward non-discriminatory inclusion. The abiding purpose of commercial international education is to make money, not provide good education to more people. But one of the spill-overs of this market is that it fosters intercultural experiences on a large scale and, arguably, brings educational opportunities to more people than would otherwise receive them, except under a relatively generous foreign aid policy. However, any tendencies in the international education market to access and non-discrimination are overdetermined by the sharply discriminatory effects of the other two relations associated with globalization in higher education: linguistic-cultural hegemony, and White Supremacy.

Cultural and linguistic hegemony

The second critique of Anglo-European globalization focuses on its enforced uniformity of cultures and languages, the ways the primacy of Anglo-American culture and science are relentlessly sustained, and the stigmatization and exclusion of everything different.

Global science is defined by the two main bibliometric collections, Scopus from Elsevier and Web of Science (WOS) from Clarivate Analytics, which are shaped by their practitioners in collaboration with leaders in the academic disciplines. Scopus and WOS are structured by an inclusion/exclusion binary that operates at two levels: first, in determining what counts as codified science, and second, in the ordering of value within it. This feeds into policy and determines performance assessments and university rankings. Most human knowledge outside Anglo-America is excluded from the global repository thus defined.

English is the first language (L1) of 378 million people, 5 per cent of the world, and the second language of 750 million (Ethnologue, 2018). Yet, because of two hundred years of British-American military, political, economic and cultural primacy, it is universal to science, having displaced Latin, French, German and Russian as world scientific languages. Of the 300,000 periodicals in Ulrich's comprehensive directory, 69 per cent are in English (UlrichsWeb, 2021). English constitutes 80 per cent of indexed journals in Scopus, 89 per cent in WOS Science Citation Index Expanded (SCIE), and 90 per cent in the Social Sciences Citation Index (SSCI) (Elsevier, 2020; WOS, 2020). Ulrichs lists 9,857 scholarly journals in Chinese; only 42 are in WOS (UlrichsWeb, 2021). In WOS, 95.37 per cent of all publications are in English; in Scopus it is 92.64 per cent. Spanish is second in WOS with 1.26 per cent, and Chinese in Scopus with 2.76 per cent (Vera-Baceta et al., 2019).

There are no standard translation protocols that bring non-English papers into English. In translation, the reverse process is at work. Almost half of all translations are from English to other languages; less than one in ten are from other languages to English (Naravane, 1999). Again, little non-English knowledge enters the common pool. In a triumphal account of global English, David Crystal (2003) remarks, in passing, that "it is possible that people who write up their research in languages other than English will have their work ignored by the international community" (p. 16). English-speaking scientists move smoothly between the local-national and global. Other scientists must deal with friction or face outright barriers.

In humanities and qualitative social science, most journals, even in English, are excluded. The globally recognized social science reflects Anglo-European (and mostly US) theories, concepts and topics. Most journal editors are from the US and UK and the definitions, validations, and exclusions are legitimated and reproduced by the Anglo-American universities that dominate global rankings, as they produce the knowledge they validate. The Leiden University (2021) ranking carries data on 2016–2019 WOS papers in the top 5 per cent by citation. Of the first 50 universities, 48 per cent were from the US and 70 per cent were Anglophone. Global university rankings are grounded in the customary profiles of the top US–UK universities: bibliometric papers, citations, number of leading researchers, Nobel Prizes, and surveys of university reputation that recycle their advantages (Marginson, 2014).

Euro-American centrism and hierarchy in knowledge draw trenchant critiques from non-English-speaking and postcolonial countries (e.g. Posholi, 2020). Hebe Vessuri et al. (2014) state that journal lists in global bibliometric collections are composed by 'self-selection,' while work in national languages is rendered invisible. Non-English-speaking jurisdictions thereby appear as relatively empty, intellectually impoverished. Yet they are full of materials (p. 654). "The mainstream has been self-built on the supposition that outside there was backwardness and lack of academic value" (Beigel, 2014, p. 619). All endogenous (indigenous) knowledge is excluded (Connell, 2014, p. 212; Nyamnjoh, 2019, p. 2).

The closure is sustained by that deep English speaker certainty that 'our' culture is not only the best but sufficient and no other insight is needed because it is necessarily inferior. Boaventura de Sousa Santos (2007) calls it a "radical denial of copresence" (p. 48), that thereby continues the colonial mindset. Sharon Stein (2021) states that "systemic forms of domination are not just national and epistemic, but also ontological – that is, they sanction particular modes of existence, and foreclose others" (p. 1779).

Global White Supremacy

The third critique of Euro-American globalization is in terms of White Supremacy. This is the dark underside of Euro-American hegemony – the embodiment of the claims to cultural superiority ('quality') in the totally unescapable facts of birth and ethnic origin. It is a reversion to determination on the basis of ancestry ('blood'), a trope of feudal society.

Global White Supremacy as a mode of thought and practice began in an older world regime, the colonial empires with their brutal record of occupation, genocide, cultural erasure and economic slavery. Claims to an essentialized superiority were maintained into the neocolonial phase after World War II and then into post-1990 globalization. The Euro-American-centric assumption of White Supremacy has become associated with English as a primary or privileged language, and the features of middle-class Anglo-American professional life. The associated cultural capital – appearance, dress, politeness rituals, and numerous cultural referents – function as default global norms of not just behavior but of being. And they can never be wholly shared by someone born un-White.

In a paper on 'Whiteness as futurity and globalization of higher education,' published in the journal *Higher Education*, Riyad Shahjahan and Kirsten Edwards (2021) show that White Supremacy and its cultural baggage are and have long been integral to the dominant forms of global higher education. In this era, globalization fosters 'a global subjectivity oriented towards Whiteness,' and no other global subjectivity presently has such power. It centers authority on the Anglo-American societies, the 'Whitest of the White.' "Whiteness, as a state of knowing and being, creates a superstructure that privileges White people, institutions, and cultural norms and orients social and political environments toward the benefit and protection of White life" (Shahjahan & Edwards, 2021). This naturalizes inequality by elevating White people above others and, through systems and structures, recycling the naturalized racial hierarchy.

Shahjahan and Edwards (2021) argue that not only do White students gain racialized advantages, investment in international higher education by non-White students is an attempt to secure what they can of a White future. Anglo-American Whiteness as the ideal form of life shapes educational aspirations and migration patterns. Status hierarchies in higher education make it economically and culturally harmful not to invest in the highest obtainable level of Whiteness. 'White credentials travel easily around the world,' though they deliver outcomes with greater certainty when the graduate is actually White.

> White nations' manipulation of global educational structures positions them as the future for which the rest of the world must aspire. Their control of educational imaginations and aspirations also evokes particular investments, which reinforce dominant nations' occupation of the center. When non-White nations explicitly adapt their educational agendas in response to global trends, they implicitly participate in the spread of White imaginations and aspirations.
>
> *(Shahjahan & Edwards, 2021)*

In this framework, the global rankings template is understood as a White institutional model that fosters desires for Whiteness and calibrates its institutional provision. "Idealizing the 'university' also Whitens aspirations, since the very concept of a university presumes the 'universality' of White institutional models" (Shahjahan & Edwards, 2021).

The Whiteness argument helps to explain the continuing overwhelming potency of both the US and the UK in international higher education, even though many other countries have developed strong domestic systems, the US is not as economically dominant as it was, and the UK confers no greater long-term career advantages than any other countries. Shahjahan and Edwards (2021) describe the imagined "futurity embedded in Whiteness" as a "compass guiding all the lateral/vertical movements we see spatially in globalization." International student flows are pre-structured by this futurity, pulled toward particular pathways by "an affective economy (i.e., of hopes and fears)?" These preferred pathways follow "modern/colonial modes of knowing, being, and relating" as Whiteness.

Mainstream analysis defines inequality only as social stratification and largely sidesteps coloniality and race or relegates this dimension to the sins of the past. Shahjahan and Edwards (2021) remark that "Scholars' long-standing preoccupation with a racist past often distracts from an analysis of Whiteness's role in the creation of the future." The hierarchies and exclusions characterizing global higher education today are in direct lineage with those sins of the past. Unless there is the necessary change in cultural norms, they will continue.

It is impossible to understand contemporary globalization without placing White Supremacy at the center. Race is as powerful in entrenching inequality, domination and control in education and knowledge as are economic wealth and social class or language and culture. The categories overlap. As Shahjahan and Edwards (2021) state, "Within the context of European colonization, Whiteness and capitalism cannot be disentangled."

However, these engines of inequality are not identical. Each explains something that the others do not. In the critique of neoliberalism, Euro-American globalization secures an exploitative and unequalizing political economy. In the critique of cultural hegemony, Euro-American globalization silences voices and excludes most human knowledge. In the critique of White Supremacy, Euro-American globalization stratifies people directly, while forcing them to invest in the system that assigns them lesser value, because exclusion is worse.

Conclusions

In abstract, globalization in higher education and knowledge has great potential. It sustains synchronous epistemic communities of unprecedented scope. It promises a move beyond the national containers that block collaborative action, for example on climate. Global convergence suggests a full and formative encounter with the diversity of human ideas, knowledge, imagination, political systems, institutions, social habits. No one country or tradition has all the answers. Most have distinctive contributions to make. That is the ideal.

In practice, global integration has not worked like this. The hopes of the 1990s for a flourishing of cultural diversity now look mistaken. There is an ever-present potential for flat, cross-border community. This has been enabling but, even within the autonomous disciplinary networks, this has been overshadowed by global hierarchy. Though globalization in higher education fosters both cultural homogenization and cultural heterogenization, it does not do so in a symmetrical fashion. It brings people face to face with different agents but on the basis of a universal template that excludes most of their perspectives, languages and learned discourse. Global university and knowledge systems largely work on the homogenizing side of the globalization dyad. They calibrate the value of people, institutions and countries by the extent to which they match the hegemonic global norms, thereby maintaining the primacy of persons, institutions and countries that embody those norms.

The neoliberal hope for the end of history, for a stable Americanized world, has faltered amid the emergence of multipolarity and fractured geopolitics. For the Anglo-American powers, global marketization is no longer the primary concern. The larger agenda is now that of containing China (an objective highly unlikely to succeed as intended). However, the neoliberal globalization project seems to have secured a longer life in higher education and research than in worldwide political economy. The outcome has been the rapid and stable expansion of international higher education and global science but on the basis of a singular language and a dominant institutional template and mix of disciplines. Potentials for the creative diversity of knowledge and approaches to higher education have been lost.

What to do? A Gramscian understanding of hegemony suggests that the struggle to pluralize knowledge is partly about language, institutions and processes. A. Joseph Mbembe (2016) suggests a 'pluriversity' in place of a university, with

> a process of knowledge production that is open to epistemic diversity. It is a process that does not necessarily abandon the notion of universal knowledge for humanity, but which embraces it via a horizontal strategy of openness to dialogue among different epistemic traditions.
>
> *(p. 37)*

Santos (2007) proposes an 'ecology of knowledges' in place of 'the monoculture of modern science.' He emphasizes "sustained and dynamic interconnections between" heterogeneous knowledges, "without compromising their autonomy" (p. 66), and intercultural translation.

> This requires renouncing any general epistemology ... not only are there very diverse forms of knowledge of matter, society, life, and the spirit, but also many and diverse concepts of what counts as knowledge and the criteria that may be used to validate it.
>
> *(p. 67)*

Santos (2007) does not want to weaken scientific knowledge. Rather, he wants to promote "the interaction and interdependence between scientific and non-scientific knowledges" (p. 70), including endogenous knowledges. This does not mean that all truths have equal status. It means that the mechanisms of structural exclusion are discarded.

One step toward epistemological diversity would be to move from sole reliance on global English to a multilingual publishing and translation regime as the primary repository in each field. English would remain the shared language but every effort would be made to bring knowledge in diverse languages to the common pool. All global field journals and leading national language journals would be available in major languages (some journals already do this). Citation counts would aggregate different versions of one text. Book publishers would facilitate online translation of books from all languages to each other.

Will the present globalization of higher education continue? No, it will not. Nothing is more certain than the fact that the present will change, for better or worse. As Gramsci remarks: "In history, in social life, nothing is fixed, rigid or definite. Nothing ever will be. New truths increase the inheritance of knowledge" (Gramsci, 1985, p. 31). And the hope for positive change, of a counter-hegemonic kind, lies, as it always does, in agency.

There is now wide recognition of the character of neo-imperial, neoliberal globalization, Euro-American cultural hegemony and the privileging of Whiteness. The global upsurge around coloniality and racism indicates the potential this has to shift. "Possibility is not reality: but it is in itself a reality", states Gramsci. What people can do, determines the boundaries of the possible. "Possibility means 'freedom'" (Gramsci, 1971, p. 360). And what people can do, politically, depends on what they do with themselves. "The only object that one can freely will, without having to take into consideration external determinations, is the self" (Foucault, 2005, p. 133). Agents in higher education can change their understanding, their capabilities, and thereby change their relations with cultural, social and material structures.

References

Appadurai, A. (1996). *Modernity at Large: Cultural Dimensions of Globalization.* University of Minnesota Press.

Baker, D., Dusdal, J., Powell, J. & Fernandez, F. (2019). The global triumph of the research university: A driving force of science production. Brookings. Retrieved 10 February 2021 from: https://www.brookings.edu/blog/education-plus-development/2018/03/29/the-global-triumph-of-the-research-university-a-driving-force-of-science-production/.

Bayly, C. (2004). *The Birth of the Modern World 1780–1914: Global Connections and Comparisons.* Blackwell.

Beck, U. (2005). *Power in the Global Age: A New Global Political Economy.* K. Cross (transl.). Polity.

Beigel, F. (2014). Introduction: Current tensions and tends in the world scientific system. *Current Sociology, 62*(5), 617–625.

Burchell, G., Gordon, C. & Miller, P. (eds.) (1991). *The Foucault Effect: Studies in Governmentality.* University of Chicago Press.

Cantwell. B. & Marginson, S. (2018). Vertical stratification. In B. Cantwell, S. Marginson & A. Smolentseva (eds.), *High Participation Systems of Higher Education* (pp. 125–150). Oxford University Press.

Castells, M. (2000). *The Rise of the Network Society.* Volume I of *The Information Age: Economy, Society and Culture* (2nd ed.). Blackwell.

Chinchilla-Rodríguez, Z., Bu, Y., Robinson-García, N., Costas, R. & Sugimoto, C. (2018). Travel bans and scientific mobility: Utility of asymmetry and affinity Indexes to inform science policy. *Scientometrics, 116*(1), 569–590.

Connell, R. (2014). Using Southern theory: Decolonizing social thought in theory, research and application. *Planning Theory, 13*(2), 210–223.

Cox, R. (1994). Approaches from an historical materialist tradition. In the forum: Hegemony and social change. *Mershon International Studies Review, 38*(2), 366–367.

Crystal, D. 2003. *English as a Global Language* (2nd ed.). Cambridge University Press.

Davies, S. & Zarifa, D. (2012). The stratification of universities: Structural inequality in Canada and the United States. *Research in Social Stratification and Mobility, 30,* 143–158.

Djelic, M. & Sahlin-Andersson, K. (eds.) (2006). *Transnational Governance: Institutional Dynamics of Regulation.* Cambridge University Press.

Drori, G., Meyer, J. & Hwang, H. (eds.) (2006). *Globalization and Organization: World Society and Organizational Change.* Oxford University Press.

The Economist. (2019, 24 January). Globalisation has faltered. Retrieved 1 October 2021 from: https://www.economist.com/briefing/2019/01/24/globalisation-has-faltered.

Elsevier. (2020). Scopus source title list. Retrieved 15 November 2020 from: https://www.elsevier.com/solutions/scopus/how-scopus-works/content.

Ethologue. (2018). *Languages of the World*. Retrieved 17 January 2021 from: https://www.ethnologue.com.

Fonseca, M. (2016). *Gramsci's Critique of Civil Society: Towards a New Concept of Hegemony*. Routledge.

Foucault, M. (1972). *The Archaeology of Knowledge*. A. Sheridan Smith (transl.). Tavistock.

Foucault, M. (2005). *The Hermeneutics of the Subject: Lectures at the College de France 1981–82*. Palgrave.

Fukuyama, F. (1992). *The End of History and the Last Man*. The Free Press.

Gramsci, A. (1971). *Selections from the Prison Notebooks*. Q. Hoare & G. Nowell-Smith (eds. and transl.). Lawrence and Wishart.

Gramsci, A. (1977). *Selections from Political Writings, 1910–1920*. Q. Hoare & G. Nowell-Smith (eds. and transl.). Lawrence and Wishart.

Gramsci, A. (1985). *Selections from Cultural Writings*. D. Forgacs & G. Nowell-Smith (eds.), W. Boelhower (transl.). Lawrence and Wishart.

Hardt, M. & Negri, A. (2000). *Empire*. Harvard University Press.

Held, D., McLew, A., Goldblatt, D. & Perraton, J. (1999). *Global Transformations: Politics, Economics and Culture*. Stanford University Press.

Kerr, C. (2001). *The Uses of the University* (5th ed.). Harvard University Press.

Lee, J. & Haupt, J. (2020). Winners and losers in US-China scientific research collaborations. *Higher Education*, 80(1), 57–74.

Leiden University. (2021). *CWTS Leiden Ranking*. Retrieved 1 October 2021 from: https://www.leidenranking.com/ranking/2021/list.

Lukes, S. (2005). *Power: A Radical View* (2nd ed.). Palgrave.

Macaes, B. (2018). *The Dawn of Eurasia: On the Trail of the New World Order*. Penguin.

Marginson, S. (2014). University rankings and social science. *European Journal of Education*, 49(1), 45–59.

Marginson, S. (2018). Equity. In B. Cantwell, S. Marginson & A. Smolentseva (eds.), *High Participation Systems of Higher Education* (pp. 151–184). Oxford University Press.

Marginson, S. (2021a). What drives global science? The four competing narratives. *Studies in Higher Education*. Advance online publication at: doi:10.1080/03075079.2021.1942822.

Marginson, S. (2021b). Global science and national comparisons: Beyond bibliometrics and scientometrics. *Comparative Education*. Advance online publication at: doi: 10.1080/03050068.2021.1981725.

Marginson, S. & Considine, M. (2000). *The Enterprise University: Power, Governance and Reinvention in Australia*. Cambridge University Press.

Marginson, S. & Rhoades, G. (2002). Beyond national states, markets, and systems of higher education: A glonacal agency heuristic. *Higher Education*, 43(3), 281–309.

Marginson, S. & Xu, X. (2021). Hegemony and inequality in science: Problems of the center-periphery model. *Comparative Education Review* (accepted 5 January 2022).

Mayo, P. (2015). *Hegemony and Education under Neoliberalism*. Routledge.

Mbembe, J. (2016). Decolonizing the university: New directions. *Arts and Humanities in Higher Education*, 15(1), 29–45.

Mettler, S. (2011). *The Submerged State: How Invisible Government Policies Undermine American Democracy*. University of Chicago Press.

Morton, A. (2007). *Unravelling Gramsci: Hegemony and Passive Revolution in the Global Economy*. Pluto Press.

Naravane, V. (1999). Fifty years of translation: The *Index Translationum* completes a half century. *Publishing Research Quarterly*, *15*(4), 23–38.

NSB (National Science Board). (2020). *Science and Engineering Indicators*. Retrieved 1 July 2021 from: https://ncses.nsf.gov/pubs/nsb20201.

Nyamnjoh, F. (2019). Decolonizing the university in Africa. In F. Nyamnjoh (ed.), *Oxford Research Encyclopedia of Politics*. Oxford University Press. doi:10.1093/acrefore/9780190228637.013.717

Olssen, M. & Peters, M. (2005). Neoliberalism, higher education and the knowledge economy: From the free market to knowledge capitalism. *Journal of Education Policy*, *20*(3), 313–345.

Ordorika, I. (2003). *Power and Politics in University Governance: Organization and Change at the Universidad Nacional Autonoma de Mexico*. RoutledgeFalmer.

Pieterse, J. (2018). *Multipolar Globalization: Emerging Economies and Development*. Routledge.

Posholi, L. (2020). Epistemic decolonization as overcoming the hermeneutical injustice of Eurocentrism. *Philosophical Papers*, *49*(2), 279–304.

Rizvi, F. & Lingard, B. (2009). *Globalizing Education Policy*. Routledge.

Rodrik, D. (2018). Populism and the economics of globalization. *Journal of International Business Policy*. Retrieved 21 April 2021 from: https://drodrik.scholar.harvard.edu/files/dani-rodrik/files/populism_and_the_economics_of_globalization.pdf.

Rose, N. (1999). *Powers of Freedom: Reframing Political Thought*. Cambridge University Press.

Santos, B. (2007). Beyond abyssal thinking: From global lines to ecologies of knowledges. *Review (Fernand Braudel Center)*, *30*(1), 45–89.

Sassen, S. (ed.) (2002). *Global Networks, Linked Cities*. Routledge.

Sayer, A. 2000. *Realism and Social Science*. Sage.

Shahjahan, R. & Edwards, K. (2021). Whiteness as futurity and globalization of higher education. *Higher Education*. Advance online publication at: doi:10.1007/s10734-021-00702-x.

Sharma, Y. (2020, 12 December). US targets China talent in drive to 'decouple' science. *University World News*. Retrieved 1 October 2021 from: https://www.universityworldnews.com/post.php?story=20201211141413735.

Smith, T. (1979). The underdevelopment of development literature: The case of dependency theory. *World Politics*, *31*(2), 247–288.

Stein, S. (2021). Critical internationalization studies at an impasse: Making space for complexity, uncertainty, and complicity in a time of global challenges. *Studies in Higher Education*, *46*(9), 1771–1784.

Tingyang, Z. (2018). *All Under Heaven: The Tianxia System for a Possible World Order*. University of California Press.

UlrichsWeb. (2021). Retrieved 12 January 2021 from: http://ulrichsweb.serialssolutions.com.

UNESCO (United Nations Educational, Social and Cultural Organisation). (2021). *Institute of Statistics*. Data. Retrieved 15 June 2021 from: http://data.uis.unesco.org.

Vera-Baceta, M., Thelwall, M. & Kayvan Kousha, K. (2019). Web of science and scopus language coverage. *Scientometrics*, *121*, 1803–1813.

Vessuri, H., Guedon, J.C. & Cetto, A. (2014). Excellence or quality? Impact of the current competition regime on science and scientific publishing in Latin America and its implications for development. *Current Sociology*, *62*(5), 647–665.

Wagner, C., Park, L. & Leydesdorff, L. (2015). The continuing growth of global cooperation networks in research: A conundrum for national governments. ed. W. Glanzel. *PLoS One, 10*(7), e0131816. doi:10.1371/journal.pone.0131816.

Wallerstein, I. (1974). The rise and future demise of the world capitalist system: Concepts for comparative analysis. *Comparative Studies in Society and History, 16*(4), 387–415.

Waters, M. (1995). *Globalization.* Routledge.

World Bank. (2021). *Indicators.* Retrieved 1 October 2021 from: https://data.worldbank.org/indicator.

WOS (Web of Science). (2020). *Web of Science Core Collection.* Retrieved 15 November 2020 from: https://mjl.clarivate.com/collection-list-downloads.

3

THE CRISIS DELUGE AND THE BELEAGUERED UNIVERSITY

Jane Kenway and Debbie Epstein

Introduction

The notion that universities are in crisis has been a constant refrain since the late 1970s when neoliberalism began its relentless march through education systems around the globe. Conventionally, the crisis commentariat start their analysis by focusing on general neoliberal shifts in government policy. Then, they consider how such shifts are manifest in government policies on university systems and how these filter down into the interstices of universities themselves. Of course, they differ on what constitutes the crisis, some arguing that the very notion of 'the university', and its purposes, are in crisis while others focus more on pragmatic matters that alter various operations of the university in undesirable ways.

Either way, the notion of crisis itself is not explained and, thus, neither is it located within any consistent theoretical paradigm. This is despite the considerable 'crisis' literature in many disciplines. Instead, the commentariat tend to mobilize various everyday notions of crisis. Crisis is used as both a descriptive and a disruptive term — as both an indictment and an incitement. Naming a problem, and framing it as a crisis, is intended to inject an air of alarm, urgency and agency. The university is 'in ruins' (Readings, 1997). It cannot remain in this ruinous state. It must change and we can and must change it for the better. Or substitute any of these — university funding, management, teaching, research or staffing — in relation to the named crisis. When the notion of crisis is applied so frequently and variably, it becomes exhausted from overuse and loses its power to indict and incite.

A crisis is commonly understood as a significant turning point, brought about by deleterious circumstances which require decisive action but "in circumstances with limited room for manoeuvre" (Campesi, 2018, p. 197). However, such

DOI: 10.4324/9781003207528-3

commonplace perceptions have their limits because the notion of crisis has different meanings and performs different functions in assorted fields. It can refer to circumstances across varying time spans and spatial scales, address the concerns of some but not others and involve different degrees of urgency and intensity. Crises can certainly have an objective reality but this reality will be felt, interpreted and addressed in various ways and in accordance with the different interests at stake.

If we are to fully consider the links between current manifestations of globalization, universities and crisis, the notion of crisis must be understood in broad historical, spatial and comparative terms. Our starting definition is as follows. Naming a crisis involves "a diagnosis of current ills, … a prognosis for the future within a philosophy of history that views the present as a moment pregnant with change and ripe for action" (Bures, 2020, p. 3). Conjunctural analysis, and associated theories of crisis and articulation, are in sympathy with this definition hence we turn to them.

We begin by explaining these concepts. Then we consider the pre-COVID-19 conjuncture, its associated crises, contradictions and nexus of articulations showing how these were expressed in universities at the time. Subsequently, we repeat the exercise for the COVID-19 conjuncture and universities. Throughout, we reference 'global North/South' disparities. This is a relational space/time concept that designates ongoing historical conditions of domination (North) and subordination (South).

Conjunctural analysis, crises and articulation

Conjunctural analysis is most commonly associated with the cultural theorist Stuart Hall. He first developed his ideas in collaboration with others in the Birmingham Centre for Cultural Studies in the 1970s. Specifically, he demonstrates the benefits of conjunctural analysis in his now-classic work written in the early days of Thatcherism (for Hall's selected political writings see Davidson et al., 2017). This work identified the various forces that, over time, came together, so potently, to shape the beginnings of neoliberalism and the systemic swerve to the right in the UK. He interpreted all this while it was happening. And, in so doing, identified the early stirrings of what was to become the global phenomena of neoliberalism.

Roughly four decades later, one of his final publications (he died in 2014) is *After Neoliberalism? The Kilburn Manifesto* (2015). This is written with his founding co-editors of the journal *Soundings* (Michael Rustin and the late Doreen Massey), which also encourages conjunctural thinking (Grayson & Little, 2017). Massey, Hall and Ruskin offer an analysis of the then-current neoliberal conjuncture which, as they demonstrate, necessitated a more global perspective than Hall's and others' work on Thatcherism. They offer a global analytic inflected by space and place and by the recognition that history and geography intersect.

A conjuncture is an historically emergent reality. Hall identifies a conjuncture as "a period during which the different social, political, economic and ideological contradictions that are at work in society come together to give it a specific and distinctive shape" (in Clarke, 2017, p. 80). As Hall observes, it "is not defined by time or by obvious things like a change of regime" but by a 'complex unity' of forces (in Clarke, 2017, p. 80). Each of these forces has its own internal, relatively autonomous, dynamics, contradictions and crises. But, Hall insists, each also provides the conditions of existence for the others.

Crises are central to conjunctural analysis. They are regarded as a driving force of history. Hall and Massey (2010, pp. 59–60) argue

> …history moves from one conjuncture to another rather than being an evolutionary flow. And what drives it forward is usually a crisis, when the contradictions that are always at play in any historical moment are condensed, … Crises are moments of potential change, but the nature of their resolution is not given.

A conjunctural crisis occurs when 'relatively autonomous' sites, with their own dynamics and contradiction, come together in the same historical moment to create a 'ruptural fusion' (Hall & Massey, 2010, pp. 59–60).

A further feature of conjunctural analysis is its focus on articulation, disarticulation and re-articulation. Focusing on articulation means identifying the forces and discourses that meld together to produce particular settlements. It asks how they do so, under what circumstances and with what consequences? Conjunctural analysis also involves a consideration of how these forces and discourses may be disarticulated and re-articulated in new combinations involving different settlements. Competing political projects and struggles are always involved.

Conjunctural analysis, then, seeks, first, to clarify the key forces of the 'complex unity' that is the conjuncture. Secondly, it unpacks these forces' characteristic features, contradictions and crises. Thirdly, it shows how these forces are mutually constituted, or otherwise, through various articulations. Fourth, it identifies the critical combinations that bring about the 'ruptural fusion' noted earlier. Finally, unless the analysis is conducted *during* the conjuncture, it observes the new settlement that has emerged. Throughout, it clarifies the political struggles of the people and groups involved and their discursive constructions of the crisis.

The crises of the pre-COVID-19 conjuncture

The pre-COVID-19 conjuncture dated from the global financial crisis in 2007–2008 and continued until 2020. It involved a conjunctural crisis consisting of five major, interwoven global crises. These were somewhat differently inflected in the Global North and South. All this led to very disquieting global settlements.

The economic crisis was most evident in the near-global meltdown of the global financial crisis (GFC or 'great recession') in 2007–2008. The behavior of financial capital power-brokers was, without doubt, morally disgraceful. Yet governments rescued the banks and even refused to reregulate them. Despite giant payouts, governments clung to the neoliberal, small-state, free-markets philosophy. The aftermath of the GFC, particularly in the Global North, included "the lethal combination of austerity, 'free trade', predatory debt, and precarious ill-paid work that characterize present-day financialized capitalism" (Fraser, 2016, p. 281). In the Global South, developing and emerging economies were "hit hard … The closer the developing countries are interconnected with the world economy, the greater the effects. The crisis was transmitted primarily by trade and financial flows forcing millions back into poverty" (Gurtner, 2010).

The severe legitimacy predicaments of national and international political systems, practices and figures were indicative of the political crisis. Around the world, and from many political standpoints, they were regarded as inadequate, inaccessible, corrupt, unaccountable and unresponsive to citizens' basic needs. Mass-based parties, parliamentarians and the political class lost much of their authority. All this led to what some call a 'crisis for democracy' and others call 'anti-politics'. For example, the common national practice of rescuing the banks and then forcing austerity onto suffering people was widely regarded as a prime example of such injurious government. And the inability of international organizations to address global crises, such as climate change and the settlement of refugees, also contributed to these legitimacy problems. Authoritarian, right-wing, populist governments burgeoned during this conjuncture (e.g. in Brazil, the UK, Poland, Hungary, and the USA). But so too did mass uprisings against governments. These often started with a particular grievance and then swelled into opposition against wider issues. In 2019, for example, these included petrol taxes in France, the cost of messaging apps in Lebanon and subway fares in Chile. They also included opposition to repressive governments, for example in Hong Kong and the Sudan.

The global ideological crisis included the so-called 'culture wars' which were waged over numerous issues. These were inflected by location but, overall, included conservatism versus progressivism, nationalism versus cosmopolitanism or globalism, common sense versus expert knowledge, everyday people versus liberal elites and one religion versus another. The right-wing press helped to fuel these wars which were accelerated, globally, by social media. Right-wing politicians and movements seemed to be winning, both ideologically and politically – but not without opposition. For example, the strident, right-wing, anti-feminist agenda met the pushback associated with the women's strikes in Poland, Argentina, Spain and Italy and the International Women's Day strike in 2019. These "reanimated the militant spirit of feminism" (Arruzza, Bhattacharya & Fraser, 2019, p. 9). They challenged austerity's shocking attacks on social reproduction – for instance, healthcare, pensions, education and housing.

Intertwined with these crises were the climate crisis and the refugee/migration crisis – crises for all humanity, the non-human and the human. The climate crisis, involving escalating gas emissions and global heating, caused dramatic rises in temperatures and in the number of wildfires, heatwaves, droughts and floods. This led to innumerable scientific reports and to international agreements setting climate targets. But these have been plagued by a lack of political will from national governments and by the failures of wealthy countries in the global North to support poor nations to make the necessary changes. Opposition to action on climate change, from the fossil fuel industry and the climate change skeptics, has been merciless. But climate change activists, most notably young people involved in global waves of school strikes, continued to say 'too little', 'too slow'. Low-lying small island states are at most risk of devastation and the geopolitics of climate change policy have, in effect, left them to sink.

The likely climate refugees from these locations are expected to add to the large numbers of refugees already trying to cross national and subnational borders to escape such horrors as war, famine and persecution. As their numbers swelled so too did the hardening of borders and the intensity of anti-immigrant sentiment. This sentiment was also fueled by the economic insecurities and fears associated with austerity policies and by associated concerns that global labor markets undermine the work opportunities perceived to belong to the national populace.

Universities and the crisis cascade

The crises of the pre-COVID-19 conjuncture found many expressions in the university sector. While each crisis had its own specificities, there was much cross-fertilization between them. And tensions, antagonisms and contradictions abounded within and between each crisis.

The financial crisis, and subsequent austerity measures, meant that the state provided even less funding than previously. University's top managers adopted a two-pronged response with many neoliberal features. First, they sought funding from non-state sources to the point that a large proportion of their income came from such sources. Second, they cut costs. The former involved increasing student fees, dramatically escalating international student numbers and intensifying the search for private partnerships, donations and bequests. The latter involved cuts to programs and courses and reconfiguring the workforce. Casual academic staff numbers rose significantly and the programs and courses deemed to have little utility value were either down-sized or dropped. Governments' austere approach to funding was accompanied by an austere notion of the university itself. This led to meager approaches to addressing the educational inequalities experienced by students from very low-income, poor migrant and state-less families, from rural areas and indigenous groups and those with disabilities.

The political institutions of the state sought to transfer their legitimacy problems to other institutions — universities included — and, thereby, to shed blame and enhance their own legitimacy. Their ruse of denigrating universities, and university expertise, helped them to justify funding cuts and to demand compliance and change via ever-increasing techniques of surveillance and intervention. Tight regulation ruled. This led to the intensification, and further bifurcation, of academic work. Expectations and workloads skyrocketed while academic morale plummeted. A new, upper-level, managerial class within the university sector sprouted and flourished. It was handsomely paid and government-compliant. This class inflicted multiple compliance regimes on reluctant, and sometimes recalcitrant, academic staff. It was instrumental in helping governments to further constrict universities' rationale to the point that the very notion and purpose of the university altered significantly.

Universities became a prime site for the ideological struggles of the culture wars. In the USA, the UK, Australia and many parts of Europe, right-wing politicians joined right-wing populist movements in their condemnation of universities, claiming they had been taken over by out-of-touch elitist ideologues who were indoctrinating students. Programs and staff, largely in the arts, humanities and social sciences, were seen as subscribing to, and pushing, cultural Marxist, post-modernist, anti-Western and gender-fluid ideas. They were thus targeted for cuts and terminations. 'Indoctrinated' students were characterized as dangerous and deficient, 'cancel culture', anti-free speech warriors. Indeed, free speech became a highly contradictory, right-wing, catch-cry — leading to increased policing of student protests on campus and, paradoxically, to attempt to clamp down on academic freedom. In various countries in the global South, ideological struggles were manifest somewhat differently. The universities' push to internationalize research, in particular, was juxtaposed against demands for indigenous knowledges. The legacies of colonialism, as were manifest in staffing, curriculum and material artifacts (e.g. statues), were also challenged via such movements as #MustFall arising in South Africa and spreading widely. Hence, the upsurge in demands to decolonize the university in the global South and North.

The climate crisis was largely acknowledged by universities and became the focus of much research which fed into various national and international policy-making and advocacy bodies. But experts in climate science, and related fields, were subject to regular diminishment in the right-wing press via such practices as elevating the views of outlier climate change denialist academics. On the other hand, to help fill funding voids, universities also accepted considerable funding from the gas, oil and coal sector, leading to questions about the extent to which research and teaching could be objective and disinterested. Nonetheless, the upper managerial class often 'green-washed' their universities' environmental practices. In North/South terms, most top climate change scientists continued to be in universities in the Global North.

The broader migration/refugee crisis was not initially seen as a crisis for universities per se. Like the climate crisis, it prompted much research and teaching and some universities developed support and advocacy programs for refugees. Largely, though, international mobility was financially essential at least for universities in the Global North. The fees arising from international student mobility constantly replenished universities' coffers as money from the state continued to diminish. Along with this, the links between higher education and global forces tightened — via such things as regional alliances, academic mobility schemes and international branch campuses. Staff were expected to grow their international research and teaching connections. And many programs for undergraduate and postgraduate students were designed to encourage, and facilitate, international experiences and imaginations. On the other hand, universities in the global South experienced, at worst, brain drain or, at best, brain circulation. Relationships with the state also tightened as universities became directly and indirectly linked to regimes involving the selection and settlement of migrants. They were also increasingly caught up in global geopolitics. As international tensions flared, the state increased its surveillance of certain students and teaching and research programs in universities. Geopolitics also contributed to racial tensions on campus.

The crises of the COVID-19 conjuncture

The pre-COVID-19 conjuncture was superseded, early in 2020, by the global COVID-19 conjuncture. The COVID-19 virus was a major historical force. It led to health, economic and political crises which, together, resulted in a conjunctural shift on a global scale. The COVID-19 conjuncture involved rather different crises, contradictions and articulations. Some crises from the previous conjuncture intensified while others drew less attention but nonetheless persisted.

Since early 2020, the health crisis has dominated all others. On March 11, 2020, the World Health Organization (WHO) declared COVID-19 a pandemic. In the face of global inaction, at the time, it stressed the need for 'urgent and aggressive action'. In late September 2021, the WHO announced that "globally, as of 3:36pm CEST, 28 September 2021, there have been 232,075,351 confirmed cases of COVID-19, including 4,752,988 deaths" (World Health Organization, 2021).

Between March 2020 and late September 2021, there was widespread infection, contagion and death — albeit varying by time and place. New, and more virulent, variants of COVID-19 emerged with expectations of more to come. In 2021, vaccines were finally developed and distributed, very unevenly, across the globe.

Little was known about COVID-19 in March 2020. Suitable health protection measures, therapeutics and vaccines had to be quickly developed and evolve as more was learned. The current 2020/21 health policy model has many intricate features which have altered according to the proportions of the population who have been vaccinated. Multi-scalar numerical information about the sick, those hospitalized, in intensive care, on ventilators, the dead and the vaccinated has been constantly provided (e.g. Worldometer's COVID-19 data). Various international, regional and global organizations, and universities, distribute and interpret such information. Some also model future scenarios. Extensive public education campaigns seek to persuade people to sanitize, practice 'social distancing', wear face masks, consider ventilation issues, register their movements and get vaccinated. Lockdowns, on various subnational scales, occur when situations are considered particularly dire. Under lockdown, public places and workplaces are closed — except for 'essential industries' and 'essential workers'. Where possible, working from home is legally required. If symptoms appear, testing is also required and the contacts and movements of those who test positive are traced. In certain circumstances, self-isolation or quarantining is mandated and heavily policed. High levels of vaccination are equated with easing time/space restrictions and opening subnational and national borders. Compulsory vaccination for certain workplaces and vaccine 'passports' are widely mooted.

The health crisis has involved many contradictions. The most obvious is the unsuitability of this dominant model, for managing the pandemic, for high-poverty countries in the global South. These often have large, highly concentrated, populations in metropolises and the countryside. Their health systems are under-resourced and struggle to deal with already existing epidemics (Shadmi et al., 2020). Accurate data gathering is difficult. To add to their difficulties, vaccines have been maldistributed by what Oxfam (2020) calls a

> broken system that protects the monopolies and profits of pharmaceutical corporations and favours wealthy nations, while artificially restricting production and leaving most of the world's population waiting longer than necessary for a vaccine.
>
> *(ibid., online)*

It was for such reasons that the WHO established the COVAX scheme which aims to ensure that vaccines are distributed to low- and medium-income countries and which encourages rich countries and pharmaceutical companies to donate. It is struggling to meet its targets. Also, there have been proposals to waive the World Trade Organization's intellectual property rules (TRIPS) for COVID-19 vaccines to enable fairer access for low-income countries. Meanwhile, many countries in the global South particularly are experiencing record numbers of deaths as the Delta variant rages through their largely unvaccinated populations.

A further contradiction is that, in so-called developed countries, the aged, the poor and poor people of color have fared worst. They have a higher prevalence of pre-existing health conditions, limited access to healthcare and endure entrenched hunger and hardship which includes cramped living conditions. People with disabilities have also fared badly in terms of contracting the virus and also rates of vaccination. A third contradiction is that, during earlier conjunctures, public hospitals and healthcare systems were starved of resources. Many were thus unable to cope with the dramatic influx of patients. Large numbers of makeshift hospitals and burial grounds resulted.

Lockdowns and border closures have damaged national economies leading to economic crises. Global supply chains, international trade partnerships and numerous businesses are seriously disrupted. Countless people have lost work or have had their working hours and wages reduced. An International Labour Organization (ILO) (2020) report identifies downward pressure on wages in many countries and notes that women and lower-paid, lower-skilled workers were disproportionally affected in the period up to June 2020. Governments have introduced various rescue packages and emergency financing for businesses, workers and households. And these have ameliorated the situation for many. For example, the ILO (2020, online) says, "[i]n countries where strong job retention measures have been introduced or extended to preserve employment, surges in unemployment have been moderated."

The richer countries have been able to provide the greatest support to their people while the poorer countries have usually required money from international organizations and other donors. Notably, the countries with right-wing governments, wealthy or otherwise, have been the least amenable to the provision of rescue packages. And, as is usually the case in crises, some sectors of the economy are making exorbitant profits. These include 'big pharma', tech. companies and retail. For example, Chase Peterson-Withron of Forbes (2021) observes that "US billionaires have gotten about $1.2 trillion dollars richer during the pandemic." Meanwhile 20 million Americans lost their jobs. Those countries that have rapidly vaccinated high proportions of their people, and have thus been able to open up their economies, have experienced quite strong economic recovery but this is fragile due to the Delta surge.

National and subnational governments have varied dramatically in their policy responses to COVID-19. For example, the UK, the USA, Brazil and India suffered terrible health consequences because their governments were *laissez-faire* denialists. In those countries where the virus appears to have been well managed, the political order has regained some legitimacy. Political leaders' approval ratings have improved even as the power of the state over people's everyday lives intensifies (e.g. Alberto Fernàndez, President of Argentina). Vaccine nationalism seems popular among voters. In some such instances, crisis management involves a mix of authoritarianism and nationalism (e.g. in Turkey and Hungary). Technological surveillance became essential for contact tracing and the police and the military are used to enforce closures and enclosures. But, as Human Rights Watch explains, there has been a great deal of 'over-reach', especially in China, Cuba, Egypt, India, Russia, Turkey, Venezuela, and Vietnam. And certainly, the pandemic has become a cover for governments to crack down on protests and dissidents of all stripes. Government legitimacy has been eroded, and consent has dissipated in those countries where the virus spread uncontrollably and where economies spiraled downwards (e.g. France and Italy). Some legitimacy has returned to such governments if they have ensured rapid, and widespread, rollout of the vaccine (e.g. the UK and the USA).

Tensions and antagonisms abound no matter what the policy settings. Health policies compete with the need for economic recovery, which is usually seen as reducing lockdowns and opening borders. Commonly, governments seek a balance between health and economic policy although the more right wing the government, the more likely it is to respond to economic pressures. From the outset, the pressure from small and large businesses alike has been intense. Further, with vaccines widely available in wealthy countries, pressure to 'open up' has intensified. Elsewhere, even where vaccination rates have been lower, the corporate world is pressuring governments to clarify an 'acceptable' level of death and illness so it can resume its activities.

The culture wars have been articulated to COVID-19. A feature of most government responses has been that experts in health science, measurement and modeling are central to public policymaking and communications. But not all governments have listened to their advice: some have selectively adopted it while others have claimed to 'follow the medical science' while doing otherwise. Whatever the case, health expertise has been widely recognized and trusted. However, and in contrast, such expertise has also been discredited as fake by right-wing, culture-war warriors. Along with anti-vaxxers, conspiracy theories have flourished to the point that the COVID-19 crisis, itself, has been declared bogus — hence the increasing flouting of health policy rules. In many countries around the world, pandemic-related and anti-government strikes and protests have flared under the banner of 'Freedom'. Everyday racism has escalated sharply, with people of certain racialized, ethnic and religious groups branded as plague bearers. Anti-Chinese, anti-Muslim and anti-immigration discourses are fused with those about the necessity of erecting hard national and subnational borders. Xenophobic nationalism is thriving (Katsambekis & Stavrakakis, 2020). At the same time, the Black Lives Matter (BLM) movement revived spectacularly in the USA in 2020 and rapidly spread around the globe, unsettling structural racism everywhere.

The migration crisis has taken on new inflections. For example, the lack of global mobility for workers has become an economic issue of concern to governments and employers. Cheap migrant labor has dried up. Migrant workers cannot readily cross national borders for work. Suddenly, the importance of such labor to many workplaces and economies became starkly evident. Special arrangements are widely canvased. And yet, despite their centrality to such economies, and despite the fact that these people are over-represented among sub-minimum- and minimum-wage workers, there is little, if any, discussion about increasing their wages. Meanwhile, the troubles of refugees largely receded from public consciousness — until Afghanistan was reclaimed by the Taliban.

For much of 2020 and 2021, the climate crisis was totally overshadowed by the health crisis. This was until, in mid-2021, intense heatwaves and fire storms across Europe, the USA, Canada and Argentina and the floods in Turkey brought it into stark relief. Then, in August 2021, the Intergovernmental Panel on Climate Change's (IPCC) Sixth Assessment Report, called *Climate Change 2021: The Physical Science Basis* (2021), was released. Amongst much, it identifies the regional and global tipping points beyond which the impacts become irreversible. And yet, despite the report's undeniable claims about the planetary dangers of climate change, this issue continues as part of the culture wars.

As further crises swamp universities

Between March 2020 and late September 2021, the global health crisis dominated the university sector, carrying forward, exacerbating and, in some cases, reconfiguring existing crises. Further, each crisis often articulated to, and aggravated, others.

In March and April 2020, senior managers of universities went into crisis-management mode and, to varying degrees, have continued to be in this mode ever since. In the first instance, they had to attend to the detailed new health policy requirements as they pertained to staff and students, while also maintaining teaching, research and administrative operations. Initially, many campuses and, where possible, student accommodation, were closed. Although certain countries were notoriously slow off the mark (e.g. the UK, USA). All courses suddenly had to be delivered online and thus had to be redesigned. If practical courses requiring face-to-face contact, such as medicine, dentistry and nursing, could not adjust they were often canceled. Staff had to work, and students had to study, at home. This swift transition from campus to home further intensified academic work. Research and service that required travel had to be reconfigured or paused. And all of this required administrative systems to adapt. Advanced, 'EdTech', higher education providers instantly spread and deepened their presence and influence in universities — initially playing an apparently palliative role but later emerging triumphantly as the apparent savior of the sector (more below).

Many of these changes had flow-on difficulties. Mental health problems climbed sharply. Morale plummeted even further among staff. Students felt estranged and many complained about the quality of online teaching, some demanding fee refunds. University entrance procedures were disrupted by the fact that schools too had been unsettled in ways similar to universities. And socio-economic and geographical inequalities intensified. 'Digital poverty' was identified as a major issue in the global South where there was a lack of access to adequate IT equipment and bandwidth and even reliable electricity supply. Under such circumstances, remote learning was difficult to say the least.

As 2021 progressed, opening up universities, in 'COVID-safe' ways, become an immediate management imperative. But with the arrival of the Delta variant, it became a stop/start affair. And, despite the development of 'COVID-Safety Toolkits', how best to open up was contentious. How should a return to campus be 'phased in'? Should vaccination and mask-wearing be compulsory? How should teaching proceed? Predictably, further use of commercially-driven, EdTech and online program management providers (OPMs) is being proposed via such notions as 'hybrid' and 'blended' learning and 'alternative delivery models'. And 'quality' is attached to each proposed approach as a reassurance — despite the care and community deficits involved.

The financial crisis has intensified during the COVID-19 conjuncture and the effects on universities are severe. International student fees, philanthropic donations and industry partnerships have plummeted. So has money from the state. This has led university senior managers to seek further ways to reduce costs — cutting to the bone. Most casual and contract staff immediately lost work when the COVID-19 crisis hit in 2020. Remaining staff were invited/required to accept wage cuts or freezes, altered entitlements and working conditions. Where programs could be further cut, they were. Again, the social sciences and humanities suffered as well as accelerator and incubator programs. Advanced EdTech systems are also being deployed as a way of reducing costs, automating such things as curriculum design, admissions, timetabling and assessments. These are contributing to the further casualization, exploitation and alienation of academic work and workers. And given the increased need for pastoral care, such approaches do not help. However, the privacy costs of EdTech companies harvesting such granular data from universities seem not have attracted any dedicated oversight or regulation. 'Digital disruption' and the 'unbundling of higher education' are spruiked as necessary but also exciting innovations.

Universities are also desperately seeking further ways to generate income. These include dramatic fee hikes for some courses but, more often, ramping up and revamping vocational courses and expanding the pool of possible students to include those who would not traditionally attend universities. In turn, this has led to modular and stackable courses, micro-credentials, 'nano-degrees' and 'bite-size content' with students supposedly mixing and matching according to the demands of the labor market. Alongside this, universities are looking to their usual sources, namely corporate partnerships and philanthropy. But such money, for example from pharmaceutical and technology companies, is usually tied to specific purposes which then steer the university in particular directions. There appears little potential for universities to 'diversify' their funding sources and so it is likely that universities will accept any, and all, comers — no matter what strings are attached.

Where government arrangements allow, the state has continued its close surveillance and command of universities. The state wants universities to further match their offerings to the so-called needs of the economy. And, under the sign of 'crisis', university management has become even more autocratic than in the previous conjuncture. Small cabals of the most senior managers have claimed extraordinary powers and are reorganizing 'their' universities without any input from academic staff who are being presented with *fait accompli*. Similarly, university senior managers are frequently expounding on the future viability of the present model of the university, asking what the 'post-pandemic university' will look like and suggesting that everything is 'open to question'. Undoubtedly, COVID-19 has raised many issues about universities' purposes and their relationship to various aspects of life. But such matters are canvassed in a rather superficial manner by senior management. Their guiding imperative appears to be expedience and survival, with IT as the 'magic bullet'. While they seem to be embracing the idea that 'with crisis comes opportunity', they tend also to be uncritically celebrating the inevitability of 'creative destruction' and 'disruptive innovation'.

And further down the food chain, in technologically well-equipped universities, extraordinary micro-management is occurring in relation both to staff working at home and their re-entry to campus. Almost constant online availability is expected/required and new surveillance mechanisms enable managers to check up on staff compliance. Overload stress and fear have engulfed many remaining staff, although some have continued to resist through their unions and with the support of student unions and activists. Some small victories have resulted. But human rights and civil society organizations in various countries have expressed concern that universities are increasingly seeking to repress student activism.

Attacks on university-based expertise are a characteristic feature of the culture wars. But, as noted earlier, health scientists from universities have been central to policy advice and in the development of tests and vaccines. Ironically, a particular notion of 'the science' and 'the medical advice' has become popular. This involves fixed truths and the expectation that all medical experts will agree. The necessary rigorous skepticism associated with scientific methods is not welcomed either by policy-makers or by a frightened public searching for certainty. On the other hand, any scientific doubt and variance has fed into the anti-science discourse of the 'culture-war warriors' and into the discourses of those policy makers who prioritize the economy over health.

The extent to which universities can contribute to society in times of crisis has become undeniable, and not just in relation to science. University-based experts from the humanities and social sciences identified the social, cultural, psychological, educational and economic consequences of COVID-19 and of various policy responses to it. The IPCC Sixth Assessment Report is one of many compelling examples. However, despite the highly visible contributions of universities, right-wing attacks on universities and on academic freedom have both continued from the previous conjuncture and accelerated. These have taken many forms which include direct government interference in university autonomy with regard to such things as appointments, promotions, forced resignations and mandated revisions to courses in order to reinstate conservative viewpoints and banning whole areas of research. Take, for example, the virulent attacks on, and attempts to censor and ban, Critical Race Theory (CRT) in universities and schools in the USA, the UK and Australia. These attacks can be seen as a backlash against the revived BLM movement. BLM and CRT have both been denounced as opposed to national values.

The migration crisis, which had not hitherto worried university management, became a mobility crisis with international education at a turning point. Given that universities had come to rely so heavily on the income generated by international students, border closures reeked financial, and other, havoc. In the early days of COVID-19, many international students returned to their home countries where possible. The minority, who did not, were often left to languish in foreign locations with only makeshift support from their universities and their host countries. Later, during 2021, some countries opened their borders earlier than others hence their universities had a jump start in attracting international students. Other universities feared the loss of their pre-COVID 'market share'. They have pressured the state to find ways to allow such students to re-enter in order to continue their studies face-to-face. But such students' loyalties have been severely tested. Delaying and switching are constantly contemplated. Many feel that the online education and care they had received, under the COVID-19 regime in 2020, was not up to standard and did not justify the high fees they normally paid. Fearing that international borders will never be as porous as in the past, universities are exploring such gimmicky options as 'internationalization at home', 'e-mobility', and 'borderless professors' — options hardly likely to appease or attract students.

Interestingly, scientific ideas have been migrating more freely during the COVID-19 conjuncture. Pushing back against scientific and vaccine national-ism and against restrictions on intellectual property rights, experts in health-related fields have worked collaboratively across national and institutional borders and moved much more to open-access publications. Initiatives encouraging such transnational and de-commodified behavior include the Open COVID Pledge (freeing up intellectual property), the European COVID-19 Data Portal (enabling rapid distribution of research) and such open-source initiatives as Against COVID-19 and COVID-19 Tech Feed.

But also, and in contrast, universities in the global South have recognized the urgent necessity for their regions to become self-reliant on all matters related to pandemic control and treatment. This view has arisen, in part, from the con-tradiction we noted earlier that global health research and related interventions do not properly attend to circumstances in the global South. The WHO has been instrumental in helping universities to develop partnerships to enable such South/South collaborations.

★★★★★★★★★★★★★

Conducting an exhaustive conjunctural analysis is far too ambitious an exercise to undertake in this chapter. Rather, its aim is to offer a glimmer of the insights about the trajectories of universities since the global financial crisis. As we have argued, the crises in/of universities are a consequence of much more than the neoliberal project. Our account of the global crises associated with the pre-COVID-19 and COVID-19 conjunctures has pointed to the complex unity of forces that long-suffering universities, staff and students have had to contend with. It has demonstrated the ruptural fusions and articulations involved and the regrettable settlements that have often resulted.

According to Lawrence Grossberg (2017, p. 110), a conjunctural crisis "calls into question a society's understanding and imagination of itself. It demands in response a vision of both the crisis and of what the society can become." His point applies equally to universities. What might they become as a result of the COVID-19 conjuncture? We have suggested that, if left in the hands of right-wing govern-ments and enfeebled senior university managers, they will be further diminished. But we also pointed out that conjunctures always involve competing political projects and struggles. We identified some. Crises are always moments of poten-tial change for better or worse. The alternative projects and struggles associated with the various crises we identified have major implications for universities. But how they might best be articulated to the struggles of university workers and students to reclaim the university for progressive and public purposes remains an important but open question.

References

Arruzza, C., Bhattacharya, T. & Fraser, N. (2019). *Feminism for the 99%: A Manifesto*, Verso.

Bures, E. (2020). When everything is a crisis, nothing is. *Foreign Policy*. Insider, August 1.

Campesi, G. (2018). Crisis, migration and the consolidation of the EU border control regime. *International Journal of Migration and Border Studies*, 4(3), 196–221. doi:10.1504/IJMBS.2018.093891.

Clarke, J. (2017). Doing the dirty work: The challenges of Conjunctural Analysis. In Henriques, J., Morely, D. & Gobiot, V. (Eds.) *Stuart Hall: Conversations, Projects and Legends*, Goldsmiths Press, pp. 79–86.

Davidson, S., Featherstone, D., Schwarz, B. & Rustin, M. (Eds.) (2017). *Selected Political Writings: The Great Moving Right Show and Other Essays*, Lawrence & Wishart.

Fraser, N. (2016). Progressive neoliberalism versus reactionary populism: A choice that feminists should refuse [Position Paper]. *NORA - Nordic Journal of Feminist and Gender Research*, 24(4), 261–284. doi:10.1080/08038740.2016.1278263.

Grayson D. & Little, B. (2017). Conjunctural Analysis and the crisis of ideas. *Soundings*, 65, Spring, pp. 59–75.

Grossberg, L. (2017). Wrestling with the angels of Cultural Studies. In Henriques, J., Morley, D & Goblot, V. (Eds.) *Stuart Hall: Conversations, Projects and Legacies*, Goldsmiths Press, pp. 107–116.

Gurtner, B. (2010). The financial and economic crisis and developing countries. *International Development Policy/Revue Internationale De Politique De Développement*, 1(1), 189–213. doi:10.4000/poldev.144.

Hall, S., & Massey, D. (2010). Interpreting the crisis. *Soundings*, 44(44), 57–71.

International Labour Organization (ILO). (2020, 30 June). ILO Monitor: COVID-19 and the World of Work. https://www.ilo.org/wcmsp5/groups/public/—dgreports/—dcomm/documents/briefingnote/wcms_749399.pdf.

Intergovernmental Panel on Climate Change. (2021). Sixth Assessment Report. *Climate Change 2021: The Physical Science Basis*, August.

Katsambekis, G. & Stavrakakis, Y. (Eds.) (2020). *Populism and the Pandemic: A Collaborative Report*, Populism Research Group at Loughborouh University.

Massey, D., Hall, S. & Rustin, M. (2015) *After Neoliberalism? The Kilburn Manifesto*, Lawrence and Wishart.

Oxfam. (2020, 17 September). *Small Group of Rich Nations Have Bought Up More Than Half the Future Supply of Leading COVID-19 Contenders*. Oxfam. https://www.oxfam.org/en/press-releases/small-group-rich-nations-have-bought-more-halffuture-supply-leading-covid–19.

Peterson, C. (2021). How much money America's billionaires have made during the Covid-19 pandemic. *Forbes*. https://www.forbes.com/sites/chasewithorn/2021/04/30/american-billionaires-have-gotten-12-trillion-richer-during-the-pandemic/?sh=77ba7c86f557.

Readings, W. (1997) *The University in Ruins*, Harvard University Press.

Shadmi, E., Chen, Y., Dourado, I., Faran-Perach, I., Furler, J., Hangoma, P., Hanvoravongchai, P., Obando, C., Petrosyan, V., Rao, K. D., Ruano, A. L., Shi, L., de Souza, L. E., Spitzer-Shohat, S., Sturgiss, E., Suphanchaimat, R., Uribe, M. V., & Willems, S. (2020). health equity and COVID-19: Global Perspectives. *International Journal for Equity in Health*, 19(104), 1–16. doi:10.1186/s12939-020-01218-z.

World Health Organization. (2021). *WHO Coronavirus Dashboard*. https://covid19.who.int/.

4

RETHINKING THE AUTHORITY OF INTER-GOVERNMENTAL ORGANIZATIONS IN EDUCATION

Johanna Kallo

Introduction

Issues relating to the authority of intergovernmental organizations (IGOs) and their capacity to steer nation states' policy priorities represent an expanding strand of research that is shaped by different schools of thought. These schools have engendered a diversity of interpretations of the leverage held by these organizations, alongside a distinct, scientific controversy concerning whether they carry out the primary agenda of their member states or whether they have ascended to the position of being actors in their own right. The latter perspective receives a subtle endorsement in education policy analyses highlighting the epistemic authority of a plurality of actors, including IGOs, in the global education policy field. However, the recent anti-internationalist tendencies that have manifested in rising populism in politics, protectionism in trade, and unilateralism in international relations affect IGOs, thus entailing a need to re-examine their authority.

This chapter seeks to rethink the authority of IGOs and their capacity to steer nation states toward certain education policy priorities. It starts with a brief outline of the notion of authority, analyzing the ways it has been redefined in recent theoretical debates. Following this outline, the authority and capacities of IGOs are discussed in view of developments that have unsettled the neoliberal imaginary of globalization. Here, the chapter attends to critical accounts of governance in international relations and analyses of the changing scope of organizational policies during crises. Finally, it visits the deliberation surrounding globalization's transformations and its implications for the future of education in view of the changing authority of IGOs.

Rethinking the work of IGOs is significant as it situates the contingent character of their authority in changing policy contexts. The activities of such

DOI: 10.4324/9781003207528-4

organizations have encroached on almost every aspect of social life and have increasingly preoccupied research on international relations. Although the scientific controversy referenced above manifests as a rather binary view of the authority held by international organizations in general, different schools of thought agree that these organizations have come to constitute an ubiquitous element in the international relations landscape (e.g., Archer, 2006; Fomerand, 2017; Jönsson, 2018). This ubiquity is demonstrated, for example, by the number of active organizations which, rising annually by about 1,200, reached over 43,000 in 2021. These figures are based on a comprehensive definition that covers diverse types of organizations, including non-governmental organizations, united by "an ordering principle and a method of conducting international relations" (Fomerand, 2017, p. 1). More narrowly, an IGO is a formal institution established by at least three sovereign states through a multilateral agreement aiming to achieve common objectives with the help of a permanent secretariat (Archer, 2006, pp. 31–32; Fomerand, 2017, p. 2; UIA, 2021). Using this more limited definition, the number of international organizations amounted to more than 10,000 in 2021, most of them non-governmental, with the number of IGOs remaining stable at 292 (UIA, 2021). Overall, the numbers above capture significantly increased and diversified activity, raising questions about what the capacity and authority of these organizations are, as well as how and by which means they aim to shape changing social imaginaries and horizons of expectations.

Theoretical traditions

The notion of authority constitutes a key element of politics. The way authority is interpreted affects understandings of what politics is and how political studies fields, including those on education politics, are constructed (Krisch, 2017). It is for these reasons that authority has been of major interest to scholarly research in political science over recent decades.

Traditionally, authority has been associated with state sovereignty. No other actor, whether foreign state or organization, has the right to intervene in the internal affairs of a sovereign state. It is the right of the state to give commands and set binding rules, including in education, giving the state political authority over its internal affairs (Zürn, 2017).

Recent accounts in political science, international relations, and education have pointed out limitations in this conventional notion of authority and have suggested a rethinking of its premises. Globalization, technological development, and the rise of the private sector have shaped the field of politics and resulted in multiple sites of governance where single authorities are ever harder to locate (Finnemore, 2014; Krisch, 2017). While the principle of non-intervention still underlies the political authority of the state, authority, as a whole, has expanded to cover emerging landscapes of international order that are increasingly multidimensional and complex. This perspective suggests that authority should not only be perceived as a right to command but also as a quality of deference that arises from the ability to provide knowledge and competitive adjustments and the capacity to shape the behavior of others. Authority of this kind is epistemic, drawing on knowledge that others do not have or are not capable of providing. Furthermore, epistemic authority is inherently ephemeral and liquid, inasmuch as it entails a continual need for recognition through social processes (Krisch, 2017).

In education policy analysis, research topics mirror the qualitative shift in the notion of authority to some extent. The epistemic culture and authority of IGOs constitute an area of growing interest (e.g. Kallo, 2020; Zapp, 2021). Particular attention has been paid to the datafication of education which, in a broad sense, refers to the way that contemporary education is increasingly defined and shaped by data, international large-scale assessments, and metrics. Research on datafication highlights that the quality of an actor's authority depends on its ability to produce and access data. It suggests that data and metrics set limits on shared understandings of what can be known and what is possible. Eventually, datafication leads to prefiguring judgments in policy-making and the authorization of metrics that support neoliberal reforms (Williamson et al., 2020). IGOs possessing the means of datafication, such as the Organization for Economic Cooperation and Development (OECD), have the capacity to define what is deemed quality in education (Kallo, 2020; Williamson et al., 2020).

Research on IGOs has generated diverse theoretical approaches that encompass different notions about source and extent of their authority. Although these approaches have unfolded in international relations studies, they have also become relevant outside that field. They underlie social science and education policy research by scholars particularly interested in epistemic authority, epistemic injustice, and organizational agenda-setting in education through data, knowledge, and policy recommendations. To discern the legacy of these different approaches and their implications for contemporary readings of the authority of IGOs in the educational field, this article examines these approaches, construing and contextualizing them.

The rivaling theoretical approaches to IGOs reflect their primary contexts — the periods of history in which they were formed and the prevailing notions of authority, decision-making, and autonomy therein. The earliest styles of reasoning conceptualized IGOs as the creations of their member states which establish such organizations to shield and promote their strategic interests in an uncertain world. Depending on the scope of analysis (scientific philosophical, political scientific), this approach was, broadly, labeled as a realist–legalistic or rationalist paradigm according to which states legitimize organizations to realize their own policies (Fomerand, 2017). These organizations implement state agenda and have little or no authority of their own. Closely associated with this style of reasoning is the view of states as principals that delegate functions to IGOs as their agents (Jönsson, 2018). This rationalist paradigm has reappeared in contemporary research (e.g., Drezner, 2020) highlighting the diverse mechanisms of the governance of IGOs, such as the OECD, and their simultaneous dependency on the largest financiers (e.g., Martens & Jakobi, 2010). It is also finding expression in works on education policies, where recent research foregrounds the temporary mandates of international organizations in education and their implications for organizational authority. For example, the OECD, possessing no permanent mandate for its activities in education, is compelled to request temporary mandates from its member countries, meaning that the content of the activities and the knowledge produced by the organization are, in turn, shaped by the contemporary priorities and concerns of those member countries (Kallo, 2020).

The changes in the world system at the turn of the 1990s, the increased number of international organizations, and their mounting activity in various fields of social policy gave rise to constructivist theoretical approaches that have continued to spark research into the 2020s. These approaches were inspired by organizational theories and sociological institutionalism, and drew particular attention to the way readings of international organizations as legal entities to which states delegate their authority seemed insufficient to interpret their growing role. Constructive approaches thus embraced these organizations as manifestations of modern bureaucracy, defining their authority as unfixed and socially constructed and re-examining the implications of using organizational authority for capacity building. The authority of organizations was understood to rely not only on legal rationality or delegated authority but, also, on other sources that allow its power to operate independently. These sources include, for example, the socially recognized, special expertise and concomitant view of organizations as repositories of knowledge (Barnett & Finnemore, 2012; Broome & Seabrooke, 2012). This inference that IGOs possess knowledge separately from their member states reinforces the organizations' moral valence and the related view that they produce knowledge that is trustworthy, depoliticized, and impartial (Barnett & Finnemore, 2012; Rizvi & Lingard, 2009a).

These two schools of thought manifest a qualitative shift in the notion of authority, as described above. They view the relations between IGOs and their member countries from divergent vantage points. The rationalist school of thought, emphasizing rational choice, postulates that member states delegate authority to organizations to gain specialized information; they provide a space for the states to promote political coordination and resolve paradoxes in collective decision-making. The states can use them to obtain institutional lock-in and to gain confidence in their own domestic policy reforms (Hawkins et al., 2006; Jönsson, 2018). Overall, the rationalist school of thought is understood to have a jaundiced eye toward the international system, perceiving it as occupied by authoritative states aiming to maximize their gains in the international system (Archer, 2006).

The constructivist paradigm, however, endorses the increased ascendancy of such organizations and identifies the epistemic sources of authority that undergird it. This paradigm presents organizations as essentially autonomous, as the mandates conferred to them never precisely correspond with social realities: the laxness of these mandates allows them to make their own policy appraisals in changing circumstances (e.g., Kallo, 2020). Indeed, the organizations seek to respond to the requirements of their member countries and facilitate states' interests. However, as the interests of member countries vary, organizations easily assume the role of mediator or, even, of major player aiming to shape policy priorities. For example, where member states have little knowledge of a given matter or simply do not care about or are unable to deal with it, the latitude of IGOs may turn out to be considerable (Barnett & Finnemore, 2012).

Moreover, the requirements and goals of the projects agreed upon by the organizations and the member states tend to change as the projects progress. Their priorities are often redefined during implementation and the final results achieved can deviate from the original objectives. Sometimes, IGOs refuse to carry out their tasks if they oppose the interests of some member states while serving the interests of others (Barnett & Finnemore, 2012). To gain adequate support for their intentions, organizations may look for sympathetic interlocutors in member countries (Broome & Seabrooke, 2012) as both benefit from this "collusion in international organizations" (Dijkstra, 2017, p. 601; Kallo, 2020). To change their policy environment, organizations may, for example, articulate their interests and create different types of norms to compensate for the absence of legislative instruments (e.g., Centeno, 2021). They shape the authoritative allocation of values in societies through the aggregation of interests and norm creation within changing social imaginaries (Rizvi & Lingard, 2009b, p. 36; see also Easton, 1965). IGOs shape and are shaped by such social imaginaries: they influence states' policy priorities which condition decisions about who gets what, when, and how.

The paradigms outlined above display rather divergent approaches in international relations; a more nuanced review also discloses other schools of thought. It is, however, beyond the scope of this chapter to provide a full account of the theoretical tradition. Two strands of research are nevertheless worth mentioning here given their seminal orientations to the research on IGOs. First of these concerns the studies in international law, which could be brought more into dialogue with educational policy research. This dialogue could help to throw light on the aspect of IGOs' work and influence on education, which seems to extend beyond their mandate and, as such, lacks adequate attention in education policy research. This dialogue between the two fields of study could bring new perspectives to education policy research as well as to the study of international law which has traditionally emphasized the importance of IGOs in promoting good intentions and related legislation in the international community. Studies in international law concentrate on the legal framework of these organizations — their constitutive documents, legal personalities, and institutional problems — and scrutiny of these ordinances could enhance the understanding of the logics that underlie the organisations' influence on education policy. From the perspective of international law, IGOs are considered capable of acting within international law to influence legislation and the dynamics of multilateral cooperation and prevailing norms, thereby shaping the identities of their stakeholders. These organizations are expected to commit to equality before the law and to further social justice (Archer, 2006, pp. 127–129; see also e.g., Burci, 2020).

The second strand of research attends to the critical approach to studies of IGOs while interrogating problems in the global education policy domain. This strand of research dissociates itself from the aforementioned theories. It rejects rationalist and constructivist readings, critiquing the former for being an advocate of the current system, thus cementing unequal global dynamics, and the latter for encouraging only minor changes within the international system. This approach is skeptical about IGOs which it perceives as the instruments of dominant players. Drawing from neo-Gramscian ideas, it destabilizes hegemonic structures by scrutinizing global governing systems and the economic clout of the privileged (e.g., Robertson, 2019; Sorensen et al., 2021). It calls for more detailed research into increasing postcolonial rifts worldwide and power blocs with shared values and interests which have become institutionalized and have achieved a position that subordinates others (Cox, 1993). These organizations, especially economic ones such as the OECD or the World Bank, provide mechanisms for enacting hegemonic norms, a phenomenon evident in education. From the perspective of the critical approach, economic organizations augment their hegemony through a variety of strategies: by advocating for continued economic growth, efficiency, and lean public management, by encroaching on competing market orders, like social democracy, and by absorbing counter-hegemonic ideas to transform them into policies that serve their interests (Andersson, 2020; Archer, 2006). All these routes coalesce into the predominance of the neoliberal imaginary.

Unsettling neoliberalism and modes of governance

Global transformation have have shaped the authority of IGOS, while these transformations, as noted below, have been shaped through the work of the IGOs. The integration of nation states, markets, and technologies progressed rapidly from the 1990s until the 2007–2008 economic crisis, with neoliberalism rising to a dominant rationality shaping ontological assumptions about social life. Neoliberalism, while advocated by the IGOS, such as the OECD and the World Bank, encroached on the social imaginary and began to undergird historically constructed and shared understandings of society. Subsequently, what is social became understood in economic terms as self-governing people exchanging goods and services (Rizvi & Lingard, 2009b; Taylor, 2003). The neoliberal social imaginary naturalized the notion of market logic, minimized states with trimmed public sectors, and spurred people to compete and strive for continued economic efficiency. It resulted in changes in the reasoning behind how public institutions, including schools, should be governed efficiently to produce a highly skilled labor force. The way neoliberal ideas infiltrated the social imaginary and influenced policy priorities has been attributed to various factors, one of which being the capacity of economic IGOs to circulate powerful ideas, promote behavior, and set trends (Rizvi & Lingard, 2009b).

Following the 2007–2008 financial crisis, globalization decelerated in the trade of goods and services, as well as in financial openness, a shift that has been characterized, for example, as a move from hyper-globalization to slowing globalization or 'slowbalization' (Titievskaja et al., 2020). Faced with the COVID-19 pandemic, globalization now appears patchy; digital interaction has multiplied whereas social distancing and restrictions on international mobility have slowed down migration and fueled protectionist intentions (Farrell & Newman, 2021; Titievskaja et al., 2020). These tendencies are expected to affect global governance and international cooperation in the long term.

In recent years, the rising awareness of inexorable climate change disaster, looming ecocatastrophes, and the deepening of social inequality have resulted in a blast of criticism toward neoliberalism and its failed promises, marking it as the one root cause of global problems. The most sanguine prognoses have declared neoliberalism dead multiple times, though the past four decades have shown its steadfast habit of re-emerging in politics (Slobodian & Plehwe, 2020). The overthrow of neoliberal market discourses would require a change in the understanding of how social consciousness is constructed and how people can critically engage in finding and promoting alternatives (Rizvi & Lingard, 2009b). Moreover, it would presuppose an undermining of the subscription to the neoliberalist market order from the settlement of high finance which rests close to public governance. This entrenchment of the neoliberal approach in politics, supported also by economic IGOs, essentializes its capacity to encroach on competing views of the liberal market order, like social democracy (Andersson, 2020; Slobodian & Plehwe, 2020). The continued predominance of neoliberal ideas, as Jens Beckert (2020) writes, contains a risk of a political impasse leading to an anomie. He attributes this to contemporary economic structures that are entwined with prevalent power constellations while significant parts of the population feel alienated from social and institutional structures(Beckert, 2020).

These neoliberal tendencies described above have been widely critiqued in recent literature. For example, postmodernist accounts, in their study of IGOs and their authority dismiss the idea of progress which they see as a metanarrative exacerbating global problems. They give no sympathy to entities, especially economic organizations, that have nurtured economic growth and the exploitation of natural resources through neoliberal policy prescriptions. Instead, they value diversity and individual action in global politics, highlighting the multilayered nature of global relations, the dwindling salience of states, and the increasing involvement of non-state actors in global agenda-setting. The governing efforts of variegated assemblies of interdependent actors, including states and IGOs, market forces, and civil society, constitute 'global governance' (Jönsson, 2018). Postmodernists scrutinize the disposition of new forms of governance, such as coordination mechanisms between IGOs, new cellular policies existing alongside vertebrate administrative structures (Rizvi & Lingard, 2009b), various hybrid administrative arrangements, and multi-stakeholder dialogues and public–private partnerships (Jönsson, 2018). The examination of authority is, therefore, not limited to nation states or organizations but is rather dispersed across subnational, national, and supranational levels. These analyses identify persistent problems, such as the democratic deficit in how decisions on global issues are, at best, enacted only by a limited consensus with a group of the population affected.

Global crises tend to sway the activities and management of IGOs, triggering diverse responses, ruptures, and cleavages. These crises are apt to concentrate executive power at the top levels. This is justified by the need to speed up the flow of information, reduce authoritative bureaucracy (which shortens the line of authority), and thereby facilitate swift policy measures (Olsson & Verbeek, 2018). The COVID-19 pandemic has been no exception in this regard. It has significantly affected the internal management of organizations, like the UN, distorting the principles of multilateral governance by delimiting spaces of negotiation and excluding important voices from meetings (Burci, 2020).

Crises and catastrophes open policy windows for the expansion of IGOs' scope and access to policy instruments although they take advantage of these unforeseen opportunities to different extents. For example, organizations may cease operations or, like the Economic Community of Central African States, provide a limited response, as in the form of a declaration. Some organizations, such as the OECD, continue to carry out their core tasks with existing instruments, while others, including the European Union (EU) and the World Health Organization (WHO), may expand their scope of activities. However, widening their scope in a crisis entails no pronounced efficiency besides the expansion of the policy areas and instruments affected by organizations' bureaucratic capacities and delegated authority (Debre & Dijkstra, 2021). These findings imply that the crisis in the international liberal order, exacerbated by the pandemic, does not influence all international organizations in the same manner. The findings leave some questions open, however, especially due to their temporal focus on the first months after the COVID-19 outbreak. Within that short period, the extent of the pandemic and its repercussions for education were hardly discernible.

Although it seems too early for any exhaustive accounts on the ramifications of the COVID-19 pandemic on the authority and capacities of IGOs regarding education, a salient feature of IGOs has been amplified by the pandemic's protracted nature: that is, their habit of constituting new forms of alliances to craft 'toolkits' and other knowledge-based solutions for solving problems in the education sector. For example, the OECD has produced an increasing number of COVID-19-related reports, surveys, and working papers to assert the need to stop learning losses and falling economic efficiency (e.g., Hanushek & Woessmann, 2020). These works illustrate the organization's sustained commitment to neoclassical economics and to what Münch (2020) labels as the education–economic legitimation of the neoliberal reform agenda in the governance of education.

This activity seems reminiscent of what Gabriel (2015) describes, metaphorically, as the work of a protagonist. The OECD's COVID-19 policy hub has encircled other international organizations and think-tanks, inviting contributions from diverse actors, including ones with little or no previous experience in education but with clout in TV and media. The Finnish-origin HundrED organization, whose founder has publicly promulgated interest in commercializing education innovations for export (e.g., Reimers et al., 2020), is just one example.

Post-pandemic global transformations

Readings in contemporary research of IGOs and globalization's transformation in the post-pandemic era are diverse. Skeptical views criticize the field for a surfeit of remarks anticipating significant global transformations, and their related effects on world politics, generated by the COVID-19 pandemic (Drezner, 2020). Opposing accounts expect the crisis to lead to a fundamental reordering of global politics. Deborah McNamara (2020) suggests that, instead of creating further controversies, it is necessary to consider whether the pandemic opens up an opportunity to study and rethink globalization and the authority of international organizations, given the vulnerability of global economic interdependence and the way globalization reshapes identities, rearranges political authorities, and creates new sites for political schisms. The COVID-19 pandemic has, indeed, resulted in a clash between the ubiquitous goal of efficiency and international interdependence; efficiency demands the constant reduction of slack, making economies vulnerable in a situation where production chains depend on individual suppliers and factories that no longer have stockpiles. The solution to this problem is expected to lead to a new kind of geopolitics of globalization, with repercussions also in the area of education, where the scale and level of political authority is becoming ever more fluid and, at the same time, more contested (Farrell & Newman, 2020; McNamara, 2020).

In view of this recent course of history, McNamara (2020) suggests that future research should focus on analyzing the transformational dynamics of globalization. This shift would require a more stringent analysis of globally-embedded structural inequalities, scrutiny of political contestations of existential ecological threats, research into the pervasiveness of digital technologies and their shaping of political identities, and an investigation into the emergence of new economic statecraft using modernized networks for strategic gains. (McNamara, 2020). These transformational dynamics manifest themselves sharply in education which, destabilized by the pandemic, will continue suffering from the structural inequalities and persistent dearth of resources that affect the teaching and learning of the disadvantaged most. Digitalization is vested with high hopes of providing enhanced opportunities of learning for all while proceeding in a manner that is not in sync with this aim. A reliance on digital learning platforms during the global pandemic revealed vast gaps between people, regions, and countries. Communications from IGOs promising to reduce the digital divide (e.g., EU, 2021) are welcome, but this change requires plans and resources for local enactment. The principles of education for sustainable development have been incorporated in IGOs' programs and curricula, shaping generational experiences; still, these principles fall short of what it would take to avoid exacerbating eco-crises in the future (Värri, 2018). Globally, the new economic statecraft, in conjunction with protectionist tendencies, could imply a rise in rationalist politics wherein state goals are driven primarily by maximizing returns from the international system. This tendency counterbalances the fact that international organizations, as 'bastions of multilateralism', are not just still standing but growing in number. They are also providing varied policy responses to the COVID-19 pandemic, demonstrating not "an impending crisis and collapse of the global order, but rather its ongoing transformation from within" (Eilstrup-Sangiovanni & Hofmann, 2020, p. 1086).

Rethinking policy futures in education

The post pandemic global transformations and their underlying social struggles open up political spaces for future contestations (e.g. Delanty, 2021). In education, multiple tendencies emerged, incrementally, out of the past and encompassed an array of transformations extending into the future. Among these is the overall economization that has affected the foundations of education, transforming its ontology (Rizvi & Lingard, 2009a).

It is within this context that the horizons of expectations about educational development beckon as sites of contestation. These contestations emanate from the tensions between equality and inequality and take place within local and national domains, which are intertwined with global developments, world economy and geopolitics. IGOs, along with their authority and capacities, have taken up the tools and methods to frame these horizons of expectations and the perceptions of what is possible and desirable in the future societies.

These acts of shaping the educational policy futures are complex, intricate, and relational processes wherein IGOs, with their repertoires of knowledge, constitute a single, albeit influential, set of players. It is suggested that IGOs can gain legitimate authority in forging the future through political plans, visions, or scenarios (Andersson, 2018). They partake in shaping and reshaping neoliberal imaginaries with a shared aim to guarantee political achievements and economic growth for their members in the future (Moisio, 2018).

In the neoliberal imaginary, the temporal quality of constructing knowledge-based economies has steered states' policies in their orientation toward the future. This ubiquitous, contemporary vision of knowledge economies is expressly future-directed (Moisio, 2018; Peters, 2013). Concomitantly, education, and the higher education sector in particular, has been treated as a breeding ground for competitiveness (Moisio, 2018). Intergovernmental organizations like the OECD have contributed to the co-creation of the neoliberal imaginary through disseminating the ideas of the knowledge-based economy. During the pandemic, IGOs like the OECD analyzed prospects for growth and emphasized the importance of continued macroeconomic support with which "policymakers can shape the recovery to boost growth, enhance resilience and inclusiveness, and improve environmental sustainability" (OECD, 2021, p. 4).

Finally, claims about the futures of education are always ambiguous and open to speculation. This uncertainty has not hindered the construction of different scenarios and forecasts but has, actually, augmented their fabrication by IGOs. The field of predictive expertise has indeed expanded in an unruly manner (cf. Andersson, 2018) (Milojevic, 2005). Sami Moisio (2018) describes this as a terrain wherein a particular interpretation of the future can become privileged or even dominant therein through a process of semiosis, in which a given imaginary, or set of imaginaries, assumes the form of a dominant imaginary and begins to re-orient economic and political thinking and resultant strategies. IGOs such as the EU, UNESCO, and the OECD play a significant role in this semiotic process, instigating intervening policy processes with their clout built upon predictive expertise (Andersson, 2008).

Overall, IGOs and other actors, such as think-tanks, with their diverse expertise in predictive methods and techniques, can forge social imaginaries by presenting plausible scenarios and the data justifying them, thereby generating their own epistemic authority (Fricker, 2017). They shape policy priorities by defining what is relevant information for future education policy-making and how it should be enacted in practice.

Concluding remarks

The construction of education policy futurity in the post-pandemic social imaginary is filled with uncertainties and optimism. Existential fears of a doomsday looming on the horizon have edged their way into the literature and have amplified dystopian reasoning. Meanwhile, anticipations of a new normality and hopes of finding solutions for wicked global problems have called for a rethinking of educational objectives and a forging of new paradigms able to oust neoliberalism (Rizvi & Peters, 2020).

The abatement of the global pandemic may signify descent into a new era of transitology at the same time as the opening of an opportunity to analyze the possible collapse of old paradigms and the construction of new political visions (cf. Cowen, 2000). This shift would be a stern test for the international community in finding alternatives to resolve the paradox embedded in the liberal foundations of market ideology. The COVID-19 pandemic has surfaced this paradox between morality and the market, culminating in a debate on the global method of market-driven triage, fraying social solidarity and leaving some groups more vulnerable than others (Barnett, 2020; McNamara, 2020). The way IGOs, with an ardent commitment to neoliberalism, continue to justify their quest for efficiency or absorb and encroach on rivaling alternative paradigms remains to be studied.

The authority that organizations have to steer national policy priorities is indeed contingent on changes in the policy environment, as organizations are habitually compelled to renew and renegotiate their authoritative establishments.

While the COVID-19 pandemic has given rise to nationalist and unilateral tendencies and has revived embedded rivalries in international politics (Farrell & Newman, 2020; McNamara, 2020), IGOs have benefited from this crisis, as they are designed to deal with cross-border problems. Large organizations, with their permanent secretariats, survive and may even expand their political sphere of action in moments of international crisis (Olsson & Verbeek, 2018). This ability to use crises as an opportunity for expanding the scope of activities and their range of devices for influence is attributed to these organizations' extensive bureaucratic capacity and the agenda-setting authority delegated to them by their member states (Debre & Dijkstra, 2021).

Finally, crises have generally been perceived as important turning points, as they change organizational processes and affect authorities and capacities (Debre & Dijkstra, 2021; Olsson & Verbeek, 2018). An essential aspect that has received little attention so far, however, is the character of the knowledge created to abate uncertainties in crises. Anticipatory practices arising during crises and the way they are incorporated into the governmentalities of education have so far remained understudied. Future research should, therefore, delve into how organizations build their epistemic authority in moments of crisis and what semiotic process exists through which scenarios and plans, entailing changes in social imaginaries, are constructed.

References

Andersson, J. (2008). *The Future Landscape*. Institute for Futures Studies. https://hal.archives-ouvertes.fr/hal-01361237/document.

Andersson, J. (2018). *The Future of the World: Futurology, Futurists, and the Struggle for the Post-Cold War Imagination*. Oxford University Press.

Andersson, J. (2020). Neoliberalism against social democracy. *The Tocqueville Review, 42*(1), 87–107.

Archer, C. (2006). *International Organizations* (3rd ed.). Routledge.

Barnett, M. (2020). Covid-19 and the sacrificial international order. *International Organization, 74*, E128–E147.

Barnett, M., & Finnemore, M. (2012). *Rules for the World*. Cornell University Press. doi:10.7591/9780801465161.

Beckert, J. (2020). The exhausted futures of neoliberalism: From promissory legitimacy to social anomy. *Journal of Cultural Economy, 13*(3), 318–330.

Broome, A., & Seabrooke, L. (2012). Seeing like an international organisation. *New Political Economy, 17*(1), 1–16.

Burci, G.L. (2020). Covid-19 and the governance of international organizations: Open challenges. *International Organizations Law Review, 17*(3), 485–491.

Centeno, V.G. (2021). The OECD: Actor, arena, instrument. *Globalisation, Societies and Education, 19*(2), 108–121. doi:10.1080/14767724.2021.1882958.

Cowen, R. (2000). Comparing futures or comparing pasts? *Comparative Education, 36*(3), 333–342.

Cox, R.W. (1993). Gramsci, hegemony and international relations. In S. Gill (Ed.), *Gramsci, Historical Materialism and International Relations* (pp. 49–66). Cambridge University Press.

Dall'Alba, G., & Barnacle, R. (2007). An ontological turn for higher education. *Studies in Higher Education, 32*(6), 679–691. doi:10.1080/03075070701685130.

Debre, M.J., & Dijkstra, H. (2021). Covid-19 and policy responses by international organizations: Crisis or liberal international order or window of opportunity? *Global Policy.* doi:10.1111/1758-5899.12975.

Delanty, G. (2021). Imagining the future: Social struggles, the post-national domain and major contemporary social transformations. *Journal of Sociology* 57 (1), 27–46. doi:10.1177/1440783320969860

Dijkstra, H. (2017). Collusion in international organisations: How states benefit from the authority of secretariats. *Global Governance, 23*(4), 601–618.

Drezner, D.W. (2020). The song remains the same: International relations after Covid-19. *International Organization, 74,* E18–E35.

Easton, D. (1965). *A Framework for Political Analysis.* Prentice-Hall.

Eilstrup-Sangiovanni, M., & Hofmann, S.C. (2020) Of the contemporary global order, crisis, and change. *Journal of European Public Policy, 27*(7), 1077–1089. doi:10.1080/13 501763.2019.1678665.

EU (2021). *Digital Education Action Plan: Resetting Education and Training for the Digital Age.* European Union. https://ec.europa.eu/education/education-in-the-eu/digital-education-action-plan_en.

Farrell, H., & Newman, A. (2020). *Will Coronavirus End Globalization as We Know It? The Pandemic is Exposing Market Vulnerabilities No One Knew Existed.* Foreign Affairs. https://www.foreignaffairs.com/articles/2020-03-16/will-coronavirus-end-globalization-we-know-it.

Farrell, H., & Newman, A. (2021). *The New Age of Protectionism: Coronavirus 'Vaccine Wars' Could Herald a Broader Retreat from the Free Market.* Foreign Affairs. https://www.for-eignaffairs.com/articles/europe/2021-04-05/new-age-protectionism.

Finnemore, M. (2014). Dynamics of global governance: Building on what we know. *International Studies Quarterly, 58*(1), 221–224.

Fomerand, J.F. (2017). Evolution of international organization as institutional forms and historical processes since 1945: 'Quis custodiet ipsos custodies?'. In N. Sandal, & R. Marlin-Bennett (Eds.), *Oxford Research Encyclopedia of International Studies.* International Studies Association and Oxford University Press. doi:10.1093/acrefore/9780190846626.013.87.

Fricker, M. (2017). Evolving concepts of epistemic injustice. In I.J. Kidd, J. Medina, & G. Pohlhaus (Eds.), *The Routledge Handbook of Epistemic Injustice* (pp. 53–60). Taylor and Francis.

Gabriel, Y. (2015). Narratives and stories in organisational life. In A. De Fina, & A. Georgakopoulou (Eds.), *The Handbook of Narrative Analysis* (pp. 275–292). Wiley.

Hanushek, E.A., & Woessmann, L. (2020). *The Economic Impacts of Learning Losses. OECD Education Working Papers No. 225.* OECD. https://www.oecd.org/education/the-economic-impacts-of-learning-losses-21908d74-en.htm.

Hawkins, D.G., Lake, D.A., Nielson, D.L., and Tierney, M.J. (2006). Delegation under anarchy: States, international organizations, and principal–agent theory. In D.G. Hawkins, D.A. Lake, D.L. Nielson, & M.J. Tierney (Eds.), *Delegation and Agency in International Organizations* (pp. 3–38). Cambridge University Press.

Inayatullah, S. (2008). Mapping educational futures. In M. Bussey, S. Inayatullah, & I. Milojevic (Eds.), *Alternative Educational Futures: Pedagogies for Emergent Worlds* (pp. 13–39). Sense Publishers.

Jönsson, C. (2018). Theoretical approaches to international organization. In N. Sandal, & R. Marlin-Bennett (Eds.), *Oxford Research Encyclopedia of International Studies*. International Studies Association and Oxford University Press. doi:10.1093/acrefore/9780190846626.013.34.

Kallo, J. (2020). Epistemic culture of the OECD and its agenda for higher education. *Journal of Education Policy*. doi:10.1080/02680939.2020.1745897.

Koselleck, R. (2004). *Futures Past: On the Semantics of Historical Time*. Columbia University Press.

Krisch, N. (2017). Liquid authority in global governance. *International Theory, 9*(2), 237–260.

Martens, K., & Jakobi, A.P., Eds. (2010). *Mechanisms of OECD Governance*. Oxford University Press.

McNamara, K.R. (2020). The big reveal: COVID-19 and globalization's great transformations. *International Organization, 74*, E59–E77.

Moisio, S. (2018). *Geopolitics of the Knowledge-Based Economy*. Routledge.

Münch, R. (2020). *Governing the School Under Three Decades of Neoliberal Reform: From Educracy to the Education–Industrial Complex*. Routledge.

OECD. (2021). *Going for Growth. Shaping a Vibrant Recovery. Executive Summary*. OECD. https://www.oecd.org/economy/going-for-growth/.

Olsson, E.-K., & Verbeek, B. (2018). International organizations and crisis management: Do crises enable or constrain IO autonomy? *Journal of International Relations and Development, 21*(2), 275–299.

Peters, M. (2013). *Education, Science and Knowledge Capitalism: Creativity and the Promise of Openness*. Peter Lang.

Reimers, F., Schleicher, A., Saavedra, J., & Tuominen, S. (2020). *Supporting the Continuation of Teaching and Learning During the COVID-19 Pandemic*. OECD.

Rizvi F., & Lingard, B. (2009b). *Globalizing Education Policy*. Routledge.

Rizvi, F., & Peters, M. (2020). Reimagining the new pedagogical possibilities for universities post-Covid-19. Postscript: Covid-19, higher education, and new possibilities. *Educational Philosophy and Theory*. doi:10.1080/00131857.2020.1777655.

Rizvi, F.A., & Lingard, B. (2009a). The OECD and the global shifts in educational policy. In R. Cowen, A. Kazamias, & E. Unterhalter (Eds.), *International Handbook of Comparative Education* (pp. 437–453). Springer.

Robertson, S. (2019). Comparing platforms and the new value economy in the academy. In R. Gorur, S. Sellar, & G. Steiner-Khamsi (Eds.), *World Yearbook of Education 2019: Comparative Methodology in the Era of Big Data and Global Networks* (pp. 169–186). Routledge.

Shore, C., & Wright, S. (2017). Privatizing the public university: Key trends, countertrends and alternatives. In S. Wright, & C. Shore (Eds.), *Death of the Public University: Uncertain Futures for Higher Education in the Knowledge Economy* (pp. 1–27). Berghahn.

Slobodian, Q., & Plehwe, D. (2020). Introduction. In D. Plehwe, Q. Slobodian, & P. Mirowski (Eds.), *Nine Lives of Neoliberalism* (pp. 1–18). Verso.

Sorensen, T.B., Ydesen, C., & Robertson, S.L. (2021). Re-reading the OECD and education: The emergence of a global governing complex – An introduction. *Globalisation, Societies and Education, 19*(2), 99–107. doi:10.1080/14767724.2021.1897946.

Taylor, C. (2003). *Modern Social Imaginaries*. Duke University Press.

Titievskaja, J., Kononenko, V., Navarra, C., Starnegna, C., & Zurner, K. (2020). *Slowing Down or Changing Track? Understanding the Dynamics of 'Slowbalisation'*. In-Depth

Analysis, European Parliamentary Research Service. https://www.europarl.europa.eu/stoa/en/document/EPRS_IDA(2020)659383.

UIA (2021). *Yearbook of International Organizations.* Brill/Union of International Organisations. https://uia.org/yearbook.

Värri, V.-M. (2018). *Kasvatus Ekokriisin Aikakaudella [Education During the Era of Ecological Crisis].* Vastapaino.

Williamson, B., Bayne, S., & Shay, S. (2020). The datafication of teaching in higher education: Critical issues and perspectives. *Teaching in Higher Education, 25*(4), 351–365.

Zapp, M. (2021). The authority of science and the legitimacy of international organisations: OECD, UNESCO and World Bank in global education governance. *Compare: A Journal of Comparative and International Education, 51*(7), 1022–1041, doi:10.1080/03 057925.2019.1702503.

Zürn, M. 2017. From constitutional rule to loosely coupled spheres of liquid authority: A reflexive approach. *International Theory, 9*(2), 261–285.

5

EMERGENT DEVELOPMENTS IN THE DATAFICATION AND DIGITALIZATION OF EDUCATION

Steven Lewis, Jessica Holloway, and Bob Lingard

Introduction

The specific focus of this chapter is the increasing datafication of schooling, including emergent developments in datafication, over the past decade. Thus, it contributes to this edited collection's remit to reflect upon, describe and analyse developments in education, and particularly education *policy*, since the publication of *Globalizing Education Policy* (Rizvi & Lingard, 2010). As sociologists of education, we recognize that these datafication developments are both situated in and articulate changing contexts of varying kinds, specifically those since 2010. One central aspect has been evolving relations between local, national and global spaces of policy-making and enactment in education. Much has occurred in that respect over the last ten or so years, including the rise of new forms of nationalism that seek to challenge globalization (see Rizvi's chapter in this collection).

As Marianne Larsen and Jason Beech (2014) and Sobe (2015) have argued, we need to go beyond regarding these relations as the global affecting the national and local in a top-down, unidirectional way. Indeed, Larsen and Beech (2014) observe that "[p]lace as local and space as global constitute 'master categories' that have dominated much of the research on the impact of globalization on local communities and places" (p. 197). Rather, the relationships between place and space need to be seen as multidirectional; that is, simultaneously bottom-up *and* top-down, as well as involving innumerable lateral relations (e.g., local to local, regional to regional). Associated with this multidirectionality are the changing imbrications of global, national and local relations (Lingard, 2021). While such relationships might be seen to reflect the rescaling of education policy, another way to think about them is as emerging through relational, or *topological*, spaces and practices (see, for instance, Amin, 2002; Decuypere, 2021; Lewis, 2020; Lury et al., 2012), meaning

DOI: 10.4324/9781003207528-5

that relations (between people, places, processes etc.) can become as significant as location. The rise and rise of the datafication of education – the so-called data deluge, the substantive focus of this chapter – must, therefore, be seen against these changing contexts and approaches to understand the global/national/local imbrications in the production and enactment of education policy.

Datafication refers to the rendering as data various aspects of experience; here, various aspects of education policy, schooling, teachers' work and the life of students. This introduces an important and long-standing philosophical issue of whether all experiences linked to schooling can be, or even ought to be, datafied (see Zuboff, 2019). What is new, however, is that the digitalization of such data potentially enables machine learning, Artificial Intelligence (AI) and big data to enhance inferential causality in relation to the 'variables' working through schooling systems, and for these to play an enhanced role in policy production and enactment, as well as school- and classroom-level practices (see Gulson in this collection on AI and education policy). Digital data infrastructures are important here, as is the significant role of the private, for-profit, edtech companies and not-for-profit organizations that have entered these digitalized and datafied schooling and policy spaces. Additionally, we have witnessed growth of the involvement of new 'shadow professionals' (Lewis & Hartong, 2021) in education systems, including data scientists, technicians and statisticians, who now play an increasingly prominent role in education and education policy processes (see also Holloway, 2020; Williamson, 2017).

Datafication does not appear in the Index to *Globalizing Education Policy*, and yet a number of related concepts and ideas do: *accountability (test-based)*, *mutual accountability (through comparison)*, *testing* and *assessment*, as well as *national* and *international large-scale assessments*. *Audit-culture* appears, as does *performativity* and *commensurability*, which is necessary to the functioning of national and international large-scale assessments. Also in *Globalizing Education Policy*'s Index are *'policy as numbers'* and *statistics*. The latter, otherwise called 'state numbers,' have long been significant in policy and the administration of school systems. The idea of policy as numbers (Lingard, 2011; Rose, 1999) picks up on the increased significance of data in the governing of school systems, the focus of this chapter.

So, what has changed in respect of numbers, data and datafication since 2010? First, our computational capacities are evidently much greater, as is the sheer volume of data that can be and frequently are collected. Much more of the work of schooling systems, schools, and teachers has been datafied and (importantly) digitalized; these two processes enable vastly more complex analyses of the data being generated, which has significant implications for how such data can inform and shape education policy. Furthermore, there are two additional and very significant changes in respect of such data, which we take up in this chapter. The first is the potential move from the collection of discrete sets of data to the collection of continuous, real-time data. The second relates to the volume of data collected, a move we might describe as the transition from the collection of *sample data* to the collection of *census data*. The sheer quantity of these census data helps to constitute what has come to be known as *big data*, which in turn facilitates different kinds of statistical analyses that enhance the capacity for drawing causal inferences from data. What is also important across these developments is the construction of socio-technical data infrastructures that enable interoperability of data (Gulson & Sellar, 2019; Lingard, 2019; Sellar, 2015). We focus on these matters in this chapter and consider how datafication actively reconstitutes teachers (Holloway & Lewis, 2021; Lewis & Holloway, 2019) and students (Bradbury, 2019; Selwyn et al., 2021) alike, as well as more broadly shaping schooling processes, practices, systems and policy.

In what follows, we provide a brief overview of how we are defining and conceptualizing the datafication of education. We then move to consider the datafication of education across three key dimensions: (i) *datafied infrastructures*; (ii) *datafied bodies*; and (iii) *datafied modes of governance*. Finally, we conclude with some thoughts on the implications for education policy and the relationships between datafication of education and changing global–national–local relations and imbrications.

Conceptualizing the datafication of education

As with other public policy domains (e.g., health, policing) that are confronting unprecedented and often unseen influences of datafication, education has become a key target of the 'data deluge' (Kitchin, 2014). With these developments, data scientists, technicians and statisticians have secured an increasingly prominent role in helping determine educational policy-making, governance and practice. At the same time, schools are now also increasingly subject to external modes of accountability that rely upon, but also produce, new forms of data. These might include large-scale assessments used for measuring school performance, value-added models used for measuring teacher effectiveness and early-warning systems designed to pre-emptively identify 'at-risk' students, as well as many other quantifying instruments used for measuring the overall and relative quality of a schooling system, school, teacher or student. These tools are not necessarily new to education but they have morphed and adapted to now incorporate available technologies alongside the rest of the increasingly 'datafied' world (de Freitas et al., 2016; Kitchin, 2014). As such, our understandings of the human and the social – such as the teacher, the student and education itself – require significant shifts in our onto-epistemic approaches and assumptions (de Freitas et al., 2016).

While postmodern theorists, such as Michel Foucault, Jacques Derrida and Pierre Bourdieu, were foundational to what many identify as the 'discursive turn' in the social sciences, Julian de Freitas et al. (2016) argue that the 'computational turn' has instead leaned more heavily on the work of Gilles Deleuze and other new materialists. These more recent contributions stress that the more discursive focus of the former is no less relevant but that earlier critiques of 'scientism', along with post-positivism, have provided a foundation upon which new materialists can respond to the rapidly shifting conditions of the current moment. With this in mind, such approaches take the 'ontology of number' in new directions that can, arguably, better account for datafication and digitalization. In a similar way, we also see the theoretical tools that were present in *Globalizing Education Policy* – a trust in numbers (Porter, 1995), policy by numbers (Grek, 2009; Lingard, 2011; Ozga, 2016; Piattoeva et al., 2018; Rose, 1999), performativity (Lyotard, 1984), et cetera – are still relevant today. In a sense, what we are thus dealing with here is the simultaneity of Foucault's disciplinary society, most notably the panopticon of control through test-based modes of accountability (national and global), with the intensification of Deleuze's control society of continuous assessments, as evidenced in the move from discrete to continuous data collection and from sample to census data.

Datafying education: infrastructures, bodies and modes of governance

Contemporary society is now characterized by the ready (and, at times, inadvertent) participation of individuals and institutions in datafied practices across a variety of *intensive* (e.g., personal health and biometric data) and *extensive* (e.g., mass public surveillance, collection of telecommunication metadata) ways. This typifies Soshana Zuboff's (2019) 'surveillance capitalism,' Nick Couldry and Ulises Mejias's (2019) 'colonisation of human life' and Steffen Mau's (2019) 'metric society'. Data collection, collation, analysis and prediction – both 'in here' and 'out there' (Hong, 2020) – now occupies a central and pervasive significance across all manner of social domains, and the datafication of education is no exception to this trend. As such, we will now detail the three key dimensions that we consider central to the datafication of education: (i) *datafied infrastructures*; (ii) *datafied bodies*; and (iii) *datafied modes of governance*.

Datafied infrastructures

Significant to the ongoing datafication of education are the new infrastructures of people and practices emerging around the increasingly datafied monitoring of schools and schooling systems. This changes not only how schooling is practiced but also, and perhaps more fundamentally, how knowledge is produced about schools and schooling systems (Sellar, 2015). We employ the term *data infrastructures* here to describe the socio-technical assemblages (i.e., people and computing hardware/software) that laboriously translate things into data. These data, in turn, provide the means to 'fabricate' supposedly objective knowledge for the purpose of governance. The increasing relevance of these data to schools and schooling systems requires their efficient and effective organization as data infrastructures. This refers to the various objects and subjects assembled around data collection, storage, visualization, and mediation between otherwise disparate, diverse and disconnected actors and spaces (e.g., schools, districts, states, systems, countries, global spaces).

Residing largely in the realm of science fiction at the time *Globalizing Education Policy* (Rizvi & Lingard, 2010) was first published, the mass datafication of schooling has required the development of complex data infrastructures to provide a systematic means of collating, analyzing and acting upon these datafied renderings of people, places and processes. Consider, for instance, the diverse data that schools and teachers collect on a daily basis. These ranges from the pedagogical, such as formative appraisals of student learning, to more formalized instances of measuring student performance on standardized tests. In addition, there are more prosaic administrative inputs that record student attendance, disciplinary infractions and class sizes. These data might have some relevance for a teacher or school administrator at the moment and site of their production but their explanatory power is significantly enhanced when such data are recombined with vast quantities of other such data generated by a given classroom, school or schooling system. This is the substantive role of data infrastructures, regardless of whether the scope and scale are more national (e.g., the *MySchool* database of school performance in Australia) or international (e.g., *Education GPS* of the OECD) in nature.

Taken collectively, these processes of data *infrastructuring* (Hartong & Piattoeva, 2021; Piattoeva & Saari, 2019) are especially significant for their ability to enable new types of datafied knowledge and, relatedly, datafied professionals, including the emergence of new professional roles and responsibilities associated with data management in schools and schooling systems (see Lewis & Hartong, 2021). This not only concerns who is allowed to produce and, particularly, decide on the quality and types of monitoring data. It also affects how these (inter)actions produce and, increasingly, normalize new datafied spaces of data measurement and governance (see, for instance, Gulson & Sellar, 2019; Hartong, 2018; Lewis et al., 2016). As Gulson and Sellar (2019, p. 350) note, the datafication of schooling has led to "changing relations of power and space in education." This reflects the escalating imbrication of the social and technical characters of digital infrastructures, where standardizing languages and expectations around data helps to bridge the distance between the technical and the human to make data legible, usable and influential. Moreover, we can see evidence of a broader logic that suggests education, teaching and learning can – and, moreover, *should* – be measured, and that policy and practice decisions should then be made on the basis of these data.

Such a focus on data also reflects a significant shift in priorities. Optimizing *data flows* within the infrastructure has become a primary concern of those who seek to know and govern schooling systems (Clutterbuck et al., 2021; Hartong & Förschler, 2019; Lewis & Hartong, 2021), rather than, for instance, the actual pedagogical practices and learning outcomes of the teachers and students notionally represented by these data. In agreement with Martin Lawn (2013, p. 8), who argues that "the creation and flow of data has become a powerful governing tool in education," we would argue the underpinning logic of a data infrastructure is its emphasis upon data flows. Put differently, the ability of data to flow in multiple directions (i.e., from places of creation to places of use, from producers to consumers, and on to subsequent consumers) becomes the definitional purpose of the infrastructure, inso-far as it enables relevant sites, people and practices to be joined to one another. This also means, however, that the data infrastructure is, both materially and figuratively, coterminous with the systems, spaces and people that it represents and enables. If data are unable to be collected from or sent to a certain person or place, then these people and places are, by definition, *excluded* from the infrastructure. The datafied space of the infrastructure is thus inscribed as perceptible, knowable and governable (Easterling, 2014; Hartong, 2018); that is, it is rendered 'real' and amenable to action.

In other words, understanding a data infrastructure's relational spatiality means con-sidering how the ongoing *flow-ability* (Lewis & Hartong, 2021) of data and ongoing processes of re/de/bordering (Mezzadra & Neilson, 2012; Robertson, 2011; Scheel, 2020; van de Oudeweetering & Decuypere, 2019) work together to constitute new spaces and relations of policymaking and governance. This is how data flows work in relation to the changing imbrications and directionalities of global–national–local relations in education policy referred to earlier. As Saskia Sassen (2007) has observed, globalization might be thought of as the creation of global infrastructures. An example in education is the ways in which international, large-scale assessments, such as the OECD's PISA, have constituted the globe as a commensurate space of measurement, based on the comparative performance of national schooling systems. Reflecting Rob Kitchin's (2014) argument that data assemblages are themselves onto-genetic, we see data infrastructures as constituting schooling spaces (i.e., *ontologically*), as well as defining the types of knowledge, expertise and discourses that are valued and authorized within those spaces (i.e., *epistemically*). Although these infrastructural spaces overlap with the other social spaces that data are derived from or fed back into, they are still signifi-cant because they comprise new relations and interactions that would otherwise be unavailable without the infrastructure (Gulson & Sellar, 2019, p. 359).

Finally, it is necessary to consider how the various aspects of schooling perfor-mance, student learning and teachers' work captured as data are then translated into a format legible to the digital infrastructure. Via 'aesthetic practices' that "purg[e] data of inconsistencies, differences and uncertainties" (Ratner & Ruppert, 2019, p. 2), data are not only made 'clean' (i.e., accurate), but are rendered in a form amenable to their ultimate use (e.g., informing decisions on teacher performance, visualizing improvement over time). These translational practices acknowledge the subjective 'messiness' of data and attempt to ensure that the data infrastructures read and make sense of data in the same way. It is arguably these 'little analytical devices' (Amoore & Piotukh, 2015) – akin to what Lawn (2013) describes as the 'hidden managers' of educational systems – that help to make big data perceptible and usable for purposes of knowing and governing social domains such as education.

Datafied bodies

One of the most significant sites implicated in the datafication of education today is that of the body. There are many types of 'body' that can be thought about here: *human bodies*, such as those of students and teachers; *professional bodies*, such as professional teacher organizations and teacher regulatory bodies; and *bodies of data*. For the purposes of this chapter, we are particularly interested in how datafication shifts the site of surveillance and control from human bodies to bodies of data. We use the case of the teacher for illustrative purposes, arguing that digital technologies have ushered in a suite of possibilities regarding how, and to what ends, teachers are both disciplined and controlled.

With digital technologies that enable the constant collection and observation of countless forms of data, the inspectoral gaze is cast upon both *human* and *data* forms of bodies to define, predict and respond to schooling matters. Over the years, policy by numbers and algorithms have progressively expanded and, in doing so, have thoroughly remade the teacher in the image of data (Lewis & Holloway, 2019). As many have argued over the past few decades, teachers and students have been subjected to, and subjects of, increasingly ubiquitous modes of quantification, evaluation and comparison. This was a fundamental argument in *Globalizing Education Policy* (Rizvi and Lingard, 2010), and it continues to be a central feature of schooling systems across countries to this day (Lingard, et al., 2017; Sellar et al., 2022; Verger et al., 2019). With various stated aims that include, for example, improving standards, quality and effectiveness of school performance, or elevating what some consider the professionalism of teachers, accountability has served as a notional solution to a myriad of 'wicked' problems. While the technical elements of accountability might look different across contexts, the logics that underpin such systems and discourses are nearly always the same. These techniques typically rely on modes of surveillance, examination and comparison to incentivize teachers and students to perform in desirable ways. Within each of these technologies, the physical body is the primary site of inspection and discipline.

Drawing on Foucault's governmentality, technologies of the self, panopticism and normalization (to name but a few), scholars have compellingly illustrated how techniques of, in particular, top-down, test-based, accountability have disciplined teachers. Teachers have been drilled to compete against themselves and their colleagues, comply with standards and performative demands, and adopt a spirit of continuous growth (Holloway, 2019; Perryman, 2009; Perryman et al., 2017; Wilkins, 2011). Indeed, the notion of teachers being deemed 'risky' subjects (Hardy, 2015; Holloway, 2019) has itself become dominant within high-stakes accountability regimes and political rhetoric. With this, teachers are discursively positioned as potential impediments to future student performance and national economic prosperity, and in need of policy interventions that might mitigate such risks. In doing so, the teacher's body serves as a site of the inspectoral gaze and is thus always exposed to scrutiny – real or perceived.

The teacher's body also serves as the site of intervention. Under threats of inspection, demotion, or public shame, the teacher is compelled to perform as a particular kind of teacher who sees metrics, competition and data-driven dispositions as valuable (and necessary) characteristics of 'good' teaching (Holloway,

2019; Thompson & Cook, 2014). The classroom is no longer the unique professional domain of the teacher, but is rather the fishbowl that exposes them to constant observation and auditing from evaluators and peers. Open-door policies, formal observations of lessons, and regular one-on-one conferences between appraisers and teachers locate the teacher's body as the exposure site of accountability. Teachers' thoughts about teaching are also no longer free from observation. Required submission of lesson plans and self-assessments are only some of the ways that teachers' opinions and beliefs have become objects of inspection, making legible the teachers' inner deliberations about their practice and sense of being. In this way, the teachers' practice is transformed but so too are their bodies, minds and souls (see Ball, 2003; Foucault, 1977).

Following such logics, compliance-based teacher accountability has become increasingly prevalent in schooling systems around the globe. At the same time, this accountability is particularly challenging to teacher professionalism. Modes of standardization, quantification and evaluation have narrowed the possibilities for teachers to rely on their professional knowledge, training, and experience (Hardy, 2021; Lewis & Holloway, 2019). Rather, teachers face increased pressure to employ numerical data (for example, from standardized literacy and numeracy tests), evaluative tools (for example, observation rubrics), and prescriptive definitions of 'what works' (Lewis, 2017, 2020) to guide their pedagogical decisions and classroom practices (Bradbury & Roberts-Holmes, 2017). While these continue to be central mechanisms for steering schools, teachers and students, the environment has been thoroughly (re)shaped by digital technologies and logics that produce entirely new conditions and possibilities. Within the digital milieu, the teacher's body continues as a site of inspection and discipline, yet the teacher's *body of data* – captured, analyzed, observed and acted upon within the digital domain – creates a new site for the inspectoral gaze.

As various parts of accountability systems migrate to digital platforms, new possibilities have emerged regarding how and to what end school subjects are monitored and acted upon (see also Manokha, 2018). Building from our argument in the previous section on data infrastructures, the digital storage and reporting of student and teacher data have created exponential growth in what and how many categories of judgment can be captured within schools and classrooms. Now, the human body is not only an object of surveillance and intervention. These same corporeal bodies are tracked and measured to amass digital *bodies of data* that shift the inspectoral gaze from classrooms to online algorithmic predictions, outputs and comparisons. While it might be tempting to view these *data-proxies* (Smith, 2016) as true representations of human bodies, the datafied body is fabricated through the data techniques and technologies available in a given context. As we know, this is always subject to the social, political, economic and historical conditions of a particular time and place.

Sometimes referred to as *dataveillance* or *liquid surveillance* (Bauman & Lyon, 2013), digital platforms create new spaces, relations and possibilities for inspection, auditing, appraisal and intervention. While teachers have been subject to metrics and constant observation for decades, the digital shift means that teachers' data can now be observed more often, by more people and from remote locations. For example, while the observation of a teacher's practice previously required someone to be inside the classroom (or else peer through a window), teacher's data that are stored electronically on a digital platform can be observed by anyone with the access code (e.g., principals, curriculum coaches, district leaders, state leaders, etc.). As technology evolves, new motivations and means for capturing various classroom events emerge. The disruptions from COVID-19, for example, have triggered an onslaught of techniques for measuring everything from online behaviors (psychodata), like scrolling speeds and mouse clicks, to remote proctoring services that watch students take exams online.

The other point we need to make here, and this links to the simultaneity of Foucault's discipline and Deleuze's control society, is that there is the possibility now for real-time, continuous surveillance of teachers and classrooms, beyond the collection of discrete, point-in-time data. The former disciplinary usage of data is extant now in most schooling systems, while the latter is still (largely) an emergent development.

Datafied modes of governance

Despite their apparently contemporary nature, datafied understandings of schools and schooling are arguably but the latest manifestation of governance processes that have long sought to know and govern education via numbers and data. Indeed, we can see this in the very origin of statistics as 'state numbers' (Rose, 1999), whereby statistics and society are both mutually known and brought into existence through 'the very act of counting' (Sætnan et al., 2011, p. 1). The thoroughly constitutive nature of such processes reflects that numerical data, far from providing an objective measure of some empirical reality, are instead deeply implicated in constructing the very phenomena they seek to measure (see Desrosières, 1998). Such logics are also evident in processes of evidence-informed policymaking (Head, 2008; Lingard, 2013), where numbers can be used to provide putatively objective 'facts' for the legitimation of policy decisions. In this way, the increasing datafication of bodies *as data*, as well as the accompanying processes of infrastructuring that have sought to arrange, format and make available these *bodies of data* as usable pieces of quantified information (Gulson & Sellar, 2019; Hartong & Piattoeva, 2021), have facilitated datafied modes of digital educational governance to emerge (Gulson et al., 2022; Williamson, 2017).

We see these developments as paralleling earlier shifts from professionally oriented modes of educational accountability that operated during the post-war, bureaucratic, welfare state, as well as more recent moves toward performative modes of accountability associated with the 'audit society' and neoliberal forms of governance (Lingard et al., 2017). This includes a significant increase in data collection, analysis and use in education globally, with numerical data now entrusted to define, measure, compare and govern the performance of students, teachers, schools and schooling systems alike (Ozga, 2016). We have thus seen an evolution of what has previously been described as policy and governance by numbers (Grek, 2009; Lingard, 2011; Rose, 1999), which enabled understandings of teacher performance to be steered in certain data-centric ways. And even while putatively 'objective' numerical measurements might be used to legitimize school or system-level policy decisions, they also clearly influence how individual teachers come to enact and value certain pedagogical practices, logics and dispositions over others (see, for instance, Hardy, 2021; Holloway & Brass, 2018; Lewis & Holloway, 2019).

Despite the pervasiveness of numerical data, we are not suggesting that the governance of schools and schooling is now determined *solely* by numbers. One need only consider recent theorizations of educational governance – such as governing by *examples* (Simons, 2015), *'best practices'* (Auld & Morris, 2016; Lewis, 2017), *national reviews* (Gorur, 2017), *socialization through reviews* (Grek, 2017), *comparison* (Nóvoa & Yariv-Mashal, 2003) and *expertise* (Grek, 2013; Lingard, 2016) – to see how these shifts in governance are, in fact, far from 'exclusively based and dependent upon the cold rationality of numbers' (Grek, 2017, p. 295). Nevertheless, these more qualitative configurations of evidence still often reference, and even complement, existing numerical data. For instance, qualitative examples of 'what works' are arguably most valued for their ability to 'improve' numerical forms of performance data (see, for instance, Lewis, 2017). Regardless of the accompanying qualitative practices, datafication has seen the unprecedented growth and use of *digital* forms of (big) data in educational governance, expressed as increasing the *volume*, *velocity*, and *variety* of data (the 'three Vs') and reflecting the 'apparent power, agential capacity and control that algorithms command of our lives' (Neyland, 2015, p. 199). In short, datafication and data infra-structuring enable an unprecedented number of people (e.g., students, teachers), institutions (e.g., schools, schooling systems) and processes (e.g., learning, pedagogy, improvement) to now be rendered as digital data, and for these data to subsequently inform decision-making around how education is understood, practiced and governed.

That being said, it is the increasingly digital(ized) nature of education data that makes datafied modes of educational governance such a stark departure from earlier forms of governance predicated on numbers. As Williamson (2016, p. 5) has observed, "[t]he monitoring and management of educational systems, institutions and individuals is taking place through digital systems that are normally considered part of the backdrop to conventional policy instruments and techniques of government." While the shift, broadly speaking, from analog to digital methods of collecting, collating and acting upon education data might merely seem a difference of degrees, new(er) types of data and analyses made possible by this move to the digital are far more substantive, and extend now well beyond the simple digitization of teacher gradebooks or student attendance. Indeed, the move from analog technologies to digital technologies (Lynch, 2015) introduces the mediation of human activity and judgment by digital software; that is, the apps, algorithms, data dashboards and statistical packages that collect and analyse data, transforming otherwise disparate and unrelated data points into authoritative correlations and compelling graphical visualizations (Decuypere, 2021; Gulson et al., 2022; Lewis, 2020). Like their earlier numerical precedents, these digital educational infrastructures remain far from objective, and instead constitute active governing devices inscribed with subjective visions of what good education, teaching and learning ought to be. As such, they do not neutrally represent educational actors (e.g., in the form of digital datasets) but, instead, actively constitute and change the actors in question and help bring them into being (Grommé & Ruppert, 2019; Hartong & Piattoeva, 2021; Jarke & Breiter, 2019).

Embedded within the digitalization of education data and systems is the wholesale move from the *discrete* to the *continuous*. Put differently, this is a move from isolated and disconnected instances of students, teachers, schools and schooling systems generating data at particular times (e.g., during annual standardized assessments) to the ability for data to be collected and analyzed on an almost continuous real-time basis and volume. Moreover, student performance data are now no longer physically recorded in teacher gradebooks or office filing cabinets that require individual in-person viewing. Rather, the shift to digital data enables remote access by teachers, as well as school- and system-level managers, via digital platforms, irrespective of time or distance from the site of data generation. Data can then be manipulated and parsed in vast quantities, not only for the purpose of auditing past performance but also, importantly, to generate speculative or predictive analytics of *future performance*, which constitutes a mode of anticipatory governance (Gulson et al., 2022). These developments are reflected in the widespread adoption by education systems of early-warning systems that monitor student progress and predict future performance to enable early intervention by teachers or other education stakeholders (see Jokhan et al., 2019).

While risk aversion and management have arguably been long-standing features of education systems (Hardy, 2015; Holloway, 2019), the predictive analytics made possible by digital data allows these practices to take place on an altogether different (temporal) scope and scale. Governance now frequently adopts an anticipatory posture, rather than being concerned with retrospective audit (Anderson, 2010; Gulson et al., 2022). Such 'technologies of speculation' (Hong, 2020) thereby risk subsuming the significance of intimately understanding and engaging with local context and people in the present to the (decontextualized) management of future data and system futures.

Concluding thoughts: the implications of datafication for education policy

There are a number of summative points we want to stress in this conclusion. The first is that, while numbers (and specifically statistics) have always been central to the management and administration of schooling systems since their creation, datafication and digitalization have significantly changed modes of governance in education. We now have far greater computational capacity and are thus able to collect much larger amounts of data. Potentially, we are able, through the digitalization of such data, to collect real-time, continuous data from classrooms. Yet, as we have noted, systems continue to collect discrete, point-in-time data for accountability purposes, changing the modes of accountability that teachers and schools are now subject to from earlier inspection models, although these continue synchronously with the new modes in some systems (e.g., England). This has predominantly been top-down, test-based accountability, where teachers and schools have been held to account by student performance data and improvement agendas, sometimes through so-called value-added models. As we have also noted, there is now the possibility for another distinct move to the collection of continuous real-time data, indicative perhaps of a move from a disciplinary to a control society. The latter approaches are only emergent in most school systems, and we would suggest these will work synchronously with the more extant mode of data use in systems.

While we have yet to see the wholesale replacement of more traditional schooling systems and their bureaucracies with modes of data-driven governance, there are now multiple spaces of educational governance, as well as residual, dominant and emergent modes linked to inspection, statistics, datafication and digitalization. Some of this is perhaps evident in a recent argument by Neil Selwyn (2021), who notes that there remain tensions in schools between a data-driven system and the tempering of such institutional data logics by teacher professionalism. However, we would argue that the research evidence used in Selwyn's analysis also clearly demonstrates how discourses associated with systemic data logics now centrally position teachers and their work. In terms of education policy, there is also the possibility that educational problems identified by datafication will become the focus of policy to the neglect of other important matters that remain outside the purview of the data/digital gaze. We are possibly witnessing the datafication of the policy cycle in education in terms of what gets onto the policy agenda, how policy is produced and responds, and how these matters are implemented and evaluated.

The final point we want to make is in respect of changing global–national–local relations in the policy cycle from agenda-setting through to enactment and evaluation. The creation of global and national data infrastructures in education enables education policy to work in and across these spaces, part of the new spatialities of globalization. These relations, though, are no longer simply unidirectional from the global to the national and then to the local. In a sense, that was the focus in *Globalizing Education Policy*, emphasizing the need to challenge methodological nationalism in policy sociology in education. Rather, we need to acknowledge that while the OECD can certainly reach into national spaces, the local can now similarly 'reach out' to the global. Consider, for instance, schools directly participating in PISA for Schools (Lewis et al., 2016), or a Prefecture in Japan that has worked with the OECD to influence national policy in Japan (Takayama & Lingard, 2021). The datafication and digitalization of schooling have enabled these topological policy developments, thereby expressing and responding to the multiple spaces and geographies of contemporary education policy-making.

References

Amin, A. (2002). Spatialities of globalisation. *Environment and Planning A, 34*(3), 385–399. doi:10.1068/a3439.

Amoore, L., & Piotukh, V. (2015). Life beyond big data: Governing with little analytics. *Economy and Society, 44*(3), 341–366. doi:10.1080/03085147.2015.1043793.

Anderson, B. (2010). Preemption, precaution, preparedness: Anticipatory action and future geographies. *Progress in Human Geography, 34*(6), 777–798. doi:10.1177/0309132510362600.

Auld, E., & Morris, P. (2016). PISA, policy and persuasion: Translating complex conditions into education 'best practice'. *Comparative Education, 52*(2), 202–229. doi:10.1080/03 050068.2016.1143278.

Ball, S. (2003). The teacher's soul and the terrors of performativity. *Journal of Education Policy, 18*(2), 215–228. doi:10.1080/0268093022000043065.

Bauman, Z., & Lyon, D. (2013). *Liquid Surveillance: A Conversation*. Polity Press.

Bradbury, A. (2019). Datafied at four: The role of data in the 'schoolification' of early childhood education in England. *Learning, Media and Technology, 44*(1), 7–21. doi:10.1080/17439884.2018.1511577.

Bradbury, A., & Roberts-Holmes, G. (2017). *The Datafication of Primary and Early-Years Education: Playing With Numbers*. Routledge.

Clutterbuck, J., Hardy, I., & Creagh, S. (2021). Data infrastructures as sites of preclusion and omission: The representation of students and schooling. *Journal of Education Policy*, 1–22. doi:10.1080/02680939.2021.1972166.

Couldry, N., & Mejias, U. A. (2019). *The Costs of Connection*. Stanford University Press.

de Freitas, E. (2017). The temporal fabric of research methods: Posthuman social science and the digital data deluge. *Research in Education, 98*(1), 27–43. doi:10.1177/0034523717723386.

de Freitas, E., & Dixon-Román, E. (2017). The computational turn in education research: Critical and creative perspectives on the digital data deluge. *Research in Education, 98*(1), 3–13. doi:10.1177/0034523717723384.

de Freitas, E., Dixon-Román, E., & Lather, P. (2016). Alternative ontologies of number: Rethinking the quantitative in computational culture. *Cultural Studies ↔ Critical Methodologies, 16*(5), 431–434. doi:10.1177/1532708616655759.

Decuypere, M. (2021). The topologies of data practices: A methodological introduction. *Journal of New Approaches in Educational Research, 9*(2), 67–84. doi:10.7821/naer.2021.1.650.

Desrosières, A. (1998). *The Politics of Large Numbers* (C. Nash, Trans.). Harvard University Press.

Easterling, K. (2014). *Extrastatecraft: The Power of Infrastructure Space*. Verso.

Foucault, M. (1977). *Discipline and Punish: The Birth of the Prison* (A. Sheridan, Trans.). Pantheon Books

Gorur, R. (2017). Statistics and statecraft: Exploring the potentials, politics and practices of international educational assessment. *Critical Studies in Education, 58*(3), 261–265. doi:1 0.1080/17508487.2017.1353271.

Grek, S. (2009). Governing by numbers: The PISA 'effect' in Europe. *Journal of Education Policy, 24*(1), 23–37. doi:10.1080/02680930802412669.

Grek, S. (2013). Expert moves: International comparative testing and the rise of expertocracy. *Journal of Education Policy, 28*(5), 695–709. doi:10.1080/02680939.2012.758825.

Grek, S. (2017). Socialisation, learning and the OECD's Reviews of National Policies for Education: The case of Sweden. *Critical Studies in Education, 58*(3), 295–310. doi:10.10 80/17508487.2017.1337586.

Grommé, F., & Ruppert, E. (2019). Population geometries of Europe: The topologies of data cubes and grids. *Science, Technology, & Human Values, 45*(2), 235–261. doi:10.1177/0162243919835302.

Gulson, K., & Sellar, S. (2019). Emerging data infrastructures and the new topologies of education policy. *Environment and Planning D: Society and Space, 37*(2), 350–366. doi:10.1177/0263775818813144.

Gulson, K., Sellar, S., & Webb, T. (2022). *Algorithms of Education*. University of Minnesota Press.

Hardy, I. (2015). Education as a 'risky business': Theorising student and teacher learning in complex times. *British Journal of Sociology of Education, 36*(3), 375–394. doi:10.1080 /01425692.2013.829746.

Hardy, I. (2021). The quandary of quantification: Data, numbers and teachers' learning. *Journal of Education Policy, 36*(1), 44–63. doi:10.1080/02680939.2019.1672211.

Hartong, S. (2018). Towards a topological re-assemblage of education policy? Observing the implementation of performance data infrastructures and 'centers of calculation' in Germany. *Globalisation, Societies and Education, 16*(1), 134–150. doi:10.1080/1476772 4.2017.1390665.

Hartong, S., & Förschler, A. (2019). Opening the black box of data-based school monitoring: Data infrastructures, flows and practices in state education agencies. *Big Data & Society, 6*(1), 1–12. doi:10.1177/2053951719853311.

Hartong, S., & Piattoeva, N. (2021). Contextualising the datafication of schooling: A comparative discussion of Germany and Russia. *Critical Studies in Education, 62*(2), 227–242. doi:10.1080/17508487.2019.1618887.

Head, B. W. (2008). Three lenses of evidence-based policy. *Australian Journal of Public Administration, 67*(1), 1–11. doi:10.1111/j.1467-8500.2007.00564.x.

Holloway, J. (2019). Risky teachers: Mitigating risk through high-stakes teacher evaluation in the USA. *Discourse: Studies in the Cultural Politics of Education, 40*(3), 399–411. doi:1 0.1080/01596306.2017.1322938.

Holloway, J. (2020). Teacher accountability, datafication and evaluation: A case for reimagining schooling. *Education Policy Analysis Archives, 28*(56), 1–12. doi:10.14507/epaa.28.5026.

Holloway, J., & Brass, J. (2018). Making accountable teachers: The terrors and pleasures of performativity. *Journal of Education Policy, 33*(3), 361–382. doi:10.1080/02680939.201 7.1372636.

Holloway, J., & Lewis, S. (2021). Datafication and surveillance capitalism: The Texas Teacher Evaluation and Support System (T-TESS). In C. Wyatt-Smith, C. Wyatt-Smith, B. Lingard, & E. Heck (Eds.), *Digital Disruption in Teaching and Testing: Assessments, Big Data, and the Transformation of Schooling* (pp. 152–165). Routledge. doi:10.4324/9781003045793-9.

Hong, S. (2020). *Technologies of Speculation: The Limits of Knowledge in a Data-Driven Society.* NYU Press.

Jarke, J., & Breiter, A. (2019). Editorial: The datafication of education. *Learning, Media and Technology, 44*(1), 1–6. doi:10.1080/17439884.2019.1573833.

Jokhan, A., Sharma, B., & Singh, S. (2019). Early warning system as a predictor for student performance in higher education blended courses. *Studies in Higher Education, 44*(11), 1900–1911. doi:10.1080/03075079.2018.1466872.

Kitchin, R. (2014). Big Data, new epistemologies and paradigm shifts. *Big Data & Society, 1*(1), 1–12. doi:10.1177/2053951714528481.

Larsen, M., & Beech, J. (2014). Spatial theorising in comparative and international education research. *Comparative Education Review, 58*(2), 191–214. doi:10.1086/675499.

Lawn, M. (Ed.). (2013). *The Rise of Data in Education Systems: Collection, Visualisation and Use.* Symposium Books.

Lewis, S. (2017). Governing schooling through 'what works': The OECD's PISA for Schools. *Journal of Education Policy, 32*(3), 281–302. doi:10.1080/02680939.2016.1252855.

Lewis, S. (2020). *PISA, Policy and the OECD: Respatialising Global Educational Governance through PISA for Schools.* Springer Nature. doi:10.1007/978-981-15-8285-1.

Lewis, S., & Hartong, S. (2021). New shadow professionals and infrastructures around the datafied school: Topological thinking as an analytical device. *European Educational Research Journal,* 1–15. doi:10.1177/14749041211007496.

Lewis, S., & Holloway, J. (2019). Datafying the teaching 'profession': Remaking the professional teacher in the image of data. *Cambridge Journal of Education, 49*(1), 35–51. doi:10.1080/0305764x.2018.1441373.

Lewis, S., Sellar, S., & Lingard, B. (2016). 'PISA for Schools': Topological rationality and new spaces of the OECD's global educational governance. *Comparative Education Review, 60*(1), 27–57. doi:10.1086/684458.

Lingard, B. (2011). Policy as numbers: Ac/counting for educational research. *The Australian Educational Researcher, 38*(4), 355–382. doi:10.1007/s13384-011-0041-9.

Lingard, B. (2013). The impact of research on education policy in an era of evidence-based policy. *Critical Studies in Education, 54*(2), 113–131. doi:10.1080/17508487.2013.781515.

Lingard, B. (2016). Think tanks, 'policy experts' and 'ideas for' education policy making in Australia. *The Australian Educational Researcher, 43*(1), 15–33. doi:10.1007/s13384-015-0193-0.

Lingard, B. (2019). The global education industry, data infrastructures, and the restructuring of government school systems. In M. Parreira do Amaral, G. Steiner-Khamsi, & C. Thompson (Eds.), *Researching the Global Education Industry* (pp. 135–155). Springer.

Lingard, B. (2021). Globalisation and education: Theorizing and resaching changing imbrications in education. In B. Lingard (Ed.), *Globalisation and Education* (pp. 1–27). Routledge.

Lingard, B., Sellar, S., & Lewis, S. (2017). Accountabilities in schools and school systems. In G. Noblit (Ed.), *Oxford Research Encyclopedia of Education* (pp. 1–28). Oxford University Press. doi:10.1093/acrefore/9780190264093.013.74.

Lury, C., Parisi, L., & Terranova, T. (2012). Introduction: The becoming topological of culture. *Theory, Culture & Society, 29*(4–5), 3–35. doi:10.1177/0263276412454552.

Lynch, T. (2015). *The Hidden Role of Software in Educational Research: Policy to Practice.* Routledge.

Lyotard, J.-F. (1984). *The Postmodern Condition: A Report on Knowledge* (G. Bennington, & B. Massumi, Trans.). Manchester University Press.

Manokha, I. (2018). Surveillance, panopticism and self-discipline in the digital age. *Surveillance & Society, 16*(2), 219–237. doi:10.24908/ss.v16i2.8346.

Mau, S. (2019). *The Metric Society: On the Quantification of the Social.* Wiley.

Mezzadra, S., & Neilson, B. (2012). Between inclusion and exclusion: On the topology of global space and borders. *Theory, Culture & Society, 29*(4–5), 58–75. doi:10.1177/0263276412443569.

Neyland, D. (2015). On organizing algorithms. *Theory, Culture & Society, 32*(1), 119–132. doi:10.1177/0263276414530477.

Nóvoa, A., & Yariv-Mashal, T. (2003). Comparative research in education: A mode of governance or a historical journey? *Comparative Education, 39*(4), 423–438. doi:10.1080/0305006032000162002.

Ozga, J. (2016). Trust in numbers? Digital education governance and the inspection process. *European Educational Research Journal, 15*(1), 69–81. doi:10.1177/1474904115616629.

Perryman, J. (2009). Inspection and the fabrication of professional and performative processes. *Journal of Education Policy, 24*(5), 611–631. doi:10.1080/02680930903125129.

Perryman, J., Ball, S. J., Braun, A., & Maguire, M. (2017). Translating policy: Governmentality and the reflective teacher. *Journal of Education Policy, 32*(6), 745–756. doi:10.1080/026 80939.2017.1309072.

Piattoeva, N., Centeno, V. G., Suominen, O., & Rinne, R. (2018). Governance by data circulation? The production, availability, and use of national large-scale assessment data. In J. Kauko, R. Rinne, & T. Takala (Eds.), *Politics of Quality in Education: A Comparative Study of Brazil, China, and Russia* (pp. 115–136). Routledge.

Piattoeva, N., & Saari, A. (2019). The infrastructures of objectivity in standardised testing. In B. Maddox (Ed.), *International Large-Scale Assessments nn Education: Insider Research Perspectives* (pp. 53–68). Bloomsbury Academic.

Porter, T. (1995). *Trust in Numbers: The Pursuit of Objectivity in Science and Public Life.* Princeton University Press.

Ratner, H., & Ruppert, E. (2019). Producing and projecting data: Aesthetic practices of government data portals. *Big Data & Society, 6*(2). doi:10.1177/2053951719853316.

Rizvi, F., & Lingard, B. (2010). *Globalising Education Policy.* Routledge.

Robertson, S. L. (2011). The new spatial politics of (re)bordering and (re)ordering the state-education-citizen relation. *International Review of Education, 57*(3–4), 277–297. doi:10.1007/s11159-011-9216-x.

Rose, N. (1999). *Powers of Freedom: Reframing Political Thought.* Cambridge University Press.

Sætnan, A. R., Lomell, H. M., & Hammer, S. (2011). Introduction: By the very act of counting: The mutual construction of statistics and society. In A. R. Saetnan, H. M. Lomell, & S. Hammer (Eds.), *The Mutual Construction of Statistics and Society* (pp. 1–17). Routledge.

Sassen, S. (2007). *A Sociology of Globalisation.* W. W. Norton and Company.

Scheel, S. (2020). Biopolitical bordering: Enacting populations as intelligible objects of government. *European Journal of Social Theory, 23*(4), 571–590. doi:10.1177/1368431019900096.

Sellar, S. (2015). Data infrastructure: A review of expanding accountability systems and large-scale assessments in education. *Discourse: Studies in the Cultural Politics of Education, 36*(5), 765–777. doi:10.1080/01596306.2014.931117.

Sellar, S., Lingard, B., & Sant, E. (2022) In the name of the nation: PISA and federalism in Australia and Canada. In D. Trohler, N. Piattoeva, & W. F. Pinar (Eds.), *World Yearbook of Education 2022: Education, Schooling and the Global Universalization of Nationalism* (pp. 153–168). Routledge.

Selwyn, N. (2021). "There is a danger we get too robotic": An investigation of institutional data logics within secondary schools. *Educational Review*, 1–17. doi:10.1080/0013191 1.2021.1931039.

Selwyn, N., Pangrazio, L., & Cumbo, B. (2021). Knowing the (datafied) student: The production of the student subject through school data. *British Journal of Educational Studies*, 1–17. doi:10.1080/00071005.2021.1925085.

Simons, M. (2015). Governing education without reform: The power of the example. *Discourse: Studies in the Cultural Politics of Education*, *36*(5), 712–731. doi:10.1080/015 96306.2014.892660.

Smith, G. J. D. (2016). Surveillance, data and embodiment. *Body & Society*, *22*(2), 108–139. doi:10.1177/1357034x15623622.

Sobe, N. W. (2015). All that is global is not world culture: Accountability systems and educational apparatuses. *Globalisation, Societies and Education*, *13*(1), 135–148. doi:10.1080 /14767724.2014.967501.

Takayama, K., & Lingard, B. (2021). How to achieve a 'revolution': Assembling the subnational, national and global in the formation of a new, 'scientific' assessment in Japan. *Globalisation, Societies and Education*, *19*(2), 228–244. doi:10.1080/14767724.2021.1878016.

Thompson, G., & Cook, I. (2014). Manipulating the data: Teaching and NAPLAN in the control society. *Discourse: Studies in the Cultural Politics of Education*, *35*(1), 129–142. doi :10.1080/01596306.2012.739472.

van de Oudeweetering, K., & Decuypere, M. (2019). Understanding openness through (in)visible platform boundaries: A topological study on MOOCs as multiplexes of spaces and times. *International Journal of Educational Technology in Higher Education*, *16*(1), 1–30. doi:10.1186/s41239-019-0154-1.

Verger, A., Fontdevila, C., & Parcerisa, L. (2019). Reforming governance through policy instruments: How and to what extent standards, tests and accountability in education spread worldwide. *Discourse: Studies in the Cultural Politics of Education*, *40*(2), 248–270. doi:10.1080/01596306.2019.1569882.

Wilkins, C. (2011). Professionalism and the post-performative teacher: New teachers reflect on autonomy and accountability in the English school system. *Professional Development in Education*, *37*(3), 389–409. doi:10.1080/19415257.2010.514204.

Williamson, B. (2016). Digital education governance: An introduction. *European Educational Research Journal*, *15*(1), 3–13. doi:10.1177/1474904115616630.

Williamson, B. (2017). *Big Data in Education: The Digital Future of Learning, Policy and Practice*. Sage.

Zuboff, S. (2019). *The Age of Surveillance Capitalism: The Fight for a Human Future at the New Frontier of Power*. Profile Books.

6

ARTIFICIAL INTELLIGENCE AND A NEW GLOBAL POLICY PROBLEM IN EDUCATION

Kalervo N. Gulson

The policy implications of Artificial Intelligence (AI) are of interest to education departments globally. The reasons for this interest relate to hopes that AI can manage the plethora of data that systems now collect, and that AI may provide new insights into enduring problems in education systems. Lee-Archer (2021) asserts, "AI is a powerful tool to augment human decision-making in analyzing and understanding the complex interactions between social determinants, which are addressed through the various arms of public policy" (p. 80). Specific to education policy, the OECD contends that AI "can contribute to the effectiveness, equity and cost efficiency of education systems" (OECD, 2021, p. 16).

AI comprises semi- and fully autonomous technologies that perform tasks with varying levels of human intervention. Rose Luckin and colleagues define AI as:

> computer systems ... designed to interact with the world through capabilities (for example, visual perception ...) and intelligent behaviours (for example, assessing the available information and then taking the most sensible action to achieve a stated goal) that we would think of as essentially human.
> *(Luckin, Holmes, Griffiths, & Forcier, 2016, p. 14)*

While AI is often discussed as an innovative, emerging technology of the twenty-first century, AI is a field where many ideas originated in the mid-twentieth century. AI rose to popularity in the 1970s with the first commercial applications in factory scheduling; applications which were based on rules for expert systems/knowledge-based systems. While expert approaches have lost commercial popularity, knowledge systems are still part of systems engineering. Indeed, such algorithms, written in the 1990s, continue to drive common education technology products such as timetable scheduling.

DOI: 10.4324/9781003207528-6

Nonetheless, AI is primarily discussed in reference to machine learning. While the rise of machine learning is attributed to the first decade of the twenty-first century with a famous paper by Geoff Hinton and colleagues on deep learning (Hinton, Osindero, & Teh, 2006), it emerged, in a long ascendance, from when 'neuron nets' were proposed at the 1955 Dartmouth Summer Research Project on Artificial Intelligence. However, machine learning did not become popular until the twenty-first century when it was seen as commercially viable with the availability of large data sets as the basis for calculations – for example, the difference between 10,000 photos and two million photos. As such, when we think of AI in contemporary applications, we are most commonly referring to a combination of sophisticated machine learning algorithms, big data sets, and substantial computing power (Boden, 2016).

With AI increasingly used across all areas of social life, there is a need for AI to be understood as more than just mathematics. As Kate Crawford proposes, we need to:

> escape the notion that artificial intelligence is a purely technical domain. At a fundamental level, AI is technical and social practices, institutions and infrastructures, politics and culture. Computational reason and embodied work are deeply interlinked: AI systems both reflect and produce social relations and understandings of the world.
>
> *(Crawford, 2021, p. 8)*

In this chapter, I work with the idea that AI is not just a technological tool or object but also includes political, cultural and social interests (Mackenzie, 2002); that AI comprises "heterogeneous sociotechnical systems, influenced by cultural meanings and social structures" (Seaver, 2019, p. 419). Thus, when we are trying to understand AI, it means we are trying to understand highly dispersed, but intricately connected, socio-technical algorithmic systems. An algorithmic system is a decision-making process in which algorithms collect and analyze data, derive information, apply this information, and recommend an action. The level of human intervention in the decision-making process varies in algorithmic systems with some automated systems using AI. In education, AI-supported algorithmic systems include semi- to fully automated "procedures in which decisions are initially — partially or completely — delegated to another person or corporate entity, who then in turn use automatically executed decision-making models to perform an action" (Algorithm Watch, 2019, p. 9). Some AI, like machine learning, is embedded in common business applications used in schools, whereas others are stand-alone products such as facial recognition technology used to take attendance. When we are looking at AI and education policy, we may be better off thinking not of robots in the classroom but of algorithms in the workflow.

My aim in this chapter is to show why it is important that we understand how AI is being used in education policy, and the challenges of trying to govern

AI supported algorithmic systems in education. My starting point is a return to what Fazal Rizvi and Bob Lingard (2010) outlined in their book, *Globalizing Education Policy*, which precedes and inspires this current collection. Rizvi and Lingard posited that linking globalization to education policy required investigating power, boundaries, the global flows of policy ideas and people, and the ways policy is created, moved and modified. It meant understanding the new spatialities of education policy. Working from Rizvi and Lingard's insights, I propose some ways of thinking about AI and education policy that cover three areas: congruence, governance and spatiality. The first part of the chapter examines the congruence of AI with the ways education is currently organized, especially through datafication and digital education governance. The second part looks at global attempts to govern AI as part of anticipatory governance, and the limitations of these attempts. The third part looks at the new spaces of AI and education policy. As a scholar of the geographies of education policy, I have a keen interest in what types of spatialities are created by AI-supported algorithmic systems, and whether the application of these systems in education policy will change existing policy spaces. I conclude the chapter by speculating on whether AI is creating a new policy problem for education.

Congruence: how AI becomes part of education policy

Artificial Intelligence is entering education policy realms as part of now-established changes to governance. In mapping the shift from government to governance, Rizvi and Lingard argued that there was a new spatiality to globalized education policy premised on understanding relationality and interconnectivity.

> The disposition for critical education policy analysis in an era of globalization requires that we recognize the *relationality and interconnectivity* of policy developments. This recognition of relationality is in response to the new spatial politics and interconnectivity within and across nations that are evident in globalization.
>
> *(Rizvi & Lingard, 2010, p. 69)*

In the decade following *Globalizing Education Policy*, policy studies examined ideas of relationality and interconnections through concepts such as topology, networks and policy mobility, drawn from geography and sociology. This work argued that some education policy-making is made beyond the nation state, with new movements of, and links between, diverse actors and organizations (Ball, 2012; Gulson et al., 2017). As Rizvi and Lingard wrote, pre-empting the extensive work that then emerged in education on network governance and new policy networks, a "new form of educational governance ... also seeks to produce new players within education" (Rizvi & Lingard, 2010, p. 138). These new players bring different expertise to policy, continuing a history of education molded by disciplines and fields, such as psychology and organization studies, from outside the realm of practice.

Rizvi and Lingard also mapped out the multiple competing values at play in education, suggesting that "educational policies are driven more by the values of the market and system efficiency than by cultural and community values such as justice and democracy" (Rizvi & Lingard, 2010, p. 116). Rizvi and Lingard posited that a focus on efficiency entrenched modes of accountability and performativity, across multiple scales from school-level practices to global organizations such as the OECD. Since *Globalizing Education Policy* was published, new methods of calculation, computation and data analytics underpin these forms of accountability; methods that are rapidly changing the nature of knowledge, practice and expertise in education policy. Along with these new methods has been both an intensification of performative accountability (quantitative evidence about how things are) and a shift to prediction (evidence about how things will be).

Prediction depends on the transformation of education policy through "policy as numbers" (Lingard, 2011, p. 357). The significance of numbers in policy is supported by datafication or the process of translating information about things and events into quantitative formats. While, on the one hand, policy as and by numbers and datafication continues the role of statistics in governing the modern nation state, including education, on the other hand, statistics has morphed into algorithmic systems. These algorithmic systems comprise emerging forms of network and digital governance in education, premised on 'computational' approaches to policy, involving the intertwining of data, software, and machines (Fenwick, Mangez, & Ozga, 2014; Williamson, 2016). AI is part of these algorithmic systems in education, from the scheduling example above to the use of machine learning in data science, and the utilization of AI proprietary software in data management systems that combine student performance and administrative data (Perrotta & Selwyn, 2019; Witzenberger & Gulson, 2021).

Now, in one sense, AI is a continuation of existing modes of statistical reasoning in education policy. For example, machine learning is based on common statistical methods such as regression. However, it is also possible to see the legions of statisticians that supported the machinery of modern mass education systems are being steadily supplanted by data scientists. Drawing on a convergence of expertise and practices from econometrics, computer science, psychology and neuroscience, data science is ushering in new computational approaches to contemporary policy-making and analysis. Data science covers data management, analytics and visualization, computational statistics, and high-performance computing and algorithms to derive patterns from large data sets (Liu & Huang, 2017). While not synonymous with data science, AI is prevalent, especially machine learning. The promise of education data science is for increased speed and scope of analysis, associated with the growing practice of using computer-based information infrastructures to integrate and use machine learning to analyse statistical information from various data sources. Data science is being used in education through the work of for-profit and not-for-profit consultancies, and through analytics sitting behind proprietary platforms (Williamson, 2017).

The efficiencies delivered by computer science and AI research may produce remarkable innovations in education. And, as is obvious, education policy and governance have led themselves to this very point by decades of practices designed to use vast amounts of data to govern. AI, in this regard, is a tool to support already existing systems. However, we must also be cognizant that datafication means that the problems of education become problems framed as solvable by AI or what Mark Andrejevic (2019) calls a series of cascading logics — from automating data collection to data processing to automating responses — that comprise a bias toward automation. As policy problems become more narrowly framed, prediction, perhaps, ends up being the question we ask in education policy, to the preclusion of others. In education policy, the implementation of AI can narrow the conditions of possibility for education policy.

Governing: global AI policy and anticipatory governance

There is global concern over the impacts of Artificial Intelligence on social and political life. Governments and non-government organizations are attempting to anticipate possible disruptions and manage the introduction of AI for economic and social benefits. In the latter part of the 2010s, and into the 2020s, there was, and is, an increasing emphasis on creating policies to both anticipate and manage AI; polices that have been termed 'algorithmic accountability mechanisms.' These mechanisms cover a "set of policies oriented toward ensuring that those that build, procure and use algorithms are eventually answerable for their impacts" (Ada Lovelace Institute, AI Now Institute, & Open Government Partnership, 2021, p. 4).

In 2019, the OECD released the *Principles of Artificial Intelligence* that aims to create international standards for the introduction of AI, noting that over fifty countries in the Global North and South have developed policies or guidelines on AI (Organisation for Economic Co-operation and Development, 2019). These policies "employ a prose of sober tech-policy, fierce national strategic positioning, and, at the same time, sketch bold visions of public goods and social order enabled through AI" (Bareis & Katzenbach, 2021, p. 2). This is not policy-making to assuage fears of sentient robots, though these fears remain. What is of more immediate concern to policy-makers is the ways that introducing AI systems will bring harm, in areas such as employment replacement and entrenching political and social inequalities (AI100, 2016).

Education policy concerns pertaining to AI tend to cover areas such as trust, transparency, bias and fairness in systems (Kizilcec & Lee, 2020). There are calls for 'core agencies' such as education to no longer use opaque or 'black-box' AI systems (Campalo, Sanfilippo, Whittaker, & Crawford, 2017), with the European Union identifying some uses of AI in education as 'high-risk' activities (European Commission, 2021). There are now global policy responses on AI and education, from the OECD, EU and specific nation-based groups[1] — with high-level expert groups often an uneasy mix of lawyers and learning analytics academics but rarely social scientists. The attempts to address the ethical issues rarely enter the political terrain; a terrain comprising tensions between the demands of nations to become competitive in using AI for education, the growing role of EdTech sectors in education, and the social impacts of using AI. So, while a policy focus on AI in education is important, I think there are some caveats we need to consider when governing AI.

The first is to identify what kinds of spatial relations and globalized policy arenas AI enters and shapes. Rizvi and Lingard suggested that the "concept of globalization is associated with increased levels of mobility, not only of capital and finance, images, information and ideologies, but also of people" (Rizvi & Lingard, 2010, p. 161). Mobility, as outlined by Rizvi and Lingard, posed policy dilemmas around dealing with cultural diversity. AI is less a problem of people moving than information, with the knowledge, expertise and technologies that make up AI being highly mobile – utilizing data and algorithms that can be created, accessed, and spread globally without the need to build supply and delivery chains. That said, algorithms always presuppose a range of debated values and ideas incorporated into code. Alex Campalo et al. (2017) remind us that "those who design, develop, and maintain AI systems will shape such systems within their own understanding of the world" (p. 18). These understandings are made mobile with and through AI.

Additionally, any of the global policy responses to AI face the challenge mobility poses to contemporary policy-making, in that it is: "both relational and territorial; as both in motion and simultaneously fixed, or embedded in place" (Cochrane & Ward, 2012, p. 7). Policies created to try and deal with a specific object (such as AI) run into two spatial problems. One, that AI itself is inherently mobile, and, two, that specific territorial concerns – social, political and cultural – end up shaping how AI policies develop and are implemented. Nonetheless, by seeing the objects of AI and global AI policy as mobile, means that "[t]he placing of policies gives them their meaning in practice, while places draw on (and draw in) a wider policy repertoire than might be available within their national as well as local boundaries" (Cochrane & Ward, 2012, p. 7)

A second issue with governing AI arises when we see AI as more than a tool. In a more expansive definition of AI, we can begin to see AI as constituting socio-political relations in education (Dixon-Román, Nichols, & Nyame-Mensah, 2020). If AI is socio-political, we can begin to ask similar questions of AI, and the algorithmic systems to which it contributes, that are posed by critical policy studies. These questions pertain especially to the need to "underline the importance of power in the construction and justification of knowledge claims" (Rizvi & Lingard, 2010, p. 47). At the least, in education policy studies, we could follow, as Crawford argues, that:

> To understand how AI is fundamentally political we need to go beyond neural nets and statistical pattern recognition to instead ask *what* is being

optimized, and *for whom*, and *who* gets to decide. Then we can trace the implications of those choices.

(Crawford, 2021, p. 9)

We could connect AI to policy through a set of political questions about who benefits, who loses, and what gets changed. In education and the use of AI, these may be questions relating to equity and access, surveillance, privacy and data issues or the role of private companies. Erica Southgate, for example, proposes that one way to locate AI as a political aspect of education is to connect the use of AI with its human rights implications (Southgate, 2021).

Uncertainty and the limits of anticipatory governance

The above policies on AI can be framed within anticipatory policy-making and governance that involve acting "on a variety of inputs to manage emerging knowledge-based technologies while such management is still possible" (Guston, 2008, p. vi). While AI in education is still in a nascent stage, it is becoming clear that it may not be easily managed. While AI promises new forms of efficiency, and finds new relationships between disparate data, it also promises a form of control that is premised on accepting uncertainty, especially when machine learning is used in opaque systems. That is, AI combines data and calculations, some of which can be easily known (e.g., rules), some of which are not so easy to know (e.g., neural networks), depending on the system used.

With some forms of machine learning, such as deep learning, the use of algorithms is now well past a simple recipe version of input in, input out. Rather, in highly complex systems what we have is "the *principle of radical complexity*. This principle says that large, interactive algorithmic systems produce emergent behavior we cannot antici-pate" (Edwards, 2018, p. 20, original emphasis). As such, 'managing' AI, in the sense of anticipatory governance, needs to deal with the idea that AI in education creates new uncertainties through unanticipated and unknowable emergent behavior. As Paul Edwards (2018) notes, "[m]achine-built systems use machine logic, not human logic" (p. 23). Delineating where these logics begin and end is part of the uncertainty of using AI systems. The good news for us is that dealing with uncertainty is a problem that education policy studies has grappled with, both ontologically and epistemologically, especially in poststructural approaches to policy analysis (see Gulson & Metcalfe, 2015).

As such, the problem of AI in education policy may not necessarily be one of understanding uncertainty – that is, a lack of knowledge about a system – but of coming to grips with a disconcerting lack of control that uncertainty brings. The philosophy of technology can provide us with possible options, that both explore why understanding of uncertainty is crucial to looking at AI and educa-tion policy, and why trying to manage AI may be fruitless.

David Roden coins the term 'new substantivism,' to understand *self-augmenting technical systems*, or what, for the purposes of this discussion, we see as AI systems.

Roden's perspective does not attribute a sentience to AI. Rather, self-augmenting techniques, such as those that use machine learning, "[do] not remove human agency but [mediate] it through networks where no single agent or collective is able to exercise decisive control over the technical system" (Roden, 2015, p. 152). These technical systems act as catalysts for further action but do not determine this action. This is an idea of technology that is *neither controllable nor in control*. As Roden suggests:

> we need not attribute agency or purposiveness to technology to explain why the evolution of technical systems eludes our control. If technology is 'out of control' it does not follow that it is 'in control' of us or under its own control.
> *(Roden, 2015, p. 160)*

The agentic combination of machines and humans is creating new conditions of possibility for what can be understood as the limits of action and control in education policy-making. Colleagues Sam Sellar and Taylor Webb and I have looked at these new conditions of possibility as part of *synthetic governance*. This is governance as an amalgamation of human classifications, calculative practices, and political rationalities, with new forms of computation and what we might consider to be non-human political rationalities or, what Edwards above calls, 'machine logic'. Synthetic governance, therefore, is not human *or* machine governance but human *and* machine governance (Gulson, Sellar, & Webb, 2022).

Spatiality: what are the old and new policy spaces of AI?

I am very interested in whether we are seeing new types of policy spatialities through either the introduction of AI into governing (i.e., changing governing itself) or through the attempts to govern AI. Conversely, are the policy spaces created more an intensification of those identified as produced by globalization? It is possible, I think, that the answer is both yes and no.

In the affirmative, governing AI occurs within a similar type of spatiality raised in *Globalizing Education Policy* around interconnectivity and relationality, and is extended in ideas of network governance. The use of AI fits seamlessly with new types of relationality and policy networks outlined in policy mobility work. For example, Jamie Peck and Nik Theodore (2015) identify what they call 'fast policy', where ideas are shared and taken up on a global scale, enabled through intensifying interconnections premised on the rapid movement of policy ideas and experts. As Ben Williamson suggests:

> current efforts to embed AI and data analytics in education exemplify how 'fast policy' is being done through edtech experts and the new power networks to which they are connected.
> *(Williamson, 2019, p. 396)*

AI, with its promise of speed, certainly fits with the notion of new kinds of compressed policy spatialities and temporalities where AI-supported policy, and attempts to govern AI, involve the movement of human and non-human actors.

That AI is just another part of network governance can be illustrated by the ways technology companies have become legitimate actors in policy-making. Overwhelmingly, AI in education, as in other fields, is being introduced as part of proprietary systems. Technology companies are playing a key role in education in two ways. First, through the introduction of AI-supported platforms, such as Google Classroom, that impact the labour of schooling and pose new governing terrains (Perrotta, Gulson, Williamson, & Witzenberger, 2021). In this way, 'certain technologies are becoming proxy policy implementation devices – or *edtech policy machines*' (Williamson, 2019, p. 396). Second, global technology companies, acting with close to monopoly power, are well embedded in all areas of education from schooling to universities. In a policy sense, these companies are both at the policy table, consulted as part of reports on using AI (e.g., OECD, 2021), and part of the governing itself, where proprietary systems provided by global and local technology corporations are used in public policy arenas. The proprietary use of AI encourages the expertise of education practitioners and administrators to be subjugated, or at least to defer, to those who build and provide algorithmic systems. Technology companies become actors in policy spaces somewhere between procurement policy and teaching and learning policy.

Legal scholars are grappling with what it means to have AI itself as a new policy actor, especially when part of a proprietary system. In this sense, the question is: What is the actor in an algorithmic system? Legal scholars try to answer this question around notions of responsibility, with some suggesting that AI systems should be considered as 'state actors.' In the US context, for example, there are possibilities of AI systems violating the constitution but with less and less accountability, for "as AI systems rely more on deep learning, potentially becoming more autonomous and inscrutable, the accountability gap for constitutional violations threatens to become broader and deeper" (Crawford & Schultz, 2019, p. 1971).

While the above are good reasons to see that AI is only one more technical introduction to, and technology companies merely one more policy actor in, education network governance, I do wonder if automation provides a different way of seeing policy spatiality. There is the materiality of AI that Crawford outlines above, which highlights how AI is a highly globally networked undertaking. And Louise Amoore provides another proposition framed as a new spatiality of algorithms. Amoore outlines how machine learning, especially neural networks or what is commonly known as deep learning, have a non-linear spatiality in which "algorithms modify themselves in and through their nonlinear iterative relations to input data" (Amoore, 2020, p. 11). Amoore suggests that trying to locate the locus of responsibility for AI is difficult. For example, where algorithmic systems are never authored by a clearly identifiable human, but rather from a composite of algorithm designers, frontline officers, the experimental models of the mathematical and physical sciences, a training dataset, and the generative capacities of machine-learning classifiers working on entities and events.

(Amoore, 2020, p. 139)

We can see Amoore's spatiality of algorithms as extending Edward's point above, that machines have a particular logic that is not a human logic.

The spaces of AI as a new global policy problem in education

In this chapter, I have tried to provide ways to think through how AI connects with education policy, and to locate this thinking in reference to Rizvi and Lingard's *Globalizing Education Policy*. I conclude by suggesting that while AI does not radically alter what Rizvi and Lingard outlined as the features of globalization and education policy, that AI does pose a new global policy problem in education.

The introduction of AI is congruent with what has already been embedded in education. Datafication, computation and new policy networks have meant that AI has intensified the means of governing around quantification and accountability. While AI can certainly identify efficiencies in education, the question really is whether these are the types of efficiencies that will allow AI to solve the enduring problems in education, such as those around inequality. I think we need to be cognizant that the very possibilities created by the introduction of AI into education may also work to erase and elide other 'conditions of possibility' (Foucault, 1970).

The introduction of AI does pose problems of governing. As the expansion of global policies to try to regulate AI show, the promises of AI are offset by the threats it poses. Such threats include that AI can draw on data and use algorithms that reinforce existing inequities, and that it is differentially applied to already marginalised, racialized, populations (Benjamin, 2019). At the least, we should make policy about AI on the understanding that AI "knowledge claims are always already embodied and socio-historically situated" (Elish & boyd, 2018, p. 73). Nonetheless, I think we run into the limits of governing AI due to new types of network governance, policy networks, and the interweaving of human/non-human actors. That is, where to intervene in algorithms when "[t]he nonhuman quality of networks is precisely what makes them so difficult to grasp. They are … a medium of contemporary power, and yet no single subject or group absolutely controls a network" (Galloway & Thacker, 2007, p. 5).

To that end, I think AI poses a new policy problem in education due to the spatiality of algorithms. This has two parts. The first relates to an intensification of existing policy spaces of interconnectedness through infrastructure and new expertise. This includes the predominance of proprietary systems and technology companies as policy actors, a feature obviously closely linked to the interconnections of network governance but one that is adding a sense of opaqueness to understanding who and where decisions about education are being made. The second aspect relates to the spatiality of algorithms, and what it means to try to understand the where of policy in an algorithmic system. This is a significant challenge when the boundaries between human and machine have been occluded in contemporary governance.

One response is to consider this policy problem conceptually. If algorithmic systems are now so embedded in and as education policy, perhaps we are at an adaptation phase of living with machines in governance. In which case, the requirement for understanding and intervening in networks means that an education politics of the twentieth century may well have reached its limits. That is, we no longer have all the right analytical tools. The types of concepts that we may need to supplement those of the twentieth century are those that see education policy and AI as part of a socio-technical system. These concepts could include some of which I have mentioned above, such as: Schultz and Crawford's proposition that proprietary AI systems are state actors; Gulson, Sellar and Webb's notion of synthetic governance; Southgate's connecting of AI to ethics and human rights; Dixon-Román and colleagues' notion that AI is socio-political; and Williamson's proposition that AI is part of EdTech policy machines. Some of these tools may be more useful than others. In a similar way to Rizi and Lingard suggesting that globalization required new policy concepts in education, these types of new socio-technical concepts may help us to better understand policy when it uses AI, and to understand policy about governing AI.

Note

1 E.g., https://ec.europa.eu/education/news/apply-expert-group-artificial-intelligence-data-education-training_en.

References

Ada Lovelace Institute, AI Now Institute, & Open Government Partnership. (2021). *Algorithmic Accountability for the Public Sector*. https://www.opengovpartnership.org/documents/algorithmic-accountability-public-sector/.

AI100. (2016). *One Hundred Year Study on Artificial Intelligence (AI100)*. Stanford University.

Algorithm Watch. (2019). *Automating Society: Taking Stock of Automated Decision-Making in the EU*. AW AlgorithmWatch gGmbH.

Amoore, L. (2020). *Cloud Ethics: Algorithms and the Attributes of Ourselves and Others*. Duke University Press.

Andrejevic, M. (2019). *Automated Media*. Routledge.

Ball, S. J. (2012). *Global Education Inc.: New Policy Networks and the Neoliberal Imaginary*. Routledge.

Bareis, J., & Katzenbach, C. (2021). Talking AI into being: The narratives and imaginaries of national ai strategies and their performative politics. *Science, Technology, & Human Values*. doi:10.1177/01622439211030007.

Benjamin, R. (2019). *Race after Technology: Abolitionist Tools for the New Jim Code*. Polity.

Boden, M. A. (2016). *AI: Its Nature and Future*. Oxford University Press.

Campalo, A., Sanfilippo, M., Whittaker, M., & Crawford, K. (2017). *AI Now 2017 Report*. AI Now.

Cochrane, A., & Ward, K. (2012). Guest editorial – Researching the geographies of policy mobility: Confronting the methodological challenges. *Environment and Planning A*, *44*(1), 5–12.

Crawford, K. (2021). *Atlas of AI: Power, Politics, and the Planetary Costs of Artificial Intelligence*. Yale University Press.

Crawford, K., & Schultz, J. (2019). AI systems as state actors. *Columbia Law Review*, *119*(7), 1941–1972.

Dixon-Román, E., Nichols, T. P., & Nyame-Mensah, A. (2020). The racializing forces of/ in AI educational technologies. *Learning, Media and Technology*, *45*(3), 236–250. doi:10. 1080/17439884.2020.1667825.

Edwards, P. N. (2018). We have been assimilated: Some principles for thinking about algorithmic systems. In U. Schultze, M. Aanestad, M. Mähring, C. Østerlund, & K. Riemer (Eds.), *Living with Monsters? Social Implications of Algorithmic Phenomena, Hybrid Agency, and the Performativity of Technology (Proceeding of the Working Conference on Information Systems and Organizations 2018)* (pp. 19–27). Springer International Publishing.

Elish, M. C., & boyd, d. (2018). Situating methods in the magic of Big Data and AI. *Communication Monographs*, *85*(1), 57–80. doi:10.1080/03637751.2017.1375130.

European Commission. (2021). *Regulation of the European Parliament and of the Council: Laying Down Harmonised Rules on Artificial Intelligence (Artificial Intelligence Act) and Amending Certain Union Legislative Acts*. https://eur-lex.europa.eu/resource. html?uri=cellar:e0649735-a372-11eb-9585-01aa75ed71a1.0001.02/DOC_1&format=PDF.

Fenwick, T., Mangez, E., & Ozga, J. (2014). Governing knowledge: Comparison, knowledge-based technologies and expertise in the regulation of education. In T. Fenwick, E. Mangez, & J. Ozga (Eds.), *Governing Knowledge: Comparison, Knowledge-Based Technologies and Expertise in the Regulation of Education* (pp. 3–10). Routledge.

Foucault, M. (1970). *The Order of Things: An Archaeology of the Human Sciences*. Tavistock.

Galloway, A. R., & Thacker, E. (2007). *The Exploit: A Theory of Networks*. University of Minnesota Press.

Gulson, K. N., Lewis, S., Lingard, B., Lubienski, C., Takayama, K., & Webb, P. T. (2017). Policy mobilities and methodology: A proposition for inventive methods in education policy studies. *Critical Studies in Education*, *58*(2), 224–241.

Gulson, K. N., & Metcalfe, A. S. (2015). Introduction: Education policy analysis for a complex world: poststructural possibilities. *Critical Studies in Education*, *56*(1), 1–4. doi:10.1 080/17508487.2015.990474.

Gulson, K. N., Sellar, S., & Webb, P. T. (2022). *Algorithms of Education: How Datafication and Artificial Intelligence Shapes Policy*. University of Minnesota Press.

Guston, D. H. (2008). The Center for Nanotechnology in Society at Arizona State University and the prospects for anticipatory governance. In N. M. d. S. Cameron, & M. E. Mitchell (Eds.), *Nanoscale: Issues and Perspectives for the Nano Century* (pp. 377–392). John Wiley & Sons.

Hinton, G. E., Osindero, S., & Teh, Y. (2006). A fast learning algorithm for deep belief nets. *18*(7), 1527–1554

Kizilcec, R. F., & Lee, H. (2020). Algorithmic fairness in education. arXiv preprint arXiv:2007.05443.

Lee-Archer, B. (2021). The relationships between humans and machines in public policy. In C. Wyatt-Smith, B. Lingard, & E. Heck (Eds.), *Digital Disruption in Teaching and Testing: Assessments, Big Data, and the Transformation Of Schooling* (pp. 75–89). Routledge.

Lingard, B. (2011). Policy as numbers: Ac/counting for educational research. *Australian Educational Researcher, 38*(4), 355–382.

Liu, M.-C., & Huang, Y.-M. (2017). The use of data science for education: The case of social-emotional learning. *Smart Learning Environments, 4*(1), 1. doi:10.1186/s40561-016-0040-4.

Luckin, R., Holmes, W., Griffiths, M., & Forcier, L. B. (2016). Intelligence Unleashed: An Argument for AI in Education. Retrieved from https://www.pearson.com/content/dam/corporate/global/pearson-dot-com/files/innovation/Intelligence-Unleashed-Publication.pdf.

Mackenzie, A. (2002). *Transductions: Bodies and Machines at Speed*. Continuum.

OECD. (2021). *OECD Digital Education Outlook 2021: Pushing the Frontiers with Artificial Intelligence, Blockchain and Robots*. OECD Publishing.

Organisation for Economic Co-operation and Development. (2019). *Artificial Intelligence in Society*. OECD Publishing. Retrieved from https://doi.org/10.1787/eedfee77-en.

Peck, J., & Theodore, N. (2015). *Fast Policy: Experimental Statecraft at the Thresholds of Neoliberalism*. University of Minnesota Press.

Perrotta, C., Gulson, K. N., Williamson, B., & Witzenberger, K. (2021). Automation, APIs and the distributed labour of platform pedagogies in Google Classroom. *Critical Studies in Education, 62*(1), 97–113. doi:10.1080/17508487.2020.1855597.

Perrotta, C., & Selwyn, N. (2019). Deep learning goes to school: Toward a relational understanding of AI in education. *Learning, Media and Technology,* 1–19. doi:10.1080/17439884.2020.1686017.

Rizvi, F., & Lingard, B. (2010). *Globalizing Educational Policy*. Routledge.

Roden, D. (2015). *Posthuman Life: Philosophy at the Edge of the Human*. Routledge.

Seaver, N. (2019). Knowing algorithms. In J. Vertesi, & D. Ribes (Eds.), *digitalSTS: A Field Guide for Science & Technology Studies* (pp. 412–422). Princeton University Press.

Southgate, E. (2021). Artificial Intelligence and machine learning: A practical and ethical guide for teachers. In C. Wyatt-Smith, B. Lingard, & E. Heck (Eds.), *Digital Disruption in Teaching and Testing: Assessments, Big Data, and the Transformation of Schooling* (pp. 60–74). Routledge.

Williamson, B. (2016). Political computational thinking: Policy networks, digital governance and 'learning to code'. *Critical Policy Studies, 10*(1), 39–58. doi:10.1080/19460171.2015.1052003.

Williamson, B. (2017). Who owns educational theory? Big data, algorithms and the expert power of education data science. *E-Learning and Digital Media, 14*(3), 105–122. doi:10.1177/2042753017731238.

Williamson, B. (2019). New power networks in educational technology. *Learning, Media and Technology, 44*(4), 395–398. doi:10.1080/17439884.2019.1672724.

Witzenberger, K., & Gulson, K. N. (2021). Why EdTech is always right: Students, data and machines in pre-emptive configurations. *Learning, Media and Technology,* 1–15. doi:10.1080/17439884.2021.1913181.

7

EDUCATION AND SHIFTS IN THE GLOBAL ECONOMY

Meritocracy and the changing nature of work

Hugh Lauder

The dominant policy view of education remains that it should enable students to be employable (Brown et al., 2020). It is a view in which it is assumed that once on the jobs ladder those with the ability and motivation to ascend it can achieve interesting, well-paid jobs. In this way, economic efficiency is linked to social justice through the idea of meritocracy. This is a powerful ideology which has sustained the legitimacy of capitalist states throughout the last century.

While this policy view has remained uncontroversial outside education research, it has now taken center stage in a firestorm flamed by a resentment of meritocracy and fanned by populism. The problem is that meritocracy does not come close to being achieved, especially in the Anglosphere countries, when compared, for example, to the relative success of Nordic and Northern European societies (OECD, 2018). This is compounded by a consistently flawed analysis which sees improving education as key to achieving a meritocratic society. While it is debatable as to whether meritocracy should be an aim of education, we need first to see that, while educational qualifications are necessary to enter the jobs competition, the fundamental problem lies in the labor market.

If we are to challenge this dominant policy discourse, we need to work through the issues relating to education, and the labor market before examining why the fractures in this relationship have influenced the rise of populism.

Education and Meritocracy

The opportunity bargain offered to achieve meritocratic outcomes is that, if young people invest in education, they will be rewarded in the labor market: those with the ability and motivation, irrespective of their social class, gender or ethnicity, can ascend the occupational ladder (Brown, 2003).

DOI: 10.4324/9781003207528-7

In striking this bargain, neoliberal governments have made several key assumptions. The first is that competition in education and in access to jobs is the central principle driving personal and national success. In countries like Britain and the United States, this view of competition is based on a Darwinian struggle in which 'natural' ability will emerge irrespective of social constraints. It is for this reason that education alone is seen as the central driver of meritocracy while social security is minimal. This primitive, capitalist assumption, which many will understand as an expression of ruling interests, explains the obsessive focus in education policy on school performance and exams. This focus measures success as expressed in testing and exams results which are deemed proof of students' and schools' worth.

At the same time, rather than seeing inequalities as social, attention has been switched, by the right, to a new version of the old and debunked Intelligence Quotient (IQ) claim that racially determined intelligence is the best explanation for social inequality. The work of Robert Plomin (2018), who developed this tradition with reference to genetics, is a good indicator of this line of research and has been endorsed by the high-profile, former English government *eminence gris*, Dominic Cummings.

When we look at comparative analyses of social mobility, we find that it is countries with a radically different form of capitalism that perform better in terms of upward social mobility. In a recent OECD report (2018), it is the North European countries where students from working-class backgrounds are more likely to be socially upwardly mobile. The difference in philosophy is stark. The present English government cavils at already meager social support, while northern European nations assume that the working-class, women and ethnic minority groups need the social support necessary for them to escape what Ceri Brown (2014) has called the binds of poverty, and to have the confidence to achieve. The picture in these countries is far from perfect but remains ahead of the United States (US) and England. That said, it needs to be acknowledged that the center-left US administration of Joe Biden is seeking to move toward the view taken in the Nordic countries.

Underlying these comparative analyses is the well-established relationship between poverty and education underperformance. Currently, there are 4.5 million children in poverty in the United Kingdom. Given what we know about the impact of poverty on educational achievement, it is clear that we do not have anything approaching the level playing field implied by the claim of meritocratic competition. In a comparative study of educational achievement, I am conducting with Andres Sandoval and Kalyan Kumar, we analyzed OECD data on achievement for 15-year-old students from the bottom 25% of the income distribution, across 63 countries. Students, from this background, in the Nordic countries had 10% more chance of succeeding in education when compared to their British counterparts and 20% better chance than US students. In the light of child poverty, this research draws attention to the need not only for financial and food security for low-income families but the restructuring of education, starting with free, early childhood education.

We should note how poverty and high-stakes testing disfigures education. In England, some of the most successful academy trusts, in terms of exam results, are those that operate a highly regimented regime in which the exclusive focus is on teaching to the exam. Given the extreme levels of child poverty, arguably the only way to provide any kind of exam success is with the forms of regimentation and control that these academies offer. But this is a Dickensian approach to education. What it does to their subsequent life chances, when they are asked to think more openly, is yet to be investigated. But, we might wonder, do we even ask university undergraduates to think openly?

From a meritocratic perspective, education is trapped between poverty and wider social class, gender and racial inequalities and a broken jobs ladder. The only way for students to have even a chance of competing for well-paid jobs is to get a degree. Here, we need to see that students are being corralled into an ever-narrowing funnel of opportunity that is, in effect, a form of social control rather than emancipation. One consequence is rising mental ill health (Brown & Carr, 2019); a view that has been dismissed by the Schools Standards Minister in England, Nick Gibb. In 2018, when asked about student mental health due to exam pressure, he said, "The way to deal with exam pressures is to make sure that young people are taking exams earlier on in their school career... so they're used to taking exams."[1] Gibb exemplifies a brutal view of young people and education.

In turn, higher education is also disfigured because, with the sole focus of enabling students to get good jobs, the wider aims of higher education relating to democracy, inequality and climate change are diminished.

The Broken Jobs Ladder

There is consensus that the fundamental problems with the labor market lie in the middle and at the bottom of the ladder. Good, working-class jobs that required apprenticeship qualifications and had status have been substituted for low-wage, insecure work. It has also been argued that the major impact of Artificial Intelligence (AI) and associated technologies has been on jobs in the middle of the income parade.

Maarten Goos and Alan Manning (2003), who first articulated the concept of a hollowed middle, argued that AI and associated technologies had substituted for routine jobs in the middle of the occupational structure. This includes process jobs in manufacturing and administrative work. In formulating this hypothesis, they pictured the labor market as an hourglass. This is a consensus built on shaky ground. Craig Holmes and Ken Mayhew (2012) have shown that, in the UK, while managerial jobs increased between 2000 and 2008, the proportion of those earning less than £400 per week increased from 37 to 58% during that period. A similar trend occurred in financial intermediation where there was an increase in managerial jobs from 2 to 10% earning over £1,500 per week at the same time as there was an increase from 24 to 30% of those earning under £400 per week. In essence, however, the analysis by Goos and Manning is misleading. Part of the problem in the analyses of these data is that the category 'manager' covers a wide range of jobs with the same job title. Rather than an hourglass, the image is more of a vase with a narrow neck and a wide base.

The wide base now comprises many in insecure, gig economy jobs. In 2015, the OECD reported that non-standard work, which includes those on temporary or zero hours contracts, part-time employees and the self-employed, was one of the major causes of inequality. Such non-standard work is now widespread and represents a significant proportion of the workforce. For example, in England, the proportion in non-standard work is 40% (OECD, 2015). Many of these jobs have been hard-wired into contemporary capitalism. To see why this is the case, we need to look at the strategies of corporations like Uber Technologies and the stock market response to them. Uber commands a high price on the stock market while it has yet to make a profit. What is going on? Uber is seeking to undercut traditional taxi firms and more recent competitors until it has a near-monopoly position. To do so, the wages of its drivers have to be low. But once it achieves a commanding market position, it would be naïve to believe that it will raise drivers' wages. Lawsuits that have been brought against its working conditions have been keenly fought in the courts by Uber because they threaten its business strategy. Here, the protection that legislation and union pressure provides is essential to enable these workers to earn a living wage. Under neoliberalism, that is less likely than in those spheres where the combination of labor market regulation and social policy reduce poverty, especially child poverty.

It could be argued that even insecure, low-wage work is the first step on the jobs ladder and that those with motivation and ability will be able to ascend it. In England, the data tell a different story. Only one in six low-paid workers secured full time, better-paid jobs between 2007 and 2017, whereas 48% fluctuated between low-paid jobs and slightly better jobs (The Social Mobility Commission, 2017). Meritocracy, for those on low pay, is a cruel hoax but when we look at the supposed privilege of graduates, we find that, even there, the rhetoric does not match reality.

The Broken Rungs for Graduate Jobs

In the debate so far, there has been a deafening silence about graduate jobs. Reference to university graduates has centered on an entrenched view that, as economic beneficiaries of a university education, students should pay fees. When the question of abolishing university fees has been raised, there have been many on the left who believe that this reinforces their privilege and is, at best, an electoral bribe. But that ignores the decline in graduate-level jobs. In *The Death of Human Capital?*, Phil Brown, Sin Yi Cheung and I have argued that human capital theory, which was supposed to describe and explain how those with a good education would be more productive and would therefore achieve higher rewards than non-graduates in the labor market, cannot accurately describe or explain the current fate of graduates in the United States and UK. Theoretically and empirically, it has led to a flawed understanding of the education economy relationship while the promise of good jobs that it offered is, for many, a chimera. Rather, we are witnessing a rupture between, on the one hand, the interests of the wealthy and their political allies and, on the other, those of graduates whose life chances in relation to good jobs are diminishing.

There is broad agreement that the top jobs in the economy are either stagnating or in decline for at least two reasons. Graduates seeking to enter global industries have to compete with their counterparts overseas in a global 'Dutch auction' in which those with equivalent qualifications who will work for the lowest wages will win (Brown, Lauder & Ashton, 2011). Often, they have the so-called 'soft skills' of being multilingual and multicultural which those educated in the Anglosphere may lack. This can give them a head start to fill the top jobs in global corporations. Despite the move toward re-creating economic nationalism, it does not automatically follow that there will be a dividend in an increasing proportion of top jobs for British or American graduates in multinational corporations.

The second concerns the advent of new technology. Major corporations, wherever they are located, have slimmed down because technology can now be substituted for labor. Gerald Davis (2016) has examined the decline in employment in what he calls the vanishing American corporation. In 2015, for example, Facebook had 1.35 billion users but only 9,199 employees and Twitter had 288 million users and 3,638 employees. This compares with old corporations like Exxon, whose 1,73,000-strong workforce in 1982 had declined, by 2012, to 77,000.

The net result is that there are not enough well-paid jobs, at all levels of educational credential. Successive governments have watched these changes to the labor market and consistently drawn the wrong conclusion, claiming the problem lies in severe skill shortages. While that may be temporarily the case right now, as a result of the pandemic, it is almost tautological to refer to skill shortages under capitalism precisely because, as Marx and Schumpeter have noted, it survives through an endemic process of creative destruction. Although there will always be some skill shortages, the fundamental problem is an absence of well-paid and interesting jobs.

Recently, 'good jobs' has entered political discourse in the facile phrase 'leveling up', yet there seems to be little appreciation of what providing such jobs entails. Good jobs cannot be created easily against the headwinds of globalization and new technology and will require state intervention in a range of initiatives that come under the rubric of industrial policy. Governments continue to assume that most of the problems in a low-wage, low-productivity economy lie on the supply side and that, if the offer of lifelong learning is taken up, more working-class jobs will be upgraded: problem solved. The demand side of this equation lies in the hope that a new green deal will be delivered by the market, as Mark Carney has argued, hence the emphasis on the supply side. Yet, there is a huge gap between the assumption that well-paid green jobs are on the way and the reality of the quality of such jobs.

While the Institute for Public Policy Research (IPPR) has documented the scale of jobs that may be created in the UK, there has been no systematic study of how such a deal will move us beyond low-wage, low-spec work. It may well eventuate but it is worth noting that the suppliers dominating the global economy in the production of green energy are not typically from the Anglosphere. Of the top ten wind turbine manufacturers, six were from China, and one each from Denmark, Germany, Spain and the United States. In all cases, their markets are global.[2] Of the leading solar panel producers, six are from China, two from Japan and one each from Canada and the United States.[3] The high-wage jobs involved in the production of this hardware is apparent; it is in their downstream application that the challenge arises.

In the meantime, the role of AI in reconfiguring or substituting good jobs is accelerating. This suggests that the broken rungs in the meritocratic ladder will not be easily replaced and we need to think through another economic basis for a new social contract to replace the promise of meritocracy.

Despite the consistent misdiagnosis of the problems raised by the education–labor market relationship, focus remains on the supply side, distorting the roles of higher and further education. Here, attention should be drawn to the way AI is unbundling the range of tasks that comprise many jobs. While there is much to criticize in the way orthodox economic theory has understood the impact technology has in raising the demand for skilled work, David Autor and his colleagues were among the first to see that the focus, in terms of labor market demand and supply, ought now be on tasks. The debate over new technology has fixated on the loss of jobs, where labor is substituted for robots. While this is an important concern, it fails to see the way jobs are already being restructured through the redesign and reallocation of job tasks. We have noted this in the debate over the hollowed middle but it applies to low-wage jobs as well as those in the middle and upper levels of the occupational structure.

These changes not only effect the decomposition of jobs; they bring, in their train, changes to education. Already, there is a debate about whether the traditional three- or four-year degree should be reduced to two years. This is not only to reduce costs but to focus university programs more closely on the changing demand for knowledge and skills. As Leesa Wheelahan and Gavin Moodie (2021) have argued, this has brought into sharp focus the salience of micro-credentials. They define them as "short courses aligned with industry which are substantive 'enough' to be counted toward a full qualification (Kato et al., 2020). In turn, micro credentials may consist of smaller units of learning, such as digital badges or digital certificates" (p. 2). They enable workers to be job ready without employers bearing the cost of training. The skills taught on these courses may address specific tasks that are in demand for a limited period before they are substituted by AI. An example may help. In England, two-year degree courses have been established in law and accountancy. Both professions have been radically restructured as a consequence of AI. Discovery work in law, which concerns identifying documentary evidence to build a case, used to be undertaken by lawyers with relatively high salaries. In the early 2000s, that work was offshored to countries like the Philippines. Now, that same work is done more efficiently by AI and a tier of the legal profession has been stripped out. It is not far-fetched to think that, in the restructured legal profession, a two-year degree will fill a temporary gap. Meanwhile, those that gain it will be trapped in the lower reaches of the profession because the leading positions will be filled by those graduating from elite universities with full-length courses.

Wheelahan and Moodie (2021) argue that micro credentials are a way of disciplining education institutions. Instead of providing a broad education that should be the intellectual basis for an economy dependent on knowledge, they are also used to downgrade the significance of education for democracy and citizenship. The problem is that, just as professions are being restructured into tiers and jobs into tasks, higher education is itself stratified. A broad, general education will be the preserve of elite institutions that will provide 'talented' labor for senior executive and managerial jobs while those in the lower tiers will focus more on credentials for general jobs.

Placed in this context, we can see how the metric of graduate employment by which universities are judged is unjust and economically illiterate. Unjust because it is inevitably the case that, in a stratified system, those at elite universities have an overwhelming advantage of being able to deliver on the jobs metric. Illiterate because the labor market is volatile, especially post the COVID pandemic, and it is difficult to match graduates to jobs for which they are qualified because we know that approximately 50% of graduates take sub-graduate jobs. The evidence also tells us that those in jobs for which they are overqualified will not typically be able to ascend the jobs ladder.

The misplaced emphasis on assuming that education can provide good jobs distorts education while failing to focus on where the problem really lies. That said, every effort should be made to create good jobs, although it will be apparent this is a long-term project with an approach to political economy which extends far from a reliance on a liberal market and low taxes characteristic of neoliberalism.

Meritocracy and Populism

The debate over meritocracy has tapped into an emerging *zeitgeist* on the center and left of politics. In two of the key critiques of meritocracy, by Michael Sandel (2021) and Daniel Markovits (2019), the question of how we value education and jobs has been central to their diagnoses. Here, moral worth is ascribed to market power. If the current pandemic has told us anything it is that the jobs that are central to our society are among the worst paid, a failure of market values equating with societal values. Mark Carney (2021) makes this point when writing about the lack of value that has been given to the natural environment: market societies have equated worth with rewards in the labor market. The idea that worth is equated with high-income jobs was first articulated by Sennett and Cobb (1972) in *The Hidden Injuries of Class* fifty years ago, where they argued that those that do not achieve educationally consider themselves worthless.

The scars left by these injuries have fed into the democratic process and the rise of populism. The sense of grievance, it is argued, is personal and enables space for the extreme right to thrive. There are differences between American and British political cultures but they share a rejection of 'experts', although the COVID crisis may have changed that for many. Daniel Markovits cites a 2017 Pew Research Centre survey which found that only 36% of Americans who supported the Republican party thought colleges and universities were good for America and 58% that they had a negative impact, while 72% of Democrats took a positive view to these higher education institutions. Erszebet Bukodi and John Goldthorpe (2021) find that it is not only a matter of social class but also of a loss of status among working-class voters that is linked to authoritarian populism.

Noam Gidron and Peter Hall (2017), in examining the politics of social status across 20 democracies, show a set of economic and cultural developments that have depressed the social status for working-class men: a decline they chart from 1987. They provide a theoretical explanation for the significance of a loss of status which has two dimensions. First, they argue that subjective status is like a positional good; that is, if one group achieves status, it is at the cost of another. Second, those who are more likely to vote for populist parties are not at the bottom of the social hierarchy but are slightly higher in economic terms, whose fear of falling means they have more to defend in terms of status. These two propositions, for which they adduce considerable empirical support, leads to ethno-nationalism and misogyny because it is feared that 'foreigners' and women will take good jobs, causing a fall in the voters' status.

In contrast, women's increasing participation in the labor market has made a significant difference to their sense of subjective status. Gidron and Hall show that, while the social status of lower-educated men has declined in most countries, for lower-educated women it is the opposite, including in Britain, the United States and Germany. These data are clearly consistent with the view that it is lower-educated men that are the driving force for authoritarian populism. The rise of Trump, Johnson and Bolsonaro is, then, no surprise.

Before we consider that authoritarian populism is wholly a function of white, working-class men, we should not forget the capitalist context for this resentment. We live in neoliberal capitalism in which reward and effort have been fractured by wealth. When house prices can outstrip wages, then, in electoral terms, economic productivity is not the primary political focus. Raising house prices is, which is why a right of center policy response to this pandemic has been to encourage house price inflation. Recent research has shown that many working-class voters who are house owners voted for populist governments. At the same time, many of the extremely wealthy in the US voted for Trump (Markovits, 2019). In Britain, Brexit was supported by the wealthy, many of whom had businesses outside of Britain; few were in the business of creating productive jobs.

In this form of capitalism, paradoxes abound. For a start, working-class resentment is not about getting a university education; rather, it is focused on the loss of good, working-class jobs, as Gidron and Hall (2017) have noted. At the same time, whatever property working-class families own, it does not compensate for a sense of resentment over the loss of good jobs which, as Angela Rayner observed, confer dignity and identity.

So, while many of the rungs of the jobs ladder have broken, populism has been particularly associated with the loss of good, working-class jobs in communities that have long suffered from the offshoring of jobs. Many of these jobs are in extractive industries that are being closed down due to the climate crisis. As these communities have been devastated, no alternative strategy for good jobs has been implemented because it was assumed that the 'market' rather than state-driven, industrial policy would address the problem.

It is only belatedly that previously neoliberal governments have started to address this problem.

The Changing Nature of Capitalism

Earlier, it was suggested that the debate over meritocracy had touched on a new *zeitgeist*. This concerned the rejection of meritocracy as the cornerstone of the social contract between the individual and the state. It has been argued that it should be retained because it has been the justification for inequality under capitalism for over a century. The problem is that there are varieties of capitalism, such as neoliberal or primitive capitalism, that have radically changed. Indeed, there is a major debate across the left, from the center to radical economists, from Piketty (2014), Reich (2015) and Zuboff (2019), through to those taking a Marxist approach, as to whether we are entering a new variant of capitalism or a new mode of production, altogether (Zacares, 2021). In terms of education and meritocracy, the idea that it is through the knowledge and skills acquired in education that aspiring individuals can be upwardly mobile needs to be heavily qualified. The fact that rises in house prices can, even for those in the least expensive houses, rise faster than annual wages tells us that twentieth century links between capitalism, the labor market, knowledge and skills no longer hold. While this is a concrete example that property owners will have experienced, the focus on much wealth creation is based on an extension of property rights to intellectual property. In turn, this has created a form of rentier capitalism which emphasizes the significance of unearned wealth through monopoly power based on intellectual property rights, land and other forms of exclusion. The American and Chinese tech corporations are paradigm examples. At the top of these corporations are executives who earn, in a year, more than an average worker earns in a lifetime: an obscene and damaging form of inequality as even the IMF recognizes. Despite the political turn to economic nationalism, the global economy remains structured as a series of oligopolies or near monopolies of which the social media giants, cars, computers and electrical goods companies are all headed by the super wealthy.

Among these forms of exclusion is private education. This was once the preserve of national ruling classes but has now been extended globally to international schools that offer elite qualifications, like the International Baccalaureate. The wealth of these elite institutions tends to foreclose on the rules determining a meritocratic competition for credentials. Access is for those who can afford the fees. Hence, they confer unwarranted property rights on the qualifications they offer. Private education has rarely entered the debate over meritocracy. As capitalism changes or is transformed, it is highly unlikely that the privilege it confers will be addressed. The nature of ruling classes may change but the inequalities remain.

In writing *Globalizing Education Policy*, Fazal Rizvi and Bob Lingard were focusing on the various global institutions that were informing policy and the processes of policy importation they facilitated under neoliberal assumptions. Neoliberalism is an exhausted doctrine because its key theoretical assumptions and the effects of its practices have been refuted (Lauder, 2020). That does not mean that some of its mechanisms of control and discipline, particularly in education, will not remain. That said, nations are now in a far more uncertain position than even in 2010, and the influence of global institutions such as the OECD, which was so important in promoting human capital theory in education, is now qualifying, if not retreating from this view. Countries now have a range of wicked problems to address and guidance for education from the market and its supporting institutions are losing their legitimacy. It is evident that many nostrums of that age no longer hold and we need to rethink the role of education in terms of a new social contract.

Toward a New Social Contract

With capitalism in transition, governed, in many countries at least in the interim, by forms of authoritarian populism, what would a new social contract involve for those who seek a progressive alternative to meritocracy?

Here we need to start with the broken jobs ladder. Policies need to be enacted in a new model of political economy which rejects the mostly widely-canvassed defense of the current model, which is that the creation of untaxed wealth is justified because it promotes innovation by rewarding risk. This is wealth that has been gained from inheritance or from rentier forms of capitalism for which innovation, according to even orthodox economists, is stifled by a lack of competition. Wealth, it is argued, trickles down to benefit everyone. This does not stand up to comparative judgments as to the best-performing economies. As Adair Turner (2001) noted two decades ago, it is political choice through conflict as to which type of capitalism is embraced.

More recently, Thomas Piketty's (2014) comparative study of what he calls the super managers shows quite clearly that this is merely an unwarranted ideology to justify wealth accumulation. More recently, economists at LSE have shown that the trickle down theory is a myth which, given that expenditure on goods can be global, is not surprising (Hope & Limberg, 2020). It is for this reason that the development of good jobs needs to be placed within a wider model in which rentier capitalism, with its super profits and rewards, is rejected for one where profit is directed to investment in good jobs alongside the funding of new forms of social contribution.

There are straws in the wind. Biden has rejected trickle down economics and has prompted a global response to the taxation of oligopolies. This is a start, albeit tenuous, because it holds out the possibility of raising funds to finance a wider understanding of social contribution at a time when good jobs are becoming scarcer. As we have seen, under neoliberalism, contribution is measured by market value. Yet, there are many forms of contribution, from the work of carers, mostly undertaken by women, to the many forms of voluntary service provided through the pandemic that should be recognized.

Given the lack of good jobs, there are at least two ways in which the state can address the twin problems of work and contribution. The first and most radical is the development of some form of universal basic income (UBI) given to all citizens which, provided it offers a genuine living wage, would enable non-market forms of contribution. It is radical because the notion of contribution through paid work is deeply ingrained within capitalism, although not that far beyond the political horizon. At the start of the pandemic, there were calls for a UBI.

An alternative would be that the state takes on the role of employer of last resort in which those who cannot find paid employment are offered good jobs that focus on forms of social contribution outside the market. This was a policy that was introduced, in many countries, in a cruder form during the Great Depression.

What role does education play in rethinking our way out of a broken system?

Rethinking Education

We can start with the view, taken by Amartya Sen, that education should enable "the expansion of human freedom to live the kind of lives that people have reason to value" (Sen, 2001). What does that mean when we have a planetary climate crisis and an authoritarian threat to democracy? We cannot choose to live on a destroyed planet and we cannot choose without democracy, even if the choices that current democracies offer are limited. Confronted by these fundamental problems, education should surely broaden its aims and curricula to include an education for democracy and for ecological sustainability, as well as providing the knowledge and skills necessary for the development of a green economy.

Is this merely a dream? Well, it is one held by millions of students who have walked out of school to protest the lack of action on the climate crisis and the misogynistic treatment of women in schools. Education policy-makers and academics focusing on the management of education treat students as if they only become aware, rational and active once they have received the prescribed knowledge and skills. This is a major error: student activism should lead to a reconsideration of how schools are run. Top-down management and the ubiquitous distributed leadership literature need to be overturned to provide schools with genuine forms of democratic participation. It was a conservative philosopher of education, Richard Peters (1966), who pointed out the inconsistency between authoritarian schooling and the development of democratic citizens.[4] We need to rethink the form, content and processes of education, while ensuring that students have access to what Michael Young et al. (2014) have called the powerful knowledge that we need as an antidote to fake news and to address the fundamental problems we confront.

Notes

1 Nick Gibb, 8 February, 2018.
2 https://www.bizvibe.com/blog/energy-and-fuels/top-10-wind-turbine-manufacturers-world/
3 https://solarpowernerd.com/top-solar-panel-manufacturers/#:~:text=10%20Top%20Solar%20Panel%20Manufacturers%20Worldwide%20%5BUpdated%202020%5D,Seraphim%20Energy%20Group.%205%20Must%20Solar.%20More%20items
4 While Peters acknowledged this inconsistency, he saw students as 'initiates' who could not make reasoned judgements until they had been educated.

References

Brown, C. (2014). *Educational Binds of Poverty: The Lives of School Children*, Routledge.

Brown, C. & Carr, S. (2019). Education policy and mental weakness: A response to a mental health crisis, *Journal of Education Policy*, *34*(2), 242–266.

Brown, P. (2003). The opportunity trap: Education and employment in the global economy, *European Educational Research Journal*, *2*(1), 142–180.

Brown, P., Lauder, H., & Ashton, D. (2011). *The Global Auction: The Broken Promises of Education, Jobs and Income*, Oxford University Press.

Brown, P., Lauder, H., & Cheung, S.Y. (2020). *The Death of Human Capital? Its Failed Promise and How to Renew it in an Age of Disruption*, Oxford University Press.

Bukodi, E. & Goldthorpe, J. (2021). Meritocracy and populism: Is there a connection? London, UKICE working paper 01/2021.

Carney, M. (2021). *Value(s)*, William Collins.

Davis, G. (2016). *The Vanishing American Corporation: Navigating the Hazards of the New Economy*, Berrett-Koehler.

Gidron, N. & Hall, P. (2017). The politics of social status: Economic and cultural roots of the populist right, *British Journal of Sociology*, *68*, S57–S81.

Goos, M. & Manning, A. (2003). *Lousy and Lovely Jobs: The Rising Polarization of Work in Britain*, Centre for Economic Performance, London School of Economics and Political Science.

Holmes, C. & Mayhew, K. (2012). *The Changing Shape of the UK Job Market and Its Implications for the Bottom Half of Earners*, The Resolution Foundation.

Hope, D. & Limberg, J. (2020). The economic consequences of major tax cuts for the rich. *International Inequalities Institute Working Papers (55)*. London School of Economics and Political Science.

Kato, S., Galán-Muros, V., & Weko, T. (2020). *The Emergence of Alternative Credentials*, OECD.

Lauder, H. (2020). Revolutions in educational policy: The vexed question of evidence and policy development, in A. Brown, & E. Wisby (Eds.) *Knowledge, Policy and Practice in Education and the Struggle for Social Justice, Essays Inspired by the Work of Geoff Whitty*, UCL Press. 179–190.

Lauder, H., Sandoval, A., & Kameshwara, K. (2021). *National Income and Educational Inequality: A Comparative Analysis*, Education Department, University of Bath.

Markovits, D. (2019). *The Meritocracy Trap*, Allen Lane.

OECD (2015). *In It Together: Why Less Inequality Benefits All*, OECD.

OECD (2018). *A Broken Social Elevator: How to Promote Social Mobility*, OECD.

Peters, R. (1966). *Ethics and Education*, Unwin University Books.

Piketty, T. (2014). *Capital in the Twenty-First Century*, Belknap/Harvard University Press.

Plomin, R. (2018). *Blueprint: How DNA Makes Us Who We Are*, Allen Lane.

Reich, R. (2015). *Saving Capitalism for the Many Not the Few*, Alfred Knopf.

Sandel, M. (2021). *The Tyranny of Merit: What's Become of the Common Good?* Penguin.

Sen, A. (2001). *Development as Freedom*, Oxford University Press.

Sennet, R. & Cobb, J. (1972). *The Hidden Injuries of Class*, Cambridge University Press.

The Social Mobility Commission (2017). *Low Pay and Labour Progression: The Great Escape*, The Social Mobility Commission.

Turner, A. (2001). *Just Capital: The Liberal Economy*, Macmillan.

Wheelahan, L. & Moodie, G. (2021). Gig qualifications for the gig economy: Micro-credentials and the 'hungry mile', *Higher Education*. doi: 10.1007/s10734-021-00742-3

Young, M., Lambert, D., Roberts, C. et al. (2014). *Knowledge and the Future School: Curriculum and Social Justice*, Bloomsbury.

Zacares, J. (2021). The noon of the rentier, *New Left Review, 129*, May/June, 47–68.

Zuboff, S. (2019). *The Age of Surveillance Capitalism*, Profile Books.

8

EDUCATIONAL PRIVATIZATION

Expanding spaces and new global
regulatory trends

Adrián Zancajo, Antoni Verger, and Clara Fontdevila

Education privatization and marketization are interconnected and globalizing phenomena. In the last three decades, numerous governments have adopted a broad range of pro-market reforms in the education sector, including freedom of school choice and competitive funding formulas, and private school provision has expanded in all world regions. However, pro-market policies are not the only driver of educational privatization. Far from being a univocal policy process, in education, privatization springs from a diverse range of mechanisms that go from the demand-driven expansion of private independent provision to government-initiated Public-Private Partnerships (PPPs) with the private school sector. Furthermore, why and how privatization has advanced and sedimented in so many educational systems vary significantly across national and sub-national contexts.

After decades of educational privatization and marketization, the impact of these trends continues to be a source of controversy. Nevertheless, in the past few years, a wide consensus about the negative effects of privatization on equity has crystallized. Comparative analysis and case studies conducted in different places have repeatedly demonstrated that the expansion of private provision tends to increase school segregation and social stratification (Alegre & Ferrer, 2010; Macpherson, Robertson & Walford, 2014). Faced with such evidence, key international organizations and civil society initiatives have advocated for adopting regulatory frameworks that allow combining the supposed benefits of private provision and school choice with certain equity standards (OECD, 2017; UNESCO, 2017; World Bank, 2017). Even civil society organizations that tend to be hostile to the very presence of private provision in educational systems consider that the public regulation debate needs to be encouraged (see The Abidjan Principles, 2019). As Rizvi (2016) points out, the current international debate "is no longer whether private actors should be allowed in education, but rather, to

DOI: 10.4324/9781003207528-8

what extent and how should their activities be regulated, and to what end" (p. 2). However, whether and how this regulatory debate manifests at the country level has not yet been examined in depth from a comparative perspective.

The main objective of this chapter is to explore how, in the past few decades, privatization policy frameworks have evolved in those educational systems with a higher presence of private schools. Specifically, we aim to find out how and to what extent equity concerns have contributed to transform the governance and regulation of private education provision. Our analysis is informed by a policy instruments perspective. This perspective departs from the assumption that the selection of policy instruments, as well as their continuous adaptation, do not always respond to pragmatic reasons or follow linear processes, but rather result from the complex and ever-evolving interaction between institutions, political and economic interests, and ideas (Capano & Lippi, 2017). This implies analyzing the set of problems associated with the choice or use of a given policy instrument, as well as the representations and problematizations involved in the reformulation of the instruments in question (Lascoumes & Le Galès, 2007).

In this chapter, we argue that the adoption of privatization policies can be motivated by a wide range of rationales, which go from fostering competition and market dynamics in education, to promoting freedom of instruction, pedagogic diversification or educational expansion. It is precisely this multiplicity of origins and policy goals that influences—and to a great extent explains—the diversity of regulatory configurations that can be observed among countries. Nonetheless, despite this diversity, over time, privatization policies have tended to be problematized due to their negative effects on social and educational equity in most contexts. Governments attempt to address these problems through the calibration and adjustment of existing regulatory instruments and through the adoption of new instruments, but less frequently through structural reforms.

To be sure, empirical evidence on the effectiveness of ongoing regulatory changes in taming market dynamics is still limited and inconclusive. This is because many of these regulatory efforts are relatively recent and, in consequence, research in this area is very much in its infancy. Likewise, the potential of regulation as a strategy to conjugate privatization with an equity agenda remains undertheorized, and the assumptions underpinning the high expectations placed on regulation often go unexamined. Nonetheless, as our chapter shows, attempts at the social re-embedding of education markets through public regulation continue to gain global momentum, contributing to the continuous transformation of privatization policies and frameworks.

Policy goals, regulatory configurations and calibrations

Privatization policies can be motivated by different policy agendas and goals, and are the result of distinct pathways and historical junctures. Accordingly, education privatization comes in many guises—far from being a unitary phenomenon, it manifests differently in different contexts, crystallizing in multiple policy instruments and regulatory configurations (Rizvi & Lingard 2009; Verger, Fontdevila & Zancajo, 2016; Rizvi & Lingard, 2009). This section delves into this heterogeneity of policy and governance frameworks by identifying and characterizing four different privatization models, corresponding to the main drivers and policy goals behind the expansion of private provision. Each model groups together those countries where privatization appears to be driven by similar rationales and to rely on policy instruments alike.

Fostering competition and choice: privatization through pro-market reforms

Chile and Sweden are two of the most emblematic cases of pro-market and privatization reforms in education. The processes of reform these countries went through aimed to foster competition between schools, as a way to undermine the so-called monopolistic position of the state in the provision of education, encourage the diversification of the education system, and favor school choice among families. The central instrument to achieve this goal was a voucher scheme, which was particularly effective at favoring the involvement of private actors in the provision of education. The voucher scheme, far from being an isolated policy intervention, became a turning point in the trajectory of the educational systems in both countries and conditioned decisively the educational debates and reforms that would have to come (Cox, 2003; Wiborg, 2015). Despite the common goals and instruments of the privatization policies in Chile and Sweden, the political economy of the respective reforms was starkly contrasting. In Chile, pro-market reforms in education were adopted in the 1980s, during a repressive military dictatorship, and in a context of structural reforms aimed to change the role of the State in the economic and social realms. In contrast, the voucher scheme in Sweden was adopted by a democratically elected conservative government, and as a continuation of a process of decentralization of public administration initiated in the late 1980s by a social democratic government (Lundahl, 2002).

In line with the objectives pursued by these reforms, in Chile and Sweden, the regulation of private subsidized provision originally followed what we could denominate as a pro-market approach (Bellei & Muñoz, 2021). This means that the PPP established with the voucher scheme was mainly guided by market rules and favored the state adopting a subsidiary role in the provision of education. Accordingly, any private school with sufficient demand was allowed to receive public funding via the voucher; the funding mechanisms of public and private subsidized schools were equivalent and distributed on a per capita basis; and private schools were allowed to obtain additional resources by charging fees to families. In this model, school choice was highly liberalized, and private subsidized schools enjoyed high levels of autonomy to establish their own admissions criteria. In line with this pro-market approach, Sweden and Chile are among the few countries in the world that have historically allowed for-profit providers to receive public funding.

Nonetheless, in the two past decades, both countries have adopted reforms through which the state has regained centrality in the governance of education and the private sector has been subject to stricter regulations. The need to reform PPP regulatory frameworks emerged mainly due to intense public and political debates around the impact of privatization policies on equity. In Chile, the high level of school segregation triggered a student-led social movement against the pro-market policies in education inherited from the dictatorship (Bellei & Cabalín, 2013). In Sweden, school segregation has also played an important role in the problematization of private subsidized provision, but the low results obtained by the country in PISA 2012 triggered an even more determinant debate due to the perceived relationship between the voucher scheme and the country's performance decline (Wiborg, 2014). Finally, in both countries, the fact that private schools can turn a profit while receiving public funding to provide a public good, such as basic education, has also been a source of controversy.

As a result of these problematic and political contested processes, Chile and Sweden have progressively revisited their PPP frameworks. Both countries have introduced relevant changes in the criteria and procedures to authorize new private schools to receive public funding. In Sweden, the authorization of a new subsidized private provider needs to consider the impact on the public schools located in the same area (Sahlgren, 2016), whereas in Chile, the new educational reform passed in 2015 requires that the new provider attends an unmet demand and offers a pedagogical approach not yet present in the local area (Ley 20845, 2015). Both countries have also banned private schools from charging fees to families—a prohibition that has been paralleled by a rise in the public funding received by these schools. The Chilean government also reformed its school choice regulation and adopted a controlled choice system directly managed by the Ministry of Education, and has prohibited for-profit providers from receiving public funding (Muñoz & Weinstein, 2019).

However, the Chilean experience demonstrates that PPP calibrations do not necessarily advance without resistances. The more recent reforms adopted by the Chilean government between 2014 and 2018 have faced important opposition by right-wing parties, private providers' organizations and even families with children attending private subsidized schools (Bellei, 2016). Many of these actors perceived stricter regulations as challenging to their privileged position in the education market (Zancajo, 2019).

Preserving freedom of instruction: the case of historical PPPs

In other countries, PPP schemes were originally adopted as a measure to guarantee the financial viability of an already existing private education supply, mainly managed by faith-based institutions. In such settings, the support for private education was initially devised as a means to preserve freedom of instruction. Generally, these PPP arrangements were adopted during the educational expansion of the twentieth century in which public provision was institutionalized. This was remarkably the case of the Netherlands, Belgium, Spain and Argentina, which went through the PPP route many decades ago, in some cases more than a century ago.

At the beginning of the twentieth century, the Netherlands adopted a generous system of public subsidies for private schools. The measure allowed for the participation of different religious groups in the provision of education and is considered a response to the religious pluralism that has historically characterized Dutch society (James, 1984). In Australia, France and Canada, efforts to protect the viability of faith-based education through PPPs were largely the result of the proactive mobilization and political pressures exerted by private providers (Angus, 2003; Fowler, 1992; Teyssier, 2011). In Belgium, Spain and Argentina, the preservation of private provision was not only oriented at preventing political conflict, but also a strategy to guarantee the sufficiency of education supply in a context of growing educational demand (De Rynck, 2005; Calero & Bonal, 1999; De Rynck 2005; Moschetti, 2018).

In many countries with historical PPPs, private provision is still publicly funded due to its perceived patrimonial value and its political weight. Nonetheless, the original goal to legitimate the adoption of this type of PPPs was to guarantee freedom of instruction. Freedom of instruction is thus a cross-cutting policy objective in historical PPPs. However, with the passage of time, some countries have attempted to conjugate freedom of instruction with advancing the equivalence between public and private-subsidized sectors. In the Netherlands, Belgium and Spain, PPP arrangements are explicitly oriented at ensuring that all publicly funded schools, regardless of their ownership, are equivalent in terms of inputs, processes and outcomes. Nonetheless, not all historical PPPs have followed the equivalence path. This divergence has translated into a bifurcation of the regulatory regimes in place.

On the one hand, we find countries with historical PPPs where 'freedom of instruction' remains the central policy goal of the partnership between the State and the private sector. In these cases, the PPP framework is oriented toward ensuring that private subsidized providers comply with some basic quality standards and have the necessary resources to continue operating autonomously. This is the case of Denmark, Canada, Argentina and Australia, where private subsidized schools enjoy considerable levels of autonomy at the organizational, educational and economic levels. In return, the public funding they receive only covers their operational costs partially—so these schools are allowed to charge tuition fees to families. Furthermore, the authorization of new private subsidized schools relies primarily on social-demand criteria, and new providers receive little to no help in order to start a new school, since these PPPs aim to guarantee the continuity of an existing private supply, but do not necessarily focus on fostering its expansion (Zancajo, Verger & Fontdevila, 2022).

On the other hand, countries such as Belgium, the Netherlands and Spain have attempted to combine freedom of instruction *with* equivalence. Accordingly, their PPP frameworks are characterized by an 'exchange logic' according to which the equalization of public funding received by public schools and private subsidized schools is paralleled by a considerable loss in the autonomy enjoyed by the latter. In these countries, the criteria guiding the human and economic resources allocation are the same for public and PPP schools, and families' contributions are prohibited or strictly regulated (De Groof, 2004; Nusche et al., 2015; Patrinos, 2013). Subsidized private schools are subject to the same accountability requirements and curricular standards as those applied to public schools. Likewise, school choice is regulated according to government-defined priority criteria, which apply to public and private subsidized schools alike. The only area in which private subsidized schools have comparatively higher levels of autonomy is the management of human resources (Eurydice, 2016).

Despite the equivalence objective to which the PPP frameworks in the Netherlands, Belgium and Spain aspire, PPPs in these countries have been problematized because of the persistent segregation and social stratification dynamics between public and private sectors. This problematization owes much to a growing body of research and comparative data (e.g., PISA) bringing to the light the relationship between private subsidized provision and high levels of school segregation of ethnic minorities and/or socially disadvantaged students (Murillo, Belavi & Pinilla, 2018; Peters & Walraven, 2011; Sierens, Mahieu & Nouwen, 2011). As consequence of the political and public debate around such questions, many of these historical PPPs have recently engaged in policy efforts to mitigate their equity problems. For instance, the French-speaking and the Flemish communities in Belgium or the Netherlands have adopted or strengthened needs-based formula funding according to which schools concentrating high numbers of disadvantaged students are allocated additional public resources. In the same spirit, most of these education systems have also established controlled school choice systems and/or prioritization criteria oriented at securing a more balanced distribution of students (Friant, 2016; Levin, Cornelisz & Hanisch-Cerda, 2013; Peters & Walraven, 2011).

Nonetheless, the reforms of the historical PPP model have not been exempted from resistance and controversy. In the case of the French-speaking community of Belgium, the adoption of a controlled school choice system was highly contested by private providers and family organizations, who considered that the new regulation was undermining families' right to choose school. Beyond the political consequences of this campaign of opposition, the fact that some key stakeholders do not legitimate the reform has negatively influenced its implementation and, accordingly, its capacity to reduce school segregation (Cantillon, 2013).

Promoting autonomy: privatization as the means for system diversification and school improvement

Different countries have embraced PPP programs as a policy expected to lead to higher levels of pedagogical, curricular and managerial autonomy. Of all of them, the charter schools programs in the US and the Academies and Free Schools policy in England are probably the most emblematic. Other countries, such as Canada, Colombia and New Zealand, have also experimented with this PPP approach through charter schools and comparable programs. However, in these countries, the programs have been completely dismantled (New Zealand) or remain small-scale and experimental (e.g., Alberta, Canada).

Here, the main policy goal is to subsidize or sub-contract private providers that are exempt from following certain regulations that apply to public schools as a means of diversifying the educational offer and of favoring school improvement and innovation within the educational system. Thus, autonomy is the cornerstone of this type of PPPs. Charter schools, Academies and Free Schools enjoy higher levels of autonomy than conventional public schools in both pedagogical and organizational terms. These schools have a great deal of autonomy as regards to the definition of the school curriculum or the school calendar, as well as in relation to staffing and budgetary decisions (Podgursky, 2006; Roberts & Danechi, 2019; Podgursky, 2006). These programs also follow an equity rationale, in the sense they are expected to give more opportunities of choice and quality education to socially disadvantaged populations (see Gorard, Siddiqui & See, 2019; Vergari, 2007).

In some cases, this high level of autonomy is not only understood as conducive to innovation and diversification, but also expected to lead to greater customization of the educational project of schools to contextual particularities. However, the autonomy enjoyed by PPP schools in these countries tends to be limited in practice by the expansion of large educational providers operating chains of schools that end up standardizing their educational product and mode of delivery. School autonomy is also restricted by high-stakes accountability measures. While the quality-assurance mechanisms usually are the same for public and private subsidized schools, evaluation and accountability instruments tend to be particularly consequential for the subsidized private school sector— since low levels of academic performance or insufficient progress in external assessments can often lead to the discontinuity of the public funding (Thomsen, 2017; Roberts & Danechi, 2019; Thomsen, 2017)). Thus, accountability pressure is especially intense in these schools, leading to a certain degree of standardization that is at odds with the autonomy goal of these PPPs. Another effect of accountability pressure is that it incentivizes charter schools and Academies to be more socially and academically selective (Coldron et al., 2008; Waitoller, 2020), contributing to school segregation and to the exacerbation of educational inequalities.

The educational systems that follow the autonomy PPP model have tended to equate the funding allocated to public and private schools over time. When first adopted in the 1990s, public subsidies did not cover the total expenses of Academies and charter schools. At the same time, these schools were not allowed to charge school fees to families; and it was expected that the private providers would resort to sponsors or philanthropic organizations to complement the public baseline funding. Nonetheless, the English PPP scheme has evolved toward equalizing Academies' and public schools' funding, whereas charter schools in most states of the US are eligible for compensatory funding oriented at supporting students with special needs (Education Commission of the States, 2018).

Regarding school admission policies, the autonomy of Academies and charter schools is rather restricted, at least according to formal regulations (Roberts & Danechi, 2019). For instance, in most US states, charter schools are obliged to select their students randomly (e.g., applying a lottery system) in the case of overdemand (Skinner, 2014). Nonetheless, in the past years, it has become obvious that both charter schools and Academies tend to enroll higher percentages of advantaged students than their counterparts from the public sector, contributing to increasing school stratification between private and public schools. In response to these concerns, the English government has reformed school admissions procedures several times, intending to homogenize the admission and prioritization criteria of public and private sectors (West, Barham & Hind, 2011). In the case of US charter schools, a prominent source of concern regarding school admissions has been the exclusion of students with special needs or disabilities (Waitoller, 2020). In response, new federal regulations have been passed requiring charter schools to provide children with disabilities with equal opportunities (National Council on Disability, 2018). New charter school regulations have been adopted at the state level as well. The state of California has been particularly active in this regard, mainly by equipping itself with new planning tools to address the fast and non-controlled expansion of charter and cyber-charter schools. However, as we have observed in relation to the previous PPP models, these regulations have been fiercely opposed by charter school organizations and families' associations, and, on occasion, have even meant the standstill of some of the Bills.[1]

Meting an expanding demand: de facto privatization

In contrast with other cases presented above, the expansion of private provision is not necessarily the consequence of an active role of governments but precisely of insufficient state intervention in the educational sector. This is, for instance, the case of the Low Fee Private Schools (LFPSs) that have mushroomed in many countries of the Global South in the past two decades.

The expansion of LFPSs is a complex and context-sensitive phenomenon. However, it is possible to identify two main factors that have led to the growth of these schools. First, the lack of an adequate state provision in areas where educational demand has grown significantly in the past years. As a consequence, LFPSs have emerged in these areas, frequently becoming the only available schooling option for many students. Second, LFPSs have catered for increasing educational demand because they have been able to meet the demands and preferences of religious or linguistic minority groups. In many countries, state provision is too uniform and, frequently, minority groups opt for LFPSs to receive an education that meets their specific needs (Härmä, 2021; Verger, Fontdevila & Zancajo, 2018).

However, the expansion of LFPSs cannot be understood without the role played by some international organizations and bilateral aid agencies. In many countries in the Global South, these international actors have played a determinant role in promoting and legitimizing LFPSs (Verger, Fontdevila & Zancajo, 2018). These actors promote LFPSs as a strategy to increase access to education in countries where the State does not have the necessary resources or technical capacity to develop a public supply capable of absorbing the growing educational demand. In addition, these organizations have also been instrumental in providing funding and credit to LFPSs—which, in turn, has contributed to increasing the interest of private companies and corporations in this sector (Srivastava, 2016).

The expansion of private independent provision in the Global South has posed several challenges in terms of equity. Despite their supposed low level of fees, LFPSs are not necessarily accessible to the poorest population. Studies in different contexts have shown that fees charged by these schools are not affordable for most socially disadvantaged groups (Ashley et al., 2014). In this regard, the combination of the lack of public provision and the prevalence of LFPSs schools has resulted in the exclusion of socially disadvantaged students from education.

The dramatic growth of LFPSs in the past decades and the concerns about their impact on equity have led an important debate about their regulation. The main objective pursued by the regulation of LFPSs is to guarantee that these schools are registered and certificated, which is considered a first and necessary step to ensure that governments are able to control the growth of this schooling sector and that LFPSs comply with, at least, basic quality standards (Härmä, 2021; Baum, Cooper & Lusk-Stover, 2018). However, the evidence available shows that the regulation of LFPSs has faced numerous challenges. For instance, many governments have failed to enforce regulations as a result of technical constraints or resource limitations (Ashley et al., 2014). Other authors have observed how LFPSs respond to stricter regulations by remaining or going unregistered, which reduces the effectiveness of public regulation (Baum et al. 2018; Härmä, 2021). Finally, corruption frequently appears as another factor that challenges the effect of public regulation since LFPSs can frequently overcome regulatory requirements by bribing government officials (Härmä, 2021). Overall, the evidence available indicates that the regulatory efforts have not been effective in mitigating the equity and quality issues associated with LFPSs (Härmä, 2019).

Other countries have opted for integrating LFPSs into PPP schemes as a means to reduce the potential negative impacts of equity. This option has received the support of international organizations like the World Bank, that considers PPP schemes suitable to overcome equity issues by facilitating the access of the poorest populations to private schooling (Dahal & Nguyen, 2014). However, the experiences of countries such as Liberia, India or Uganda show that the public funding of private schools is not necessarily exempt from problems and risks in terms of equity. In many cases, private schools continue to charge fees to families (despite receiving public funding) or to exclude socially disadvantaged students (Crawfurd, 2017; Walford, 2013).

Discussion and conclusions

The privatization of education has the gift of ubiquity. It is simultaneously a globalizing and a highly contextual phenomenon. The diversity of pathways toward education privatization that we have shown in this chapter is largely reflected in the variegated objectives sought by pro-private sector policies in education. To a great extent, education privatization models vary significantly depending on why, by whom and under which circumstances pro-privatization policies and instruments have been adopted. Nonetheless, privatization trends do not follow a clear-cut pattern in terms of conventional institutional variables, such as types of welfare regimes or governmental ideologies. The fact that the most drastic pro-market reforms in education have been adopted by countries with both (neo)liberal and social-democratic welfare state traditions, as Chile and Sweden respectively have, illustrates well this idea.

Regardless of their social and political origins, education privatization policy frameworks are constantly moving, something that adds an additional layer of complexity to the study of the phenomenon. Continuous processes of problematization are key to understand this dynamic. Four decades after the emergence of privatization in the global education agenda, there is consensus on the numerous risks that the penetration of private actors and market principles in education pose to equity. Independently of the model, it is increasingly clear that privatization policies across the board tend to reproduce educational inequities—and that, more often than not, they directly lead to the exacerbation of social class division and the erosion of social cohesion. This is so as the coexistence of public and private subsidized schools, and the expansion of school choice that frequently complements PPP arrangements, is conducive to higher levels of social stratification between schools, and leads to an inequitable distribution of school resources. In response to these concerns, the idea that the ultimate impact of privatization policies depends largely on the specifics of certain policy options and regulations has also been gaining ground. It is increasingly assumed that more effective public regulations could prevent privatization and pro-market policies from undermining equity. Indeed, as we have shown in this chapter, many governments have reformed their PPPs in order to mitigate phenomena such as school segregation. In most cases, these calibration processes have consisted of increasing the role of the state while curtailing the role of the market in the governance of education.

Despite optimistic views on the potential of the regulatory reforms of PPPs, evidence about the impact of this strategy is still scarce and inconclusive. The limited number of impact studies shows that regulatory reforms have had, at best, modest effects in improving equity. Two main factors could explain why regulatory reforms do not necessarily achieve the expected results. First, regulatory reforms are not necessarily able to tackle the ultimate causes of inequality in highly privatized and marketized education settings. The available evidence demonstrates that the complex mechanisms through which privatization and pro-market policies negatively affect equity (e.g., social closure, 'white flight', etc.) are not necessarily related to how these policies are designed or calibrated.

The second factor that could explain the lack of effectiveness of public regulations is related to the political economy of educational reforms. The regulatory reforms of PPPs aimed at favoring equity usually face open resistance from a wide range of actors that perceive the status quo is better aligned to their own interests. In fact, this resistance tends to come from constituencies—including private providers' associations or families' representatives— that have emerged and/or been empowered at the dawn of the same PPP policies they are trying to protect. Their resistance can result in the most disruptive elements of the reforms not being retained in the system. Nonetheless, even when pro-equity regulations are adopted, their effectiveness may be low because key actors who do not see the new measures as legitimate try to bypass them. In other cases, the lack of consensus around these reforms makes them vulnerable to changes in the ideological orientation of national or regional governments.

The factors outlined above suggest that there are important limits to the transformative power of policy regulation when education privatization has advanced substantively. Once market forces have been unleashed, they produce structural transformations that are difficult to address by simply adjusting public policy instruments or through light-touch regulatory interventions. Privatization policies inevitably end up creating vested interests, and altering the subjectivities of families, students and schools (Rizvi, 2016). Tackling the inequities produced by privatization is not possible without addressing these structural transformations—that is, without generating new forms of engagement with and within education, and altering the structure of incentives created by market mechanisms. It follows from this that, if not accompanied by a broader reflection on the ultimate goals and interests being served by pro-private provision policies, calibration efforts are unlikely to lead to the social re-embedding of education systems.

Note

1 See California Charter Association (2021). *Charter Nation unites to defeat AB 1316.* Available on: https://info.ccsa.org/blog/charter-nation-unites-to-defeat-ab-1316

References

Alegre, M. A., & Ferrer, G. (2010). School regimes and education equity: Some insights based on PISA 2006. *British Educational Research Journal, 36*(3), 433–461.

Angus, M. (2003). School choice policies and their impact on public education in Australia. In D. N. Plank, & G. Sykes (Eds.), *Choosing choice: School choice in international perspective* (pp. 112–141). New York, NY: Teachers College Press.

Ashley, L. D., McLoughlin, C., Aslam, M., Engel, J., Wales, J., Rawal, S., Batley, R., Kingdon, G., Nicolai, S., & Rose, P. (2014). *The role and impact of private schools in developing countries: A rigorous review of the evidence. Final report* (EPPI-Centre Education Rigorous Literature Review No. 2206). London, UK: Department for International Development.

Baum, D. R., Cooper, R., & Lusk-Stover, O. (2018). Regulating market entry of low-cost private schools in Sub-Saharan Africa: Towards a theory of private education regulation. *International Journal of Educational Development, 60*, 100–112.

Bellei, C. (2016). Dificultades y resistencias de una reforma para des-mercantilizar la educación [Difficulties and resistances of a reform to diminish the market dynamics of education]. *RASE: Revista de la Asociación de Sociología de la Educación, 9*(2), 232–247.

Bellei, C., & Cabalín, C. (2013). Movimientos estudiantiles chilenos: Lucha sostenida para transformar un sistema educativo orientado al mercado [Chilean student movements: Sustained struggle to transform a market-oriented educational system]. *Current Issues in Comparative Education, 15*(2), 108–123.

Bellei, C., & Muñoz, G. (2021). Models of regulation, education policies, and changes in the education system: A long-term analysis of the Chilean case. *Journal of Educational Change.* Advance online publication. doi: 10.1007/s10833-021-09435-1

Calero, J., & Bonal, X. (1999). *Política educativa y gasto público en educación: aspectos teóricos y una aplicación al caso español* [Educational policy and public spending on education: Theoretical aspects and an application to the Spanish case]. Barcelona, Spain: Pomares-Corredor.

Cantillon, E. (2013). Mixité sociale: Le rôle des procédures d'inscription scolaire [Social diversity: The role of school enrolment procedures]. In P. Maystadt, E. Cantillon, L. Denayer, P. Pestieau, B. Van der Linden, & M. Cattelain (Eds.), *Le modèle social belge: Quel avenir?* (pp. 847–864). Charleroi, Belgium: Éditions de l'Université Ouverte.

Capano, G., & Lippi, A. (2017). How policy instruments are chosen: Patterns of decision makers' choices. *Policy Sciences, 50*(2), 269–293.

Coldron, J., Tanner, E., Finch, S., Shipton, L., Wolstenholme, C., Willis, B., Demack, S., & Stiell, B. (2008). *Secondary school admissions (Research Report DCSF-RR020).* London, UK: Department for Children, Schools and Families.

Cox, C. (2003). Las políticas educacionales de Chile en las últimas dos décadas del siglo XX [Chile's educational policies in the last two decades of the 20th century]. In C. Cox (Ed.), *Políticas educacionales en el cambio de siglo: La reforma del sistema escolar de Chile* (pp. 73–146). Santiago de Chile, Chile: Editorial Universitaria.

Crawfurd, L. (2017). School management and public–private partnerships in Uganda. *Journal of African Economies, 26*(5), 539–560.

Dahal, M., & Nguyen, Q. (2014). *Private non-state sector engagement in the provision of educational services at the primary and secondary levels in South Asia: An analytical review of its role in school enrollment and student achievement* (World Bank Policy Research Working Paper No. 6899). Washington, DC: World Bank-South Asia Region, Education Unit. https://openknowledge.worldbank.org/bitstream/handle/10986/18786/WPS6899.pdf?sequence=1&isAllowed=y

De Groof, J. (2004). Regulating school choice in Belgium's Flemish Community. In P. J. Wolf, S. Macedo, D. J. Ferrero, & C. Venegoni (Eds.), *Educating citizens: International perspectives on civic values and school choice* (pp. 157–186). Washington, DC: Brookings Institution Press.

De Rynck, S. (2005). Regional autonomy and education policy in Belgium. *Regional & Federal Studies, 15*(4), 485–500.

Education Commission of the States. (2018, January). *Charter schools: How is the funding for a charter school determined? (50-S Com).* http://ecs.force.com/mbdata/mbquestNB2C?rep=CS1716

Eurydice. (2016). *Teachers' and school heads' salaries and allowances in Europe—2015/16.* Luxembourg: Publications Office of the European Union.

Fowler, F. C. (1992). School choice policy in France: Success and limitations. *Educational Policy, 6*(4), 429–443.

Friant, N. (2016). *NESET Country Report: Belgium (Unpublished manuscript)*. *Université de Mons*. https://halshs.archives-ouvertes.fr/halshs-01392996

Gorard, S., Siddiqui, N., & See, B. H. (2019). The difficulties of judging what difference the Pupil Premium has made to school intakes and outcomes in England. *Research Papers in Education, 36*(3), 355–379.

Härmä, J. (2019). Ensuring quality education? Low-fee private schools and government regulation in three sub-Saharan African capitals. *International Journal of Educational Development, 66*, 139–146.

Härmä, J. (2021). *Low-fee private schooling and poverty in developing countries*. London, UK: Bloomsbury Publishing.

James, E. (1984). Benefits and costs of privatized public services: Lessons from the Dutch educational system. *Comparative Education Review, 28*(4), 605–624.

Lascoumes, P., & Le Galès, P. (2007). Introduction: Understanding public policy through its instruments? From the nature of instruments to the sociology of public policy instrumentation. *Governance, 20*(1), 1–21.

Levin, H. M., Cornelisz, I., & Hanisch-Cerda, B. (2013). Does educational privatisation promote social justice? *Oxford Review of Education, 39*(4), 514–532.

Ley 20845. (2015). *de inclusión escolar que regula la admisión de los y las estudiantes, elimina el financiamiento compartido y prohíbe el lucro en establecimientos educacionales que reciben aportes del Estado* [School inclusion law, 20845, 2015, which regulates student admission, eliminates shared financing and prohibits profit-making in educational establishments that receive State funding]. https://www.bcn.cl/leychile/navegar?idNorma=1078172

Lundahl, L. (2002). Sweden: Decentralization, deregulation, quasi-markets–and then what? *Journal of Education Policy, 17*(6), 687–697.

Macpherson, I., Robertson, S., & Walford, G. (Eds.). (2014). *Education, privatisation and social justice: Case studies from Africa, South Asia and South East Asia*. Oxford, UK: Symposium Books.

Moschetti, M. (2018). Alianzas público-privadas en educación. Un análisis de la política de subvenciones a escuelas privadas en barrios desfavorecidos de la Ciudad de Buenos Aires (Doctoral thesis). Universitat Autònoma de Barcelona). https://www.tdx.cat/handle/10803/665450

Muñoz, G., & Weinstein, J. (2019). The difficult process in Chile: Redefining the rules of the game for subsidized private education. In C. Ornelas (Ed.), *Politics of education in Latin America. Reforms, resistance and persistence* (p. 72100). Leiden, The Netherlands: Brill.

Murillo, F. J., Belavi, G., & Pinilla, L. M. (2018). Segregación escolar público-privada en España [Public–private school segregation in Spain]. *Papers. Revista de Sociologia, 103*(3), 307–337.

National Council on Disability. (2018). *Every student succeeds act and students with disabilities*. Washington, DC: National Council on Disability.

Nusche, D., Miron, G., Santiago, P., & Teese, R. (2015). *OECD Reviews of School Resources: Flemish Community of Belgium 2015*. Paris, France: OECD Publishing.

OECD. (2017). *School choice and school vouchers: An OECD perspective*. Paris, France: OECD Publishing.

Patrinos, H. A. (2013). Private education provision and public finance: The Netherlands. *Education Economics, 21*(4), 392–414.

Peters, D., & Walraven, G. (2011). The Netherlands: Interventions to counteract school segregation. In J. Bakker, E. Denessen, D. Peters, & G. Walraven (Eds.), *International perspectives on countering school segregation* (pp. 131–150). Anvers, Belgium /Apeldoorn, The Netherlands: Garant.

Podgursky, M. (2006). Teams versus bureaucracies: Personnel policy, wage-setting, and teacher quality in traditional public, charter, and private schools. Education Working Paper Archive. https://eric.ed.gov/?id=ED509018

Rizvi, F. (2016). *Privatization in education: Trends and consequences (Education Research and Foresight Working Paper No. 18)*. Paris, France: UNESCO.

Rizvi, F., & Lingard, B. (2009). *Globalizing education policy*. London, UK: Routledge.

Roberts, N., & Danechi, S. (2019). *FAQs: Academies and free schools* (Briefing Paper No. 07059). London, UK: House of Commons Library.

Sahlgren, G. H. (2016). *Regulation and funding of independent schools. Lessons from Sweden*. Vancouver, British Columbia: Fraser Institute.

Sierens, S., Mahieu, P., & Nouwen, W. (2011). The desegregation policy in Flemish primary education: Is distributing migrant students among schools an effective solution? In J. Bakker, E. Denessen, D. Peeters, & G. Walraven (Eds.), *International perspectives on countering school segregation* (pp. 151–171). Anvers, Belgium/Apeldoorn, The Netherlands: Garant.

Skinner, R. R. (2014). *Charter school programs authorized by the Elementary and Secondary Education Act (ESEA Title V-B): A primer*. Washington, DC: Congressional Research Service.

Srivastava, P. (2016). Questioning the global scaling up of low-fee private schooling: The nexus between business, philanthropy, and PPPs. In A. Verger, C. Lubienski, & G. Steiner-Khamsi (Eds.), *World Yearbook of Education 2016: The global education industry* (pp. 248–263). New York, NY: Routledge.

Teyssier, R. (2011). The organizational and electoral determinants of the provincial funding of private education in Canada: A quantile regression analysis. *Canadian Journal of Political Science/Revue canadienne de science politique, 44*(4), 829–857.

The Abidjan Principles. (2019). *Guiding Principles on the human rights obligations of States to provide public education and to regulate private involvement in education*. https://static1.squarespace.com/static/5c2d081daf2096648cc801da/t/5dc414bb9f409d285dc9abf2/1573131454068/Online+version_A4_WEB_COUV%2BTEXTE_THE-ABIDJAN-PRINCIPLES_Nov_2019.pdf

Thomsen, J. (2017). *Charter school accountability under ESSA*. Denver, Colorado: Education Commission of the States.

UNESCO. (2017). *Global Education Monitoring Report 2017/18. Accountability in education: Meeting our commitments*. Paris: UNESCO.

Vergari, S. (2007). The politics of charter schools. *Educational Policy, 21*(1), 15–39.

Verger, A., Fontdevila, C., & Zancajo, A. (2016). *The privatization of education: A political economy of global education reform*. New York, NY: Teachers College Press.

Verger, A., Fontdevila, C., & Zancajo, A. (2018). Constructing low-fee private schools as an educational model for the Global South: From local origins to transnational dynamics. In A. Verger, M. Novelli, & H. K. Altinyelken (Eds.), *Global education policy and international development: New agendas, issues and policies* (2nd ed.) (pp. 255–276). London, UK: Bloomsbury.

Waitoller, F. R. (2020). *Excluded by choice: Urban students with disabilities in the education marketplace*. New York, NY: Teachers College Press.

Walford, G. (2013). State support for private schooling in India: What do the evaluations of the British Assisted Places Schemes suggest? *Oxford Review of Education, 39*(4), 533–547.

West, A., Barham, E., & Hind, A. (2011). Secondary school admissions in England 2001 to 2008: Changing legislation, policy and practice. *Oxford Review of Education, 37*(1), 1–20.

Wiborg, S. (2014, September 9). The big winners from Sweden's for-profit 'free' schools are companies, not pupils. *The Conversation*. https://theconversation.com/the-big-winners-from-swedens-for-profit-free-schools-are-companies-not-pupils-29929

Wiborg, S. (2015). Privatizing education: Free school policy in Sweden and England. *Comparative Education Review, 59*(3), 473–497.

World Bank. (2017). *World Development Report 2018: Learning to realize education promise.* Washington, DC: The World Bank.

Zancajo, A. (2019). *Drivers and hurdles to the regulation of education markets: The political economy of Chilean reform* (National Center for the Study of Privatization in Education Working Paper No. 239). New York, NY: Teachers College Press.

Zancajo, A., Verger, A., & Fontdevila, C. (2022). The instrumentation of public subsidies for private schools: Different regulatory models with concurrent equity implications. *European Educational Research Journal, 21*(2), 440–470. Advance online publication. doi. 10.1177/14749041211023339

9

THINKING ABOUT SOCIAL INEQUALITIES AND MARGINALIZATION IN EDUCATION UNDER SHIFTING GLOBAL CONDITIONS

Tero Järvinen

Introduction

In this chapter, I examine the connections between education policies, social inequality and marginalization under changing global conditions. I begin by exploring the relationship between education and social inequality before linking the concept of social inequality to identities. By referring to the concept of the 'marginal man' (sic) proposed by Robert E. Park (1928), I conceptualize marginalization as an identity conflict that is rooted in cultural transitions. Although this view of marginalization originates from the early twentieth century, I consider it a useful theoretical idea for understanding the impact of various cultural transitions on individuals' inner conflicts in today's rapidly changing globalized world. Last, I examine social inequality and marginalization in relation to educational policies. By focusing specifically on the situation of today's youth, I argue that it is crucial for the educational policies that aim to reduce inequality and marginalization to recognize the ways in which global developments are reflected in the identity formation and identity conflicts of young people. Instead of being based on ideas such as the prevalence of the standardized 'normal' life course and the homogeneity of citizens, the policies should be built on an understanding of the complexities, diversities and instabilities that are the primary features of contemporary social life.

Education and social inequality

In essence, the idea of social inequality refers to the hierarchical differences that exist between groups of people. In scholarly literature, this topic has traditionally been approached from two viewpoints. The distributional view of social

DOI: 10.4324/9781003207528-9

inequality considers the hierarchical distribution of social, political, cultural and economic resources in a given society, whereas an equality of opportunity perspective focuses on the extent to which individuals and social groups have access to these resources and valued positions in a society (Blackburn, 2008; Habibis & Walter, 2015). According to the equality of opportunity view, social inequality exists when some people have greater opportunities than others to develop and exercise whatever potential they may have (Lupton, 1992). The framework of equality of opportunity is widely used in studies on educational inequality, particularly in large-scale quantitative studies (e.g. Barone & Ruggera, 2018; Erikson, 2020).

In meritocratic societies, the intention is to design societal institutions to ensure that social position and wealth are not based on privilege but, rather, on individual ability and effort (Habibis & Walter, 2015). In line with meritocratic thinking, the objectives of reducing inequalities associated with privilege have been widely adopted in educational policies across the world since World War II. In the name of social justice and societal efficiency, the key policy aim has been to provide equal educational opportunities for all individuals irrespective of their gender, religion, ethnicity and cultural or socioeconomic backgrounds. The overall aim of these policies has been to promote the equal and just treatment of all individuals and social groups and to establish an agenda of improving the life opportunities and living conditions of the disadvantaged and discriminated groups of a society (Järvinen & Silvennoinen, forthcoming).

However, despite all the equalizing policy initiatives and implementations executed over the past fifty years, research shows that the educational attainment gap between the advantaged and disadvantaged has barely narrowed (Erikson, 2020; Järvinen & Silvennoinen, forthcoming). Research and statistics indicate persistent inequalities with regard to educational opportunities and outcomes both between and within countries. Although education has expanded rapidly in developing countries, there remain significant differences between the richer and the poorer parts of the world regarding educational enrollment and completion. While the primary school completion rate is 99 per cent in Europe and North America, the corresponding figure is 65 per cent in Sub-Saharan Africa. Global inequality is even greater at the level of lower secondary education, with completion rates being 97 per cent in Europe and North America, while being only 49 per cent in Sub-Saharan Africa (UNESCO, 2020). Further, within countries, socioeconomic inequalities in terms of educational achievement and outcomes have remained high until recently(Erikson, 2020; Lagravinese et al., 2020; Triventi et al., 2020).

In the field of sociology of education, the relationship between one's socioeconomic status and educational achievement and outcomes has been one of the major themes of research. According to the conflict theorists in the field of sociology of education, such as Bourdieu and Passeron (1977), the fundamental feature of education is that it is one of the main causes of social inequality and, at the same time, it is seen as the primary solution for the same inequalities. Since a key societal function of education is to allocate individuals to positions in the labor market and social hierarchy, it is not possible for all individuals to succeed equally in school (Labaree, 2012). In this context, the primary question from the point of view of social inequality is regarding how fairly the education system serves its function of allocating individuals to positions in a social hierarchy. The educational inequalities associated with socioeconomic status have been explained by stating that the linguistic, cultural and pedagogical practices of schools reflect the values of the middle and upper classes of society, and thus favor children belonging to these classes. Bourdieu and Passeron (1977) famously argue that, instead of being fair, education serves the interests of the privileged groups by rewarding cultural capital. That is, certain cultural and linguistic competences and dispositions of the children belonging to upper classes are prized while those of children from disadvantaged backgrounds are devalued. This manifests in the cultural demands that school sets for students, as well as in institutional practices of the school, such as allocating students into hierarchically different tracks and, thereby, providing them with unequal opportunities for further education. From this point of view, education systems are embedded in the production of inequalities. Furthermore, since individuals are allocated to the positions in the societal hierarchy based on their educational attainment and credentials, education is a crucial mechanism by which the inequalities are legitimated (Bourdieu & Passeron, 1977).

Intersectional view on social inequality

In the context of an industrial society, particularly in the first decades after World War 2 (WW2), class-division based on the distribution of economic resources was considered a primary source of social inequality. This view was reflected in educational policies, where economic maldistribution between social classes was seen as the main obstacle to educational equality. Thus, policy objectives were aimed at eliminating financial barriers so that children from disadvantaged socioeconomic backgrounds could have access to more than just compulsory education (Power, 2012). In response to changing social conditions, the theoretical understanding of social inequality has subsequently changed. Under the conditions of post-industrialism, globalization and multiculturalism, the notion of class being the primary determinant of social inequality has been challenged. As globalization progressed, and the economy moved away from industrial production to service delivery, these changes raised the criticism toward the traditional class-based understanding of social inequality. Increased immigration and the subsequent rise of multiculturalism after WW2 further fragmented the illusion of a homogeneous class structure in many countries. Further, feminist critiques pointed out that class is not a gender-neutral concept and suggested that it was gender, not class, that was the most enduring and significant source of inequality (Habibis & Walter, 2015).

The inequalities between men and women in terms of educational attainment have remarkably reduced in the long run. The growth among women with regard to participation in higher education has been rapid which has reversed gender inequalities in tertiary-level educational attainment in almost all OECD countries. At the same time, there is significant segregation between men and women in terms of their field of study. From the perspective of inequality, it is crucial to note that, regardless of the field of study women choose, their earnings still lag behind those of men. Even when women hold the same degree as men, they earn less on average than men in all fields of study and in all OECD and partner countries (OECD, 2020). Moreover, global statistics show that, even though most countries have achieved gender parity in primary education enrollment, disparities that disadvantage girls persist in many countries, particularly in Africa, the Middle East and South Asia. In secondary education, the patterns of disadvantage are, however, more complex. In contrast to primary education, the gender disparity appears to disadvantage boys in many countries. The largest gender gaps that disadvantage girls, in turn, are observed in Sub-Saharan Africa. In Chad, for example, only 62 girls are enrolled in lower secondary school for every 100 boys. Girls not only face social and economic exclusion more often than boys, but they are also vulnerable to being forced to marry early with attendant health risks, such as adolescent childbearing (UNICEF, 2020).

Due to global migration, the population of many countries is becoming diverse. At the same time, social inequalities within countries have increased. Newly arrived immigrants often have difficulties with gaining access to education to receive the knowledge, skills and certificates needed to participate in the labor market and, thus, may remain unemployed or be stuck with low-paid unattractive jobs that other people tend to avoid (Blackburn, 2008), even if they have a higher education certificate from their country of origin (Kyhä, 2011).

These days, under the conditions of globalization, migration and multiculturalism, the prevailing sociological outlook toward social inequality is characterized by an intersectional emphasis on multiple positions, where inequality is understood as being multidimensional and involving the interaction of diverse variables, which include gender, ethnicity and class. Consequently, identity has replaced class as the primary concept for understanding social inequality (e.g. Wilson, 2013). This does not mean, however, that the socioeconomic view on social inequality has lost its importance. The extent of inequality in this respect is enormous around the world (United Nations, 2020). The stark contrast between the rich and poor countries, the emergence of new groups of poor in wealthy countries and the persistent and, sometimes, worsening circumstances of disadvantaged groups around the world indicate that the traditional view of social inequality is still important in today's post-industrialized and globalized world.

The concept of identity is used to explore individual subjectivities through a criticism of the traditional, class-based understanding of inequality. Identity itself is considered to be formed from multiple sources rather than one essential variable such as class or gender. While the importance of class-based politics aiming to redistribute economic, social and political resources has declined, new forms of social movements, such as feminism and environmentalism, have emerged (Habibi & Walter, 2015). Subsequently, there have been identity-based movements and struggles with an emphasis on recognizing social diversity in many countries. Many of these movements have highlighted the inequalities that stem from cultural differences and, thus, differentiated themselves from class-based movements, wherein class-based inequality were seen as the fundamental source of exploitation and oppression (Bernstein, 2005). Further, there has been a theoretical shift from the simplistic focus on race or gender toward the idea of intersectionality as multiple disadvantage. This increasing complexity includes not only recognizing more identity-based groups and dimensions of individual difference but also acknowledging their convergence in intersectional forms of discrimination (Vertovec, 2012).

Inequality as a socio-historical construction

The view of social inequality based on the idea of equal opportunity has also been criticized because it entails a logical contradiction (Blackburn, 2008). If equal opportunities are understood as chances for moving up a society's structure of stratification, there has to be a structure of inequality. The existence of the structure of inequality, in turn, means that social positions, occupations and, ultimately, individuals in these positions and occupations are judged against this structure, a historically formed, social construction in itself (Vanttaja & Järvinen, 1998).

When the hierarchical classification of social positions and, by extension, the hierarchy of individuals in these positions are taken for granted, a value judgment of what is considered important and desirable in life is created. When we routinely use categories such as upper and lower class or high and low socioeconomic groups, we implicitly evaluate one kind of lifestyle as being more valuable and desirable than another. Unnoticed, these classifications may be internalized in the minds of individuals and the ways in which they see the world. We may start to think it is natural for one to behave differently toward different people, to pay them different wages for their work and to expect certain kinds of behavior or opinions from them (Vanttaja & Järvinen, 1998). Along the way, the classification which, from the aforementioned point of view, is a socio-historical construction by nature, starts to appear as an objective description of reality (Berger & Luckmann, 1966).

There is a risk that well-intentioned equalizing policies disregard the subjective experiences of individuals. It is possible, for example, that low-educated people do not consider their lack of education problematic. It may be that they have never attempted to pursue higher education degrees or occupational positions that are highly valued in society. They may want to use social arenas other than education to develop and exercise their human potential. This can be understood by utilizing the idea of culture as a historically constructed, shared view of a given group regarding what is good and desirable in life and all the associated aspects. This view does not entail the hierarchical classification of people based on their life values and ways of living but, rather, the recognition of the differences and diversities among people and social groups. In this regard, cultures can be said to differ from each other horizontally instead of vertically. They consist of values, norms and practices that form the basis of the social relationships within their cultural groups. The preferences of individuals who have grown up under the influence of different cultures differ from each other, since these people have adapted different life goals and different ways to express themselves or handle their feelings, et cetera. (Clarke et al., 1976; Therborn, 1991).

It is difficult to impact on culturally internalized values, norms, worldviews and modes of thought using external means, as Berger and Luckmann (1966) propose. According to their discussion of primary socialization, every individual is born into a community in which they encounter people who are responsible for caring for them. Typically, this refers to one's parents, who cannot be chosen. A child internalizes the culture of the persons responsible for their upbringing and does not adopt their perception of the world as one of those possible ones but, instead, as the only possible one that can exist. During the years of primary socialization, an individual experiences things as meaningful and inescapable that, in reality, are accidental and dependent on the particular environment and milieu in which the individual happens to be born. According to Berger and Luckmann (1966), the worldview that is internalized during the years of primary socialization is embedded in an individual's consciousness to a much greater extent than that which is internalized during the later stages of the socialization process. Despite the fact that, these days, the influence of secondary socialization can already be seen in people's lives from an early age, one can argue that the basic values and norms that create the basis of an individual's life are acquired from their family's social circles and cultural environment during their formative years.

From the equal opportunity perspective, social positions are considered hierarchical by nature and social mobility can occur either downwards or upwards. From an individual's point of view, upward social mobility tends to be seen as a positive development. If education has played a significant role in this process, education is regarded as having had a positive impact on the life course of an individual. However, individuals do not necessarily experience social mobility as a positive development in their life. Individual social mobility usually implies some kind of cultural transition which may cause an identity conflict for that individual. An identity conflict, in turn, can lead to them experiencing marginalization. Individuals may feel alienated from their culture of origin while, simultaneously, feeling incapable of adapting to the values, norms and the modes of practice of the new culture.

Marginalization as an identity conflict

To understand marginalization as an identity conflict, the discussion begins with the classic studies conducted by members of the Chicago School of Sociology in the early twentieth century. In his well-known article, Robert E. Park (1928) introduced the concept of the 'marginal man', which was later brought to the fore by his student Everett Stonequist (1965). Referring to a certain type of person and personality through this admittedly gendered concept rooted in the patriarchal sociology of Park's time (Kharlamov, 2012; Marotta, 2006), Park and Stonequist described an individual whose life is impacted by two distinct cultures and who adopts the contradictions of these cultures as his own. According to their work, this kind of marginalization was caused by immigration and diaspora in particular. People who are disconnected from their origins and are placed in an environment that has new values, norms and cultural expectations do not feel accepted as equal members (Park, 1928; Stonequist, 1965).

Park and Stonequist used the concept of marginalization to specifically refer to the experience of being an outsider. They considered it to be a consequence of a cultural transition that one experiences at some point in life. Certain events, such as immigration or leaving a closed religious community for the secular world, may cause an inner conflict because of a person's inability or unwillingness to abandon their cultural background or due to difficulties with finding a sense of place, culturally, and a reference group to identify with in a new cultural environment. (Järvinen & Jahnukainen, 2016). The experience of marginalization can either be temporary or more permanent. The latter occurs when the individual becomes so intensely aware of the cultural conflict that it forms a part of their identity.

A similar kind of an interpretation of marginalization is present in Berry's (1992) typology regarding the different acculturation strategies employed by immigrant groups. Following the research tradition of cross-cultural psychology, Berry was interested in determining what happens to individuals who have grown up in a certain cultural context when they attempt to re-establish their lives in another one. The starting point for his acculturation theory is that cultural groups and their individual members have to find a balance between cultural maintenance and establishing relationships with other cultural groups. Individuals can choose to orientate themselves to their traditional culture, the wider society, to both or to neither. It has been argued that the conflict between the demands of their native culture and the new host culture migrants often experience is likely to have negative psychological and social consequences which may create an identity conflict for them. In this respect, marginalization refers to the incompatibility of multiple identities (Ward, 2008).

The risk of marginalization in the abovementioned context can be assumed to be greater among young people than in other age groups. Youth is a transitional phase and can be viewed as a marginal position in itself: one is no longer a child but is not yet fully integrated into society and adulthood either. Recent cultural and societal changes have introduced new types of uncertainties into the lives of young people. Today's young generation have more difficulties with fulfilling many of the traditional expectations of adulthood than previous generations. This is particularly true for migrant youths. Compared with individuals belonging to the dominant cultural groups of a society, migrant youths may experience discrimination and struggle to find a place in the labor market which can inhibit their reaching the status of an independent adult (Järvinen & Jahnukainen, 2016).

Globalization, identities and marginalization

As a result of the massive immigration and the opportunities for communication and networking enabled by new technologies, such as the internet and smartphones, that have occurred in the past few decades, the meaning and experience of diaspora for immigrant groups are not the same as they were a century ago when Park published his classic article. The experience of migration does not disconnect individuals from their cultural origins in the same way it did before. Instead, globalization has brought about an increasing interdependence between different people, regions and countries and the weakening of national boundaries. Under current global conditions, geographical distance no longer necessarily equates with social distance (Beck & Beck-Gernsheim, 2009). At the same time, the issue of developing cultural identity has become more complex: it is no longer a question of becoming an adult in one culture but a task of navigating both local and global cultures (Kharlamov, 2012).

In particular, the internet and the spread of smartphones have fostered the establishment of a new global culture that offers an endless supply of role models for identity construction and negotiation for young people all over the world. It is argued that we should disconnect the sociological concept of generation from its national frame of reference and understand it in a broader global framework (Beck & Beck-Gernsheim, 2009; Edmunds & Turner, 2005). The growth of global media, with the accompanying increased importance of social media, have made it possible for localized traumatic events, such as terrorist attacks or environmental crises, to be experienced globally, effectively creating a global generational consciousness. However, the shared experiences of today's global generation are not restricted to traumatic events, as in the classic Mannheimian view (Mannheim, 1952). Rather, they increasingly consist of events, images, trademarks and symbols which spread through markets, migration and media.

Today, the impact of media, particularly social media, on young people's identities is enormous. The information transmitted by media spreads across countries and continents, reaching metropoles and the remotest of places alike. It means that young people everywhere look at and evaluate their lives through the images and identity models offered by the media, comparing the world presented in the media to their own. The internet, specifically, has globally become the reference frame for young people's perception of the world. At the same time, however, there are growing inequalities between young people from different parts of the world in terms of life chances. There is a huge gap in the material resources and, by extension, the life opportunities available to the young people growing up in wealthy countries and those growing up in poor ones. Therefore, as Ulrich Beck and Elizabeth Beck-Gernsheim (2009) argue, the global generation should not be treated as a single, homogeneous generation with a unique and universal consciousness. Instead, one should pay attention to the multiplicities within the global generation that appear as a set of intertwined, transnational, generational constellations.

The experienced inequality in life chances may lead to young people growing up in the poorer parts of the world moving to a different part of the world in search of better life chances (Beck & Beck-Gernsheim, 2009). At the same time, in the wealthier parts of the world such as in Europe, individual trajectories from youth to adulthood have also become more volatile. Despite the enormous educational expansion that has occurred since WW2 and the fact that young people in Europe are more educated than previous generations, youth unemployment rates are persistently high in many European countries. There is a plethora of empirical studies, conducted across Europe and beyond on the school-to-work transitions of young people, which illustrate that these transitions have become more extended, fragmented and uncertain (e.g. Buchmann & Kriesi, 2011; Isoniemi, 2017; Pilz et al., 2015). Among these, Robert Pryor and Jim Bright (2013) begin their theory of career formation under the influence of a constantly changing work life with the premise that both stability and instability are inherent properties of the world and that emerging stable orders must be considered in relation to instability and uncertainty. Today, it is widely held that the careers of an increasing number of young people will be non-linear and consist of successive transitions. Career choices, in turn, have to be made in a systemic context that is characterized by complex interactions, constant changes, uncertainties and unplanned incidents and episodes that lie beyond the control of individuals.

The structural transformation of work life we have witnessed during recent decades has had consequences for not only individuals' biographies, but also their identities. However, as analyses concerning the Nordic countries reveal (Jørgensen et al., 2019), despite the recent de-standardization of life courses, educational and employment policies may still be based on the assumed prevalence of the linear, standardized, 'normal' life course. Moreover, a lack of jobs, particularly a decline in low-skilled jobs, has resulted in intensified competition among individuals for the available vacancies in the job market. Young people who have struggled with education, which includes immigrant youths as newcomers in particular, may lose faith in finding their place in society. This is due to a lack of faith in their own ability to compete for jobs that pay decently and a lack of faith in there being opportunities for such jobs made available to them (Rinne et al., 2020). At the same time, in policy discourse, structural problems of society are individualized and young people are increasingly expected to take responsibility for their own employability and to become self-governing, enterprising and proactive (Jørgensen et al., 2019; Lundahl & Olofsson, 2014).

One can argue that increasing insecurity is becoming the basic experience of the global generation of young people at the same time as transnational identities are emerging (Beck & Beck-Gernsheim, 2009). Globalization has further altered the conditions for marginalization understood as an identity conflict. This particularly affects young people who are forced to construct their identities in a global 'risk society' (Beck, 1992) characterized by uncertainties, instability of institutions and cultural and ethnic conflicts. The COVID-19 pandemic during 2020 and 2021 is an example of the global risks that the institutions of modern society cannot control comprehensively. Within a few months, the pandemic also changed the course of globalization in an unpredictable manner. When faced with this previously unknown threat, we witnessed people clinging to nation states and abandoning global solidarity. Further, the crisis strengthened the anti-globalization populist politics in many countries. For young people, the economic and social consequences of the epidemic, such as the massive drop in employment security and growing economic polarization, will challenge their transition from youth to adulthood in new and unpredictable ways. It can also be argued that, suddenly, young people across the world—the global generation—dropped to a marginal position in relation to time, where the past and future are disconnected from the present. In this regard, marginalization entails a break in individual narratives. For today's young people, it seems to be even harder to find answers to the questions of 'Who am I?' and 'What is my place in the world?' This indicates marginalized identities will become more common among the contemporary global generation. Simultaneously, as global inequalities continue to increase, identities are becoming more and more important arena of power struggles in a globalized world. Remembering Robert E. Park's idea of the 'marginal man', one can argue that what was once related to the life histories of the few individuals who have experienced migration and diaspora is becoming a common feature of human existence.

Conclusion

The developmental trends and characteristics of our times presented in this chapter pose a challenge for policies, including educational policies that aim to reduce social inequality and marginalization. In mainstream policy thinking since WW2, the class-division of a society has been seen as a primary source of social inequality. In line with this, reducing educational inequalities associated with socioeconomic status position has been widely adopted in education policies across the world. The understanding of marginalization, in turn, has typically been based on a monocultural notion of marginalization which assumes the existence of a single reference culture that has a normative center and a periphery (Kharlamov, 2012). From this viewpoint, marginal groups of young people, such as school dropouts, the unemployed or those engaged in asocial or subcultural lifestyles, are seen as deviating from the normative ideal of social living and thus being on the fringes of a 'good society'. The main objectives of equalizing education policies based on the above views have been to reduce inequalities in educational opportunities between socioeconomic groups of a given society (Järvinen & Silvennoinen, forthcoming) and to get those people whose life courses do not follow an ideal standardized life-course model 'back on track' (Jørgensen et al., 2019; Rinne et al., 2020).

However, recent societal changes have significantly altered the operational environment of education policies. The economy has moved away from industrial production to service delivery, and increased immigration and the subsequent rise of multiculturalism have resulted in the situation where the population in many countries is becoming more diverse. Moreover, rapid technology development and the increased influence of the global media, and the internet in particular, have brought about an increasing interdependence between people and established the new global culture that offers an endless supply of role models for young people's identity negotiation.

The abovementioned trends and changes have challenged the illusion of a homogeneous class structure in many countries and suggested that social inequality should be understood not only as a class-based phenomenon but as a wider cultural and identity issue. Marginalization, in turn, should be approached, as Park and Stonequist did, from a polycultural standpoint that emphasizes the existence of multiple cultures that come into contact and integrate with each other. In this sense, marginal does not refer to peripheral but to existing in a boundary zone between cultures. Such a view is a more valid standpoint under the current conditions of globalization and the increase of cultural contacts, transitions and conflicts (Kharlamov, 2012).

Instead of designing and implementing policies based on the taken-for-granted assumptions and value judgments of what is considered 'normal' and thus desirable in life, subjective experiences of individuals should be taken into account when designing and implementing policies aimed at reducing social inequality and marginalization. Moreover, education policies should recognize the ways in which certain global developments, such as the emergence of global media culture and extensive immigration, are reflected in young people's identity formation and identity conflicts. Many of the difficulties young people face when growing up are intersectional by nature and thus require intersectional political solutions. Instead of employing ideas such as the prevalence of the standardized 'normal' life course, the homogeneity of citizens and the taken-for-granted view on static social structures, policies should be built on an understanding of the complexities, uncertainties and instabilities forming the primary features of contemporary social life. How successful future policies will be depends on how dynamic, reflexive and culturally sensitive these policies are in serving their function of supporting young people through their multiple life journeys within the context of the complexities, uncertainties and instabilities of our globalized, post-industrialized and multicultural world.

References

Barone, C. & Ruggera, L. (2018). Educational equalization stalled? Trends in inequality of educational opportunity between 1930 and 1980 across 26 European nations. *European Societies, 20*(1), 1–25. doi: 10.1080/14616696.2017.1290265

Beck, U. (1992). *Risk Society: Towards a New Modernity.* SAGE.

Beck, U. & Beck-Gernsheim, E. (2009). Global generations and the trap of methodological nationalism for a cosmopolitan turn in the sociology of youth and generation. *European Sociological Review, 25*(1), 25–36. doi: 10.1093/esr/jcn032

Berger, P. & Luckmann, T. (1966). *The Social Construction of Reality. A Treatise in the Sociology of Knowledge.* Penguin Books.

Bernstein, M. (2005). Identity politics. *Annual Review of Sociology, 31,* 47–74. doi: 10.1146/annurev.soc.29.010202.100054

Berry, J.W. (1992). Acculturation and adaptation in a new society. *International Migration,* 30(Si), 69–85. doi: 10.1111/j.1468-2435.1992.tb00776.x

Blackburn, R.M. (2008). What is social inequality? *International Journal of Sociology and Social Policy, 28*(7–8), 250–259. doi: 10.1108/01443330810890664

Bourdieu, P. & Passeron, J.-C. (1977). *Reproduction in Education, Society and Culture.* SAGE.

Buchmann, M. & Kriesi, I. (2011). Transition to adulthood in Europe. *Annual Review of Sociology, 37,* 481–503. doi: 10.1146/annurev-soc-081309-150212

Clarke, J., Hall, S., Jefferson, T. & Roberts, B. (1976). Subcultures, cultures and class, in S. Hall & T. Jefferson (Eds.), *Resistance Through Rituals. Youth Subcultures in Post-War Britain* (pp. 9–80). Hutchinson.

Edmunds, J. & Turner, B.S. (2005). Global generations: Social change in the twentieth century. *The British Journal of Sociology, 56*(4), 559–577. doi: 10.1111/j.1468-4446.2005.00083.x

Erikson, R. (2020). Inequality of educational opportunity—The role of performance and choice. *European Review, 28*(1), 44–55. doi: 10.1017/S1062798720000897

Habibis, D. & Walter, M. (2015). *Social Inequality in Australia: Discourses, Realities and Futures.* Oxford University Press.

Isoniemi, H. (2017). *European Country Clusters of Transition to Adulthood.* University of Turku.

Järvinen, T. & Jahnukainen, M. (2016). Now which of us are excluded? Conceptual examination of marginalization and social exclusion, in T. Hoikkala & M. Karjalainen (Eds.), *Finnish Youth Research Anthology 1999–2014* (pp. 547–564). Finnish Youth Research Society/Finnish Youth Research Network.

Järvinen, T. & Silvennoinen, H. (forthcoming). Educational policies, lifelong learning and social diversity, in M. Berends, B. Schneider & S. Lamb (Eds.), *The SAGE Handbook on the Sociology of Education.* SAGE.

Jørgensen, C.-H., Järvinen, T. & Lundahl, L. (2019). A Nordic transition regime? Policies for school-to-work transitions in Sweden, Denmark and Finland. *European Educational Research Journal, 18*(3), 278–297. doi: 10.1177/1474904119830037

Kharlamov, N.A. (2012). Boundary zone between cultural worlds or the edge of the dominant culture? Two conceptual metaphors of marginality. *Journal of Intercultural Studies, 33*(6), 623–638. doi: 10.1080/07256868.2012.735111

Kyhä, H. (2011). *Koulutetut Maahanmuuttajat Työmarkkinoilla. Tutkimus Korkeakoulututkinnon Suorittaneiden Maahanmuuttajien Työllistymisestä Ja Työurien Alusta Suomessa* [Educated Immigrants in Employment Markets. A Study on Higher Educated Immigrants' Employment Opportunities and Career Starts in Finland]. University of Turku.

Labaree, D.F. (2012). *Someone Has to Fail: The Zero-Sum Game of Public Schooling.* Harvard University Press.

Lagravinese, R., Liberati, P. & Resce, G. (2020). The impact of economic, social and cultural conditions on educational attainments. *Journal of Policy Modeling, 42*(1), 112–132. doi: 10.1016/j.jpolmod.2019.03.007

Lundahl, L. & Olofsson, J. (2014). Guarded transitions? Youth trajectories and school-to-work transition policies in Sweden. *International Journal of Adolescence and Youth, 19*(1), 19–34. doi: 10.1080/02673843.2013.852593

Lupton, G. (1992). Aspects of social inequality, in G. Lupton, P.M. Short & R. Whip (Eds.), *Society and Gender. An Introduction to Sociology* (pp. 67–92). Palgrave.

Mannheim, K. (1952). The problem of generations, in P. Kecskemeti (Ed.), *Essays on the Sociology of Knowledge* (pp. 276–320). Routledge & Kegan Paul.

Marotta, V. (2006). Civilization, culture and the hybrid self in the work of Robert Ezra Park. *Journal of Intercultural Studies*, 27(4), 413–433. doi: 10.1080/07256860600936911

OECD. (2020). How have women's participation and fields of study choice in higher education evolved over time? *Education Indicators in Focus*. March #74. doi: 10.1787/22267077

Park, R.E. (1928). Human migration and the marginal man. *The American Journal of Sociology*, 33(6), 881–893. https://www.jstor.org/stable/2765982

Pilz, M., Schmidt-Altmann, K. & Eswein, M. (2015). Problematic transitions from school to employment: Freeters and NEETs in Japan and Germany. *Compare*, 45(1), 70–93. doi: 10.1080/03057925.2013.835193

Power, S. (2012). From redistribution to recognition to representation: Social injustice and the changing politics of education. *Globalisation, Societies and Education*, 10(4), 473–492. doi: 10.1080/14767724.2012.735154

Pryor, R.G.L. & Bright, J.E.H. (2013). The chaos theory of careers (CTC): Ten years on and only just begun. *Australian Journal of Career Development*, 23(1), 4–12. doi: 10.1177%2F1038416213518506

Rinne, R., Silvennoinen, H., Järvinen, T. & Tikkanen, J. (2020). Governing the normalisation of young adults through lifelong learning policies, in M. Parreira do Amaral, S. Kovacheva & X. Rambla (Eds.), *Lifelong Learning Policies for Young Adults in Europe. Navigating Between Knowledge and Economy*. Policy Press.

Stonequist, E.V. (1965). *The Marginal Man. A Study in Personality and Culture Conflict*. (2nd ed.) Russell & Russell.

Therborn, G. (1991). Cultural belonging, structural location and human action: Explanation in sociology and in social science. *Acta Sociologica*, 34(3), 177–191. https://www.jstor.org/stable/4194726

Triventi, M., Skopek, J., Kulic, N., Bucholz, S. & Blossfeld, H.-P. (2020). Advantage 'finds its way': How privileged families exploit opportunities in different systems of secondary education. *Sociology*, 54(2), 237–257. doi: 10.1177%2F0038038519874984

UNESCO. (2020). *Global Education Monitoring Report 2020. Inclusion and Education: All Means All*. https://en.unesco.org/gem-report/report/2020/inclusion

UNICEF. (2020). *Gender and Education*. https://data.unicef.org/topic/gender/gender-disparities-in-education/

United Nations. (2020). *World Social Report 2020. Inequality in a Rapidly Changing World*. United Nations: Department of Economic and Social Affairs. https://www.un.org/development/desa/dspd/world-social-report/2020-2.html

Vanttaja, M. & Järvinen, T. (1998). Koulutus, eriarvoisuus ja koettu marginaalisuus [Education, inequality and experienced marginalization]. *Yhteiskuntapolitiikka* [*Society and Politics*], 63(4), 350–356. http://urn.fi/URN:NBN:fi-fe201209116441

Vertovec, S. (2012). 'Diversity' and the social imaginary. *European Journal of Sociology*, 53(3), 287–312. doi: 10.1017/S000397561200015X

Ward, C. (2008). Thinking outside the Berry boxes: New perspectives on identity, acculturation and intercultural relations. *International Journal of Intercultural Relations*, 32, 105–114. doi: 10.1016/j.ijintrel.2007.11.002

Wilson, A. (Ed.), (2013). *Situating Intersectionality. Politics, Policy and Power*. Palgrave Macmillan.

10

RETHINKING ACADEMIC MOBILITY THROUGH EMERGING GLOBAL CHALLENGES

Suvi Jokila, Arto Jauhiainen, and Marja Peura

Introduction

Since spring 2020, the global mobility of people has been severely disrupted by the COVID-19 pandemic in an unforeseen manner. This followed the previous decades' steady increase in the number of people moving across national borders for a host of reasons, including seeking refuge, migrating, for education, employment, tourism among other purposes. Despite the disruption caused by the pandemic, the motives for people to move across national borders have not disappeared. After COVID-19, both forced and voluntary mobility is expected to again accelerate, globally, with the directions of flows remaining unequal, in line with earlier patterns. Over the past three decades, the conflicts in Syria, Iraq and Afghanistan had given impetus to extensive refugee flows. According to the UN Refugee Agency (UNHCR, 2021), from the 82.4 million forcibly displaced people abroad, the majority come from just five countries. Forces driving such mobility have not vanished. Nor have its outcomes, resulting, for example, in a major demographic crisis in Europe.

The presence of an increasing number of mobile people continues to create much public and political turmoil, giving impetus to populist and nationalist sentiments. Two major outcomes of the increased global flows of people were Brexit in the UK and the election of Donald Trump as the president of the United States. These developments have, arguably, transformed the political and economic conditions affecting the local population's sense of their living conditions. The political rationality linked to mobility has also had a significant effect on the imaginary space of opportunities for mobile people or groups. These dynamics have inevitably affected the experiences of the mobile people residing within the receiving countries.

DOI: 10.4324/9781003207528-10

Mobility of people is, however, not only linked to migration experiences but has also become a major part of academic work and student life. International mobility for the purpose of studying, often defined as a form of voluntary mobility, has surged from over 2 million in 2000 to 5.7 million in 2018 (UIS, 2021). Within this period, the study destinations (in terms of both countries and educational institutions) have widened, while the modes of mobility have moved from short-term exchange to degree studies. Mobility has also been encouraged through various organizational arrangements that include joint educational programs and educational hubs. Despite the significant increase in numbers, policies and programs designed to make mobility multidirectional, the global space for academic mobility has remained predominantly unbalanced and hierarchical.

In this chapter, we discuss issues of academic mobility at the intersection of national policies, politics and governing structures, as well as the challenges posed by the global transformations that have taken place over the past decade. We argue that academic mobility has entered a time where its profound values and modes need rethinking in order to facilitate a more equal and sustainable future in an era in which the processes of globalization are acquiring new forms. We begin with a theoretical discussion of the processes of globalization and policy responses to them. Next, we will discuss some of the major trends and challenges associated with the shifting forms of mobility and conclude with a discussion of the implications of these developments for the future of academic mobility.

Globalization and the politics of mobility

Globalization processes have been widely analyzed for decades. However, finding a single definition for comprehending the complexities and contingencies of the concept has proved impossible. Globalization can be seen as a complex process of social, political and economic transformations (Bishop & Payne, 2021). In the late 1990s, David Held et al. (1999) provided their analysis on globalization by distinguishing three perspectives: hyperglobalists, skeptics and transformationalists. Their underlying interest was in national and global governing structures. Hyperglobalists, they argued, perceive a decline in the role of the nation state while skeptics find globalization as an ideological construction. Transformationalists are in between these two poles, accepting that globalization transforms social and power relations while acknowledging it has a historical contingency.

While other interpretations of globalization are possible, globalization has predominantly been characterized by a neoliberal imaginary stressing its economic aspects (Rizvi & Lingard, 2010). However, globalization itself is not merely a neoliberal economic project but also refers to issues of spatiality, such as those involved in the mobility of ideas, money and, of course, people. Neoliberal globalization has, for instance, enabled a wider population to travel and find a job abroad (Bishop & Payne, 2021).

Matthew Bishop and Anthony Payne (2021) have argued that what has changed since Held et al.'s analysis is the counter-processes of globalization. The wider social, political and economic problems caused by the neoliberal interpretation of globalization has attracted much criticism (ibid.). As a result, some political movements have questioned the globalization paradigm itself (Flew, 2020), in favor of a post-globalist interpretation that has highlighted the renewed significance of the nation state. Since the early 2000s, such a post-globalist interpretation has given rise to right-wing populism, drawing support across Europe, including Western and former socialist countries, and North America. Expansion of immigration, the rise of economic and social disparities as well as a critical attitude toward national and transnational (supranational) political institutions like the EU are among the reasons for the rise of populism (Weimer & Barlete, 2020).

Right-wing populism takes different forms depending on the country, its history, culture and current social circumstances. One, and perhaps the most important, feature is neo-nationalism, which has been a trademark of right-wing, populist, political parties (e.g. the Law and Justice Party in Poland, the Finns Party in Finland, the Sweden Democrats in Sweden, the Fidesz Party in Hungary, and the National Rally in France). It is important to note, however, that these parties are by no means functioning in their national 'bubbles'; rather, they are ideologically and concretely connected to each other (Öniş & Kutlayb, 2021). While not all populists are extremists, some right-wing populists have manifested themselves through radical nationalist (far-right) groups and organizations like neo-Nazi organizations acting beyond the laws (Greven, 2016). In Europe, Brexit can be seen as a result of the triumph of right-wing populism, as indeed can be the rise of Trump presidency in the US (Greven, 2016).

As we have already noted, a key aspect of globalization is mobility. Mobility is, of course, not a new phenomenon. However, under the conditions of globalization, the number of mobile people has greatly increased, as indeed has the impact on societies and their infrastructures. Migration has always been a profoundly global phenomenon that is governed nationally. Yet, there is no global policy framing, as such, to govern mobility and migration across borders: national borders and policy contexts continue to play a significant role in governing mobility flows. Sandro Mezzadra and Brett Neilson (2013) argue that borders are "instruments for managing, calibrating, and governing global passages of people, money, and things" (p. 3). Not surprisingly, therefore, global mobility of people represents a space of political contestations. Referring to Saskia Sassen's work, Antoine Pécoud (2021) notes that the current migration governance is an illiberal anomaly—illiberal in its reliance on national border controls and an anomaly in the ways the ideas of control contradict the globalization processes. As a response to Bishop and Payne's (2021) call to reconceptualize globalization as re-globalization, Pécoud (2021, p. 104) argues that "any substantive process of re-globalization is a long way off in the area of migration, simply because neither the globalization *of* governance nor its subsequent deglobalization has happened in what is an undeveloped governing regime."

Illustrating the complex relations between global and national interests in migration governing approaches, Pécoud (2021) identifies five contrasting lines of political contestation: (1) those focusing on national sovereignty insist that mobility is a national issue, (2) anti-immigration movements demand the need to limit immigration, (3) rights-based immigration groups refer to global agreements on human rights, (4) states increasingly prefer global immigration to be driven selectively to serve particular purposes of meeting gaps in the national labor market, and (5) those who advocate free movement of people without any specific governing structures.

Compared to other mobility groups, the mobility of academics and international students are governed in a slightly different way than those that relate to migration. Even though universities directly recruit their students and staff, academic mobility is widely encouraged by the national governments and simultaneously coordinated through national governing structures. According to Christopher Ziguras and Grant McBurnie (2015), countries vary in their governing practices. While some countries govern through funding mechanisms like internships or direct funding, others have regulatory measures in place. These measures particularly target fee-paying international students.

International students are often positioned as a desired group because they produce financial gains or, in the case of doctoral students, contribute to nation-building through their research and innovation capacity. To support academic recruitment, governments differentiate various mobility groups; implementing segregated processes, for instance, in handling visa procedures. Fast-track citizenship is encouraged through selective migration practices for those that are regarded as 'super talents', such as top scientists and academics (Shachar & Hirschr, 2013). At the same time, however, in the university context, an academic deficit narrative is at times attached to international students instead of regarding them as co-contributors to knowledge and equal learners (Lomer & Anthony-Okeke, 2019).

In the prevailing populistic discourses, when migration is often positioned at the center of the political critique, there are, inevitably, consequences for the experience of academic mobility. Populist discourses often build on the ideologies of 'othering', categorizing people into 'us' and 'other'. The constructions of 'others' vary across different national contexts, from seeing them as the 'corrupted elite'—domestic or foreign (like in Brexit)—to regarding them as 'underserving' minorities, such as occurs with Mexicans and other immigrant groups from Latin America in American populism. These groups are typically represented as a threat to 'us', with xenophobia becoming one of the driving forces for national populism (Rodrik, 2020; Weimer & Barlete, 2020). Even though international students and researchers belong to a, comparatively, more desired mobility group, they nonetheless become incorporated into the larger xenophobic discourses, and are sometimes equally subjected to racism and discriminatory practices in their host country. Jenny Lee and Charles Rice (2007) have noted that the forms of racism that international students experience vary and depend on their ethnic background, allowing Lee and Rice to interpret their findings through a neo-racism theory that interprets discriminatory practices on the basis of skin color or culture.

What this analysis implies is that the mobility of international students needs to be understood in spatio-temporal terms, within the context of particular political, economic and societal landscapes at different times. Within the past two decades, for example, Rahul Choudaha (2018) has pointed out the 9/11 terrorist attack, the global recession in 2008, Trump becoming the president of the US and Brexit as significant events that have greatly shaped the policies relating to international student mobility, as well as the experiences that the students have. The COVID-19 pandemic can be added to the list of major transformations that have the potential to transform the nature and extent of academic mobility.

Globally stratified mobility patterns

Global higher education space has always been segregated, hierarchically structured and reflective of the wider economic and political structures (Brooks & Waters, 2011). The value of education, globally, is defined at the intersections of university reputation, degrees obtained and financial conditions—all of which have significant variations. These differences are visible in international mobility structures. An example of these global structures is that high-income countries more often host international students, while middle- and low-income countries pay for the education (UIS, 2021). Also, in terms of degree structures, international doctoral education, in particular, is highly concentrated in relatively few universities globally, resulting in benefits for a limited group of nations and institutions (Van der Wende, 2015). These stratified higher education structures are reproduced in the process. This is evident in global rankings that are subjective productions and representations of inequalities of the global higher education space. Global rankings are used for the purpose of governing individual decision-making while embedding power constellations (Jöns & Höyler, 2013).

Until recently, the focus of the attention in relation to academic mobility has been on the prestigious American and European universities. Now, the attention has extended to include some leading Asian universities, specifically in China. With their extensive policy initiatives, China aims to establish 'world-class' universities within its hierarchical university system. Also, within the Asian context, several countries, such as Singapore, have begun to create schemes to support the region's cooperative ties. Through initiatives such as the Belt and Road Initiative (BRI), established in 2013, China is seeking to develop infrastructure and cooperative ties with countries along the old Silk Road, as well as on maritime routes. BRI aims "to promote peace and cooperation, openness and inclusiveness, mutual learning and mutual benefit among the more than sixty-five countries that comprise the land and sea routes linking Eurasia" (Peters, 2020, p. 586). One of BRI's priorities is people-to-people communication through academic exchange facilitated through scholarship programs. This initiative has resulted in a 12 percent increase in the number of international students in China from BRI countries, to 317,000 in total (Wu & Chan, 2019).

As a policy response to the widening opportunities in international education and the aim to create 'world-class' universities, countries, particularly in Asia, are developing higher education hubs with the aim to attract a growing number of international students to their campuses. These policies closely intersect with wider, nationally-specific, socio-political interests, particularly economic ones. Yet this instrumental approach has the potential to contradict, or at least draw attention away from, a more ethical understanding of international education, including a focus on culturally-just forms of cosmopolitan learning (Soong, 2020).

Over the past two decades, the Bologna Process has been another example of a regional initiative facilitating student mobility by harmonizing degree structures in participating countries. Eva-Marie Vögtle and Michael Windzio's (2016) network analysis within OECD countries shows a rather stable, spatial domination of leading destinations, including in the United States (US), the United Kingdom (UK), France and Germany. A shared border is perceived to positively support the possibilities of student exchange flows. Within the European Union, the Erasmus Programme is also widely regarded as a success since it has provided structures and funding for the mobility of already 3.3 million tertiary students (European Commission, 2015). In the aftermath of Brexit, some changes to the Erasmus Programme are inevitable, but such is the value attached to student mobility that Great Britain is also initiating its own Turing Scheme to support British students' international mobility.

Rachel Brooks and Johanna Waters (2011) have argued that national policy-makers play a significant role in framing the mobility policies despite the significance of international organizations such as the European Union. Within a national context, the issue of hosting (more) international students is, however, in itself a kind of 'illiberal anomaly' (Pécoud, 2021) as national pro-mobility educational policies and other public policies do not necessarily align (Sá & Sabzalieva, 2018). While mobility is symbolically supported in policy texts, tension from this misalignment often results in international students encountering various barriers; for instance, through visa regulations and access to the labor market. Nation states continue to struggle to adjust their policies and regulations to meet and handle the mobility flows as well as to retain the students while remaining conscious of the local backlash against cultural diversity that global mobility produces.

The prospect of hosting international students is framed by national regulations, policies and the status of the higher education system (Ziguras & McBurnie, 2015). National motivations to attract and retain international students involve several factors that are not new, nor de-contextual, including attempts to recruit and retain international students as skilled labor reflecting the central role of knowledge and the appreciation of its commercial value in contemporary societies (Välimaa et al., 2016; Ziguras & McBurnie, 2015), as well as 'soft power' policies (Haugen, 2013). For instance, international education has significantly boosted the economies of the US, the UK and Australia, traditional study abroad destinations.

While academic mobility has, in recent decades, been perceived to have a global character, actually, mobility experiences and perceptions are strongly nationally and locally embedded. According to Jade Lansing and Rebecca Farnum (2017), even though the aims of mobility underline the importance of cosmopolitanism and global mindedness, the marketing and experiences of study abroad remain rather state-centric. In the process, study abroad reveals itself to be problematic, contributing more to statecraft rather than global citizenship. Martin Myers and Kalwant Bhopal (2021) provide an example of how nationally-produced cosmopolitan brands of elite universities in the UK and the US often deliver social and cultural capital to a selected range of students. These brands are produced and used by both the institutions and the students in their narratives. Sharon Stein and Vanessa Andreotti (2016) argue that the international student recruitment policies rely on a global imaginary embedded in the hierarchical positionalities of Western supremacy, entailing racist ideas of knowledge and knowing. They connect the ideas of Western supremacy to rationales for international student recruitment and to students' racist experiences.

Despite recognition of the unequal and hierarchical structures of academic mobility, issues of inequalities involving international students are not widely examined. These issues point to the very question of what counts as education which is at times reduced to a question of who should pay for education rather than its broader purposes. Simon Marginson (2018) has unpacked the contribution of higher education to society through a set of dichotomies: individualized and collective goods and national and global goods. Within these two poles, he has stressed the importance of 'common goods.' The poles show the complex inter-dependencies of the meanings education has, simultaneously, to different actors. This question of *whose interests* are served by academic mobility is particularly important in international education, especially when international students are, in many respects, treated in a manner different to home students.

Stuart Tannock (2018) has analyzed the perceptions of education equality among UK university staff with respect to international students. He has shown how these perceptions are not shared by all. Neither is there a common understanding of what is meant by equality in the context of international students nor how similar objectives to equality might apply to international students. Clearly, differentiated tuition fee structures and visa permits set them apart (Tannock, 2018). These findings further highlight nationally-embedded meanings of equality, leading Tannock (2018) to conclude that international students are de-located from social, economic and political contexts and perceived as being active choice-makers to whom the equality ethos does not similarly apply.

Beyond the bodily movement of people, technological developments have significantly affected the forms and politics of international mobility and interchange. A variety of technological equipment and digital platforms facilitate academic mobility and interactions including information sharing, maintaining social relations and providing platforms for taking a degree. Digital platforms also provide a commercial infrastructure that facilitates the international students' recruitment and living in their host country. For instance, information is not only bound to official information providers but is shared through unofficial channels (e.g. Jayadeva, 2020). Various commercial actors have also emerged; for instance, to provide digital platforms that can facilitate digital course provision (e.g. Pearson's OPM). While providing these tools, the platforms produce micro-processes that make markets of mobility and reshape higher education and its activities (Williamson, 2021).

Fran Martin and Fazal Rizvi (2014) argue that many international students are now living transnational lives, where the 'back home' and 'out here' binary collapses and allows co-presence in different spaces simultaneously. These spaces are enabled by digital technologies, resulting in new patterns of communication across spatial divides. Xinyu Zhao (2021) provides an analysis of Chinese international students' digital usage and how this supports transnational commercial practices. He identifies a complex pattern of digital usage and private work within student communities, able to develop enterprises both within and across national borders. Student transnationalism is also relevant to an understanding of the role of the state. Shanti Robertson (2013) shows, for example, how student-migrants are transnational migrants that have particular kinds of migration trajectories. These trajectories are characterized by precariousness and a particular relation to the host state that takes different forms in line with the migration process.

Magali Ballatore and Martha Ferede (2013) find that the students in Erasmus Programmes represent a selected group, with more travel experience and higher socio-economic backgrounds compared to their immobile counterparts. Although international students are often assumed to represent an elite, Renee Luthra and Lucinda Platt (2016) argue that, partly as a consequence of the 'massification' of international student mobility, they in fact constitute an increasingly diversified student body in terms of their ethnic origins, skills, academic, class and social backgrounds, and their future goals for employment and migration. Hence, international students' experiences are structured around a multiplicity of heterogeneities related to socio-economic background, gender, nationality, and the stage of education or career, resulting in an unequal positioning in terms of both access to and outcomes of mobility (Bilecen & Van Mol, 2017).

While some students are well supported by their families, others are financially limited and rely heavily on various temporary precarious jobs. Robertson (2013) problematizes their elite positionalities. She argues that international students often find themselves in precarious working conditions, having to work in low-skilled work, without any guarantee of a path toward permanent residence or migration. These students can be referred to as the middling transnationals (Luthra & Platt, 2016), linked to a phenomenon that problematizes the processes of skilled labor rationalization. Besides the issues of equal educational opportunities for international students, the issues of their transition to the labor market after graduation are also challenging (Bilecen & Van Mol, 2017; Lomer, 2018). This can be a result of an imbalance between the language of instruction in the university (English in most cases) and the local language that is often required for employment (Saarinen, 2020).

Within higher education policy and practice, international students are often treated differently from the local student body through the use of 'international' or 'foreign' as an adjective before the word 'student', which emphasizes borders or other citizenship positionalities. Elspeth Jones (2017) has problematized the consequences of this dichotomy between international and domestic students, which is often employed for administrative and research purposes but also has cultural effects. Jones argues that many issues attached to international students also apply to domestic students but, in many cases, the domestic–international distinction may not support the educational needs of either of the student groups. For social inclusion to become an important policy priority on campuses, these kinds of categorizations may not always be helpful.

Emerging challenges reconfiguring international mobility

In recent years, the politics and possibilities of academic mobility have become much more complex. Illustrative of the complexities, and the challenges they pose, are the issues of climate change and the current health crisis that is expected to have long-term consequences. The outbreak of the COVID-19 pandemic in early 2020 designates the most extensive global disruption in international student mobility numbers ever seen. For instance, in the Fall of 2020, US higher education institutions experienced a decrease of 16 per cent in the number of international students (Baer & Martel, 2020). In addition, the pandemic has challenged the market orientation of higher education prevalent in some countries heavily reliant on international students' tuition fees (Pan, 2020).

This health crisis has reconfigured the global space and brought to the surface some underlining inequalities not visible earlier. During the pandemic, many international students were living within differentiated spatial and temporal configurations shaped by their current host locality, host's national (non-)restrictions and the circumstances in their home country. In practice, the policy measures set to prevent the mitigation of the COVID-19 crisis, including border closures, quarantines and online teaching, affected the mobility and everyday living condition of both academics and international students. This meant significant disruption of earlier-imagined mobility spaces enabling, for instance, the possibility of keeping transnational family ties alive as well as some tourism elements attached to student mobility.

Combating COVID-19 involved a global scientific effort to understand the nature and effects of the virus and also develop vaccines. As impressive as the scientific achievements have been, they have also demonstrated the inequities within systems of multilateral cooperation whereby the national interests of richer countries have been invariably prioritized (Lee & Haupt, 2021). The growing geopolitical tensions between the US and China have also run alongside attempts at scientific cooperation during the pandemic. Although pre-pandemic conditions had shown some restrictions in the cooperation between China and the United States, the scientific cooperation and co-publishing, as measured by co-authored papers, nonetheless has persisted. This has led Lee and Haupt (2021) to conclude that, during the pandemic, both scientific globalism (referring to the global generation of knowledge) and scientific nationalism (emphasizing national interests) may exist simultaneously. They assert that, although politicians may opt for nationalism, the scientific community has a more global orientation and an overriding interest in the creation of new knowledge.

The policies and practices of academic mobility are further challenged by climate change and the need to strive toward the achievement of sustainability goals. Until recently, in the field of international education, the issues of sustainability had not been widely raised but UNESCO's Sustainable Development Goal 4 for education has driven the field to pay more attention to the need to increase mobility scholarships to enable the least developed countries to participate in the knowledge creation systems. However, almost no attention is paid to the unsustainable aspects of bodily mobility in the damage it causes to the environment. While higher education is often noted for its positive contribution to sustainable development goals through cultural exchange and in increasing access to higher education, to name but a few, Robin Shields (2019) has attempted to move the discussion toward the problematic environmental burden caused by international travel, especially when long distances are involved. Meanwhile, the pandemic forced scientific and academic communities to seek alternatives to face-to-face meetings. For instance, while the Comparative and International Education Society (CIES) already had a plan to pilot a virtual conference in line with sustainable development goals (Silova et al. 2020), this plan was hastened by the pandemic. Due to border closures and travel restrictions from the pandemic, the annual meeting of CIES for 2020–2021 *had* to be held online if it was to go ahead and it is likely that fully online or hybrid conferences will become a common practice.

The pandemic has also sped up the transfer from on-campus to remote and virtual modes of teaching and meeting of research groups which were, to an extent, unimaginable previously. Many events that, prior to the pandemic, took place within a physical institutional setting have now become open and free for the wider community to participate in. Online events, such as conferences and workshops, have also become financially accessible since they do not require expensive travel. Yet neither the scientific or academic community nor online mobility function in a fully transparent and equal system. Restrictions to access remain and the platforms are not yet 'out there' for everyone to reach.

Academic mobility in post-pandemic times?

In this chapter, we have discussed how international mobility is entangled with broader political, economic and social processes as well as national and global interests. The ongoing global crises, such as the pandemic and climate change, have created new challenges yet have also opened new possibilities, establishing a need to reassess where academic mobility is heading and what are the underlying rationales behind its policies and practices.

As we have noted, international mobility is embedded in hierarchical power structures, both global and national. Individual mobility decisions are made within wider meso- and macro structures that may, for instance, support mobility to certain, often highly ranked destinations by those who are less well positioned within the global economic and political system. As mobility has become a major policy priority in the academic world, and the success of higher education institutions is determined in terms of their ability to attract international students, mobility decisions invariably reproduce already existing structures of inequalities.

It should be noted, moreover, that higher education remains nationally funded and steered by national governments. This means that issues of international academic mobility are articulated with national interests in mind. Hence, since interpreting higher education as a global common good (Marginson, 2018) does not appear likely in the near future, policy-makers continue to be challenged by conflicts over multiple purposes of academic mobility. Fundamental to these challenges are questions of whether there is common ground for national and global interests in mobility and how intercultural communication can be supported while mobility decisions remain trapped within the logic of non-humanistic, instrumental values espoused by the neoliberal corporate universities.

In recent years, considerable ideological and political shifts (e.g. neo-nationalism) have taken place in many countries around the world. These shifts have given rise to a range of complex issues. For example, since the values the global academic community has traditionally shared, and that underlie its mobility practices, such as individual freedom, democracy, tolerance, respect for human rights, critical thinking and respect for truth, appear currently to be under threat, how can these values be protected? We may speculate that the fields of academic mobility may become divided into two distinct camps: (intellectually) free and less free or even open and closed spheres (and societies), as was the case during the Cold War era. The question of who might be major decision-makers on the nature of academic mobility also arises. How might these decisions reflect students' points of view: their positions, aims, preferences, personal values and worldviews? Instead of brain circulation, which is one of the key aspirations of mobility, how might we prevent mobility from becoming brain drain for one and brain gain for others (see Van der Wende, 2015)? Issues of brain drain and, at the same time, academic, forced, parallel or one-way mobility into universities (of a kind of intellectual refugee) may also arise. Anxieties about academic mobility cannot be directly equated with the concerns of immigration and they are not governed in a similar manner. However, since academics do not live in a vacuum that escapes the political and social realities of the surrounding (global) world, how can they negotiate these realities in ways that are both critical and creative?

It is not possible to unravel the elements of inequality and injustice hidden within mobility structures until we perceive nations, institutions and individuals as equals rather than the objects of our interests in an inevitably competitive world. According to Jacques Hallak (2000, 25), three types of actors or players can be distinguished in globalization: "those who globalise and those who are globalised and those who are left out of globalisation." As long as academic mobility and higher education institutions are framed within the logics of academic capitalism and competition between states some will inevitably benefit more than others.

With increasing attention paid to the challenges of climate change and sustainability, the justifications of people and material being mobile have been questioned in recent years. For instance, if international travel (especially air traffic) is to be restricted permanently and it becomes substantially more expensive in the future, many questions will arise about mobility: Who will have the opportunities to be mobile? Will 'internationality' become an even more significant factor contributing to inequality between individuals, institutions and countries? What kind of possible hierarchies might then be formed with regard to mobility? What modes of academic mobility might become dominant? If who pays for the mobility will determine who benefits from the mobility then the question arises as to how mobility flows might be conceptualized and managed differently.

Despite national and international policy-makers having the responsibility for more equal mobility structures and flows, individual researchers, and perhaps also students, may need to examine these important questions critically. They might also need to consider how they could prevent the realization of the negative consequences of mobility and threats to its sustainability.

Understandably, there is no single answer to these various questions and concerns. However, it is clear that cooperation and dialogue across different national and cultural spaces must continue between academics and institutes in different countries, regardless of the complexities and headwinds facing intergovernmental relations.

In order to reconsider the relationship between higher education and mobility beyond nationally crafted rationales, academics face numerous dilemmas in reconciling national strategic interests with their wider, global, humanistic understanding of the world in an attempt to reposition international academic mobility within a rapidly changing global context. Indeed, to reimagine academic mobility in an equitable and sustainable way, the discussion needs to be extended beyond the national, or even regional, perspective. Indeed, we need to rethink mobility as an important ethical practice that involves transnational collaboration, and as a driving force for the creation of a truly global academic community, committed to working through the emerging challenges to be faced in both human and non-human futures.

References

Baer, J. & Martel, M. (2020). *International Student Enrolment Snapshot*. IIE. https://www.iie.org/Research-and-Insights/Open-Doors/Fall-International-Enrollments-Snapshot-Reports.
Ballatore, M. & Ferede, M. K. (2013). The Erasmus Programme in France, Italy and the United Kingdom: Student mobility as a signal of distinction and privilege. *European Educational Research Journal, 12*(4), 525–533. doi: 10.2304/eerj.2013.12.4.525

Bilecen, B. & Van Mol, C. (2017). Introduction: International academic mobility and inequalities. *Journal of Ethnic and Migration Studies, 43*(8),1241–1255.doi:10.1080/1369183X.2017.1300225

Bishop,M.L.& Payne,A.(2021).The political economies of different globalizations:Theorizing reglobalization. *Globalizations, 18*(1), 1–21. doi: 10.1080/14747731.2020.1779963

Brooks, R. & Waters, J. (2011). *Student Mobilities, Migration and the Internationalization of Higher Education.* Palgrave Macmillan.

Choudaha, R. (2018).Three waves of international student mobility (1999–2020). *Studies in Higher Education, 42*(5), 825–832. doi: 10.1080/03075079.2017.1293872

European Commission. (2015). *Erasmus: Facts, figures & trends. The European Union support for student and staff exchanges and university cooperation in 2013–2014.* European Commission. https:// ec.europa.eu/assets/eac/education/library/statistics/erasmus-plus-facts-figures_en.pdf

Flew, T. (2020). Globalization, neo-globalization and post-globalization:The challenge of populism and the return of the national. *Global Media and Communication, 16*(1), 19–39. doi: 10.1177/1742766519900329

Greven, T. (2016). The rise of right-wing populism in Europe and the United States. *Friedrich-Ebert-Stiftung.* https://library.fes.de/pdf-files/id/12892.pdf

Hallak, J. (2000). Globalization and its impact on education. In T. Mebrathu, M. Crossley & D. Johnson (Eds.) *Globalization, Educational Transformation and Societies in Transition* (pp. 21–40). Symposium Books.

Haugen, H. Ø. (2013). China's recruitment of African university students: Policy efficacy and unintended outcomes. *Globalization, Societies and Education, 11*(3), 315–334. doi: 10.1080/14767724.2012.750492

Held, D., McGrew, A., Goldblatt, D. & Perraton, J. (1999). *Global Transformations: Politics, Economics and Culture.* Polity.

Jayadeva, S. (2020). Keep calm and apply to Germany: How online communities mediate transnational student mobility from India to Germany. *Journal of Ethnic and Migration Studies, 46*(11), 2240–2257. doi: 10.1080/1369183X.2019.1643230

Jones, E. (2017). Problematising and reimagining the notion of 'International student experience'. *Studies in Higher Education, 42*(5), 933–943. doi: 10.1080/03075079.2017. 1293880

Jöns, H. & Höyler, M. (2013). Global geographies of higher education:The perspective of world university rankings. *Geoforum, 46,* 45–59. doi: 10.1016/j.geoforum.2012.12.014

Lansing, J. & Farnum, R. L. (2017). Statecraft and study abroad: Imagining, narrating and reproducing the state. *International Journal of Development Education and Global Learning, 9*(1)3–17. doi: 10.18546/IJDEGL9.1.02

Lee, J. J. & Haupt, J. P. (2021). Scientific collaboration on COVID-19 amidst geopolitical tensions between the US and China. *The Journal of Higher Education, 92*(2), 303–329. doi: 10.1080/00221546.2020.1827924

Lee, J. J. & Rice, C. (2007). Welcome to America? International student perceptions of discrimination. *Higher Education, 53*(3), 381–409. doi: 10.1007/s10734-005-4508-3

Lomer, S. (2018). UK policy discourses and international student mobility:The deterrence and subjectification of international students. *Globalization, Society and education, 16*(3), 308–324. doi: 10.1080/14767724.2017.1414584

Lomer, S. & Anthony-Okeke, L. (2019). Ethically engaging international students: Student generated material in an active blended learning model. *Teaching in Higher Education, 24*(5), 613–632. doi: 10.1080/13562517.2019.1617264

Luthra, L. & Platt, L. (2016). Elite or middling? International students and migrant diversification. *Ethnicities, 16*(2), 316–344. doi: 10.1177/1468796815616155

Marginson, S. (2018). Public/private in higher education: A synthesis of economic and political approaches. *Studies in Higher Education, 43*(2), 322–337. doi: 10.1080/03075079.2016.1168797

Martin, F. & Rizvi, F. (2014). Making Melbourne: Digital connectivity and international students' experience of locality. *Media, Culture & Society, 36*(7), 1016–1031. doi: 10.1177/0163443714541223

Mezzadra, S. & Neilson, B. (2013). *Border as Method, or, the Multiplication of Labor.* Duke University Press.

Myers, M. & Bhopal, K. (2021). Cosmopolitan brands: Graduate students navigating the social space of elite global universities. *British Journal of Sociology of Education* 42 (5–6), 701–716. doi: 10.1080/01425692.2021.1941763

Öniş, Z. & Kutlayb, M. (2021). The global political economy of right-wing populism: Deconstructing the paradox. *The International Spectator, 55*(2), 108–126. doi: 10.1080/03932729.2020.1731168

Pan, S. (2020). COVID-19 and the neoliberal paradigm in higher education: Changing landscape. *Asian Education and Development Studies, 10*(2), 322–335. doi: 10.1108/AEDS-06-2020-0129

Pécoud, A. (2021). Philosophies of migration governance in a globalizing world. *Globalizations, 18*(1), 103–119. doi: 10.1080/14747731.2020.1774316

Peters, M. A. (2020). China's belt and road initiative: Reshaping global higher education. *Educational Philosophy and Theory, 52*(6), 586–592. doi:10.1080/00131857.2019.1615174

Rizvi, F. & Lingard, B. (2010). *Globalizing Education Policy.* Routledge.

Robertson, S. (2013). *Transnational Student-Migrants and the State: The Education-Migration Nexus.* Palgrave.

Rodrik, F. (2020). Why Does Globalization Fuel Populism? *NBER Working Paper Series Economics, Culture, and the Rise of Right-Wing Populism.* National Bureau of Economic Research. Working Paper 27526. http://www.nber.org/papers/w27526

Sá, C. M. & Sabzalieva, E. (2018). The politics of the great brain race: Public policy and international student recruitment in Australia, Canada, England and the USA. *Higher Education, 75*(2), 231–253. doi: 10.1007/S10734-017-0133-1

Saarinen, T. (2020). *Language and New Nationalism in Higher Education.* Springer.

Shachar, A. & Hirschr, R. (2013). Recruiting "super talent": The new world of selective migration regimes. *Indiana Journal of Global Legal Studies, 20*(1), 71–107. doi: 10.2979/indjglolegstu.20.1.71

Shields, R. (2019). The sustainability of international higher education: Student mobility and global climate change. *Journal of Cleaner Production, 217*(20), 594–602. doi: 10.1016/j.jclepro.2019.01.291

Silova, I., Millei, Z., Goebel, J., Manion, C. & Read, R. (2020). Beyond the human: Rethinking education and academic conferencing during the times of climate crisis. *Comparative Education Review, 64*(4), 749–752. doi: 10.1086/710774

Soong, H. (2020). Singapore international education hub and its dilemmas: The challenges and makings for cosmopolitan learning. *Asia Pacific Journal of Education, 40*(1), 112–125. doi: 10.1080/02188791.2020.1725433

Stein, S. & Andreotti, V. D. O. (2016). Cash, competition, or charity: International students and the global imaginary. *Higher Education, 72*(2), 225–239. doi: 10.1007/s10734-015-9949-8

Tannock, S. (2018). *Educational Equality and International Students: Justice Across Borders?* Palgrave Macmillan.

UIS. (2021). *UIS Statistics*. UIS. http://data.uis.unesco.org/

UNHCR. (2021). *Figures at a Glance*. UNCHR. https://www.unhcr.org/figures-at-a-glance.html

Välimaa, J., Papatsiba, V. & Hoffman, D. (2016). Higher education in networked knowledge societies. In D. Hoffman & J. Välimaa (Eds.) *Re-Becoming Universities? Higher Education Institutions in Networked Knowledge Societies* (pp. 13–39). Springer.

Van der Wende, M. (2015). International academic mobility: Towards a concentration of the minds in Europe. *European Review, 23*(S1), S70–S88. doi: 10.1017/S1062798714000799

Vögtle, E. M. & Windzio, M. (2016). Networks of international student mobility: Enlargement and consolidation of the European transnational education space? *Higher Education, 72*(6), 723–741. doi: 10.1007/s10734-015-9972-9

Weimer, L. & Barlete, A. (2020). The rise of nationalism: The influence of populist discourses on international student mobility and migration in the UK and US 2020. In L. Weimer & T. Nokkala (Eds.) *Universities as Political Institutions* (pp. 33–57). Brill.

Williamson, B. (2021). Making markets through digital platforms: Pearson, edu-business, and the (e)valuation of higher education. *Critical Studies in Education, 62*(1), 50–66. doi: 10.1080/17508487.2020.1737556

Wu, X. & Chan, W. K. (2019). Integrating international student mobility in the belt and road initiative: From state-dominated to state-steering? *Higher Education Evaluation and Development 13*(1), 33–47. doi: 10.1108/HEED-03-2019-0010

Zhao, X. (2021). Digital labour in transnational mobility: Chinese international students' online boundary work in Daigou. *New Media & Society 23*(9), 2554–2574. doi: 10.1177/1461444820934096

Ziguras, C. & McBurnie, G. (2015). *Governing Cross-Border Higher Education*. Routledge.

11

GLOBAL BIOPOLITICS OF CLIMATE CHANGE

Affect, digital governance, and education

Marcia McKenzie

A recent survey of 10,000 young people from around the world found that over 80 per cent were moderately to extremely worried about climate change (Marks et al., 2021). Just under half said the way they feel about climate change negatively affects their day-to-day lives, and over half of global youth surveyed indicated they believe that 'humanity is doomed' due to anthropogenic climate change. There are also high levels of concern and anxiety about climate change across the general population, for example with 64 per cent of 1.2 million respondents over 50 countries indicating climate change is an emergency (UNDP, 2021).

However, there has also been a global increase in climate denial over the past decade. By recent counts, under 60 per cent of the United States (US) population believes climate change is mostly caused by human activities; this denial is also enmeshed with affective registrars of fear and hopes for the future (Sinatra & Hofer, 2021). Gallup Poll findings indicate a widening gap in the US between Democrat and Republic sentiments on climate change (Saad, 2021). For example, 67 per cent of Democrats 'now consider global warming a serious threat to themselves,' compared with just 11 per cent of Republicans (a 56 point difference, in contrast to a 38 point difference in 2016, and 16 points in 2001). The US is not alone in having growing segments of climate denialists (and other forms of science denial, including regarding COVID-19), with "the affective politics of the 'post-truth' era" (Boler & Davis, 2018, p. 75) causing increasing political polarization and large partisan gaps in sentiments on issues critical to human and planetary life.

It used to be possible to talk about a more consistent 'structure of feeling' of a particular place during a given era (Williams, 1961). However, through the globalizing effects of digital and migrational infrastructures, collective affect is now networked more globally, based on cross-national political and ideological communities and affinities, and less exclusively centered in geographic localities

DOI: 10.4324/9781003207528-11

(e.g., Kahan, 2012). Despite having the scientific knowledge and technological advances to prevent catastrophic climate change, progress is also reliant on these global webs of affective politics. Many overlapping factors contribute to the flows of (mis)information and conflicting 'feeling rules' that are at the heart of our global inability to take the significant action needed to curb climate change within the necessary timelines. These include global, corporate, fossil fuel lobbying; growing algorithmic governance and its role in political polarization within and across nations; anti-globalization and increased national populism; widened wealth gaps; and historical and ongoing colonial and extractivist policies (Boler & Davis, 2018; IPCC, 2018; Moffat, 2020).

This chapter explores this terrain, examining how the global affective mobilities enabled by corporate, algorithmic, and political modalities are a sizable barrier to addressing climate change, as we have also seen with COVID-19. It also discusses how affect is mobilized through the weather events caused by an already changed global climate, as another globally circulating influence in shaping collective affect and orientations to climate change. The chapter ends by asking how our approaches to climate change might be informed through further examining how these digital and climatic biopolitics are shaping our global climate futures, and implications for broader forms of communication and education, including education policy.

Affective biopolitics

As exemplified by the study on young people's feelings about climate change above, the relationship between climate change and emotions is a burgeoning area of concern. Recent book titles on this nexus include: *A Field Guide to Climate Anxiety, Climate Psychology: On Indifference to Disaster, Environmental Melancholia,* or *Psychological Roots of the Climate Crisis* (Hoggett, 2019; Jaquette Ray, 2020; Lertzman, 2015; Weintrobe, 2021). The American Psychological Association (APA) recognizes climate change as a growing issue for mental health (APA, 2019), with a proliferating host of networks, associations, and businesses aimed at addressing the growing mental health impacts of climate change (e.g., the Good Grief Network based on the 12 step AA program, or the Climate Psychology Alliance). Much of this work is being led by psychologists, and takes as its focus the individual psychological and emotional effects of climate change, along with relatively individualized points of intervention and action (e.g.,'10 steps to personal resilience and empowerment').

However, as Sara Ahmed (2004) describes in a paper on 'collective feelings', "[r]ather than seeing emotions only as psychological dispositions, we need to consider how they work, in concrete and particular ways, to mediate the relationship between the psychic and the social, and between the individual and collective" (p. 27). Social relations can be understood as "imbued with affect – our ways of operating in society held together, and attached to, by invisible registers, habits, and excesses of feeling" (McKenzie, 2017, p. 4). Collective affect can be viewed as not separate from individual felt experiences but, rather, as also encompassing the broader contextual and cultural milieus, the 'feeling rules' and 'affective atmospheres' in which those emotions are embedded, and their social and political effects (Anderson, 2009; Hochschild, 1983). Thus, individual emotive responses to climate change can be understood as embedded within broader collective affective orientations, which are increasingly shared in and across nation states, globally, through digital and climatic means.

Geographical work on affect seems particularly helpful for thinking through the spatial characteristics of collective affect, including uneven global mobilities. As geographer David Bissell (2010) writes, "Since affect emerges as a relation between bodies, objects, and technologies, it has distinctly spatial characteristics" (p. 272). He, along with others (e.g., Anderson, 2009), has previously used the term 'affective atmospheres' to connote the spatialized aspects of affect – created and maintained in relation, moving between and among bodies and objects locally, but also globally. Zizi Papacharissi (2015) has articulated something similar in the 'affective publics' enabled by technology, defined as "networked publics that are mobilized and connected, identified, and potentially disconnected through expressions of sentiment" (p. 311).

However, the conceptualization of 'affective atmospheres', especially, has been critiqued for a lack of attention to how individual and shared experiences of collective affect will also be shaped by prior affective experiences which change the body's capacity to affect and be affected (Wetherell, 2013). As Ahmed (2004) writes, "it is not simply my perception [e.g., of an atmosphere], but involves a form of 'contact' between myself and others, which is shaped by longer histories of contact" (p. 31). In relation to climate change and climate justice, this includes histories of colonial, racial, gendered, and Global North–South contact which render the spatialization of collective affect uneven, globally, as well as uneven in particular places.

Ben Anderson's more recent (e.g., 2014) work has been especially helpful for conceptualizing affect as encompassing both shared affective conditions and the differentially experienced bodily felt, as well as the biopolitical techniques that mediate between the two (see also McKenzie, 2017). As Anderson (2012) writes, "the affective life of individuals and collectives is an 'object-target of' and 'condition for' contemporary forms of biopower" (pp. 28–29), such as the corporate and algorithmic influence on our collective orientations to climate change, as will be discussed further below. However, Anderson also points to the possibilities invoked in Foucault's original use of the concept of biopower; in that it does not assume life is completely governed by the techniques introduced to shape it: it also "constantly escapes them" (Foucault in Anderson, 2012, p. 29). In yet later work, Anderson (2014) explores how bodily experiences between people, for example, can enable affective experiences that mediate or resist the affective interventions of 'apparatuses of power,' and can also migrate outwards to influence broader collective affective conditions. This has been extended to bodily experiences with place, for example with "the river and the watershed and then the Sturgeon" (fish) leading to collective affect and actions regarding the Nechako River in British Columbia, Canada (Pitton & McKenzie, 2020, p. 11). In a collection on the 'sites and spaces of affective governance', Eleanor Jupp, Jessica Pykett, and Fiona Smith (2016) also attend to both the politically constraining and enabling aspects of affect, in considering both "how emotions create and sustain new relationships of power and modes of governing, but also how they might disrupt governance regimes, surface in unexpected ways and places, generate new identifications and solidarities, and perhaps shift policy and politics" (p. 3).

In what follows, the biopolitics of affect are discussed more specifically, including in relation to collective orientations to climate change. The chapter then explores the global flows of the corporate and algorithmic governing of collective affect on climate change, as well as affective encounters with climate change through weather events. It closes by asking what the roles of communication and education might be in mediating or contributing to these forms of global affective governance, including in the mobilities and polarizations of education policy.

Digital governance of climate change affect

In better understanding new global conditions as they impact on whether and how climate change is addressed, including in education, it has become evident that the affective politics of digital governance is important. Indeed, it may be increasingly influencing the relative action or inaction of national governments on climate change. While member countries convene annually for Conference of the Parties (COP) on the United Nations Framework Convention on Climate Change (UNFCCC, 1992) and the more recent Paris Agreement (UNFCCC, 2015), progress is impeded by the lack of ambition of powerful countries' governing parties, in most cases elected by country citizens. As Greta Thunberg conveyed in a recent speech to the Youth4Climate summit in the run up to COP26, it is too often a matter of 'blah, blah, blah' speeches and posturing, rather than the concerted and urgent action that is needed. This extends to the inclusion of communication and education on climate change in such intergovernmental forums and related target-setting, with minimal ambition to further engage these approaches to inform and increase public support for climate action (McKenzie, 2021; UNESCO, 2021). The US withdrawal from the Paris Agreement under the Trump administration, and its now underwhelming re-engagement under Biden, exemplifies how intergovernmental action is hamstrung by the ideological leanings of member party representatives and their electorates.

The basis for these leanings and their national and global circulation and impact in intergovernmental spheres and beyond is, then, of interest for climate action; including their relationship to what is possible via education. A breadth of disciplinary research has identified the ways that orientations to climate change rest largely on affinity groupings, including ideological belonging and political affiliation, as well as other types of social and cultural affinity, such as religion, cultural identity, national identity, vocation (e.g., Calliston, 2014; Kahan, 2012). Variously described in these diverse literatures as dependent on values, narratives, cultural frames, and so on, a collective affective orientation to the issue is inherent in affinity groups' likelihood to 'believe in' and have a capacity to support action on climate change. For example, as Kari Norgaard (2011) describes in her well-known study of parallels in what shapes responses to climate change across the US and Norway, there is a 'social organization' to our responses to climate change, shaped through assemblages of 'symbols, stories, rituals, and world-views,' in which affect plays a large part. She writes, "norms of behavior from conversation, feelings, and attention shape and reinscribe what is considered 'normal' to think about, talk about, and feel. And these local cultural norms are in turn connected to larger political economic relations" (p. x). This chapter is focused on the increasingly global forms of 'social organization' shaped through the circulations of collective affect within and across both national borders and localized cultural norms and their role in our climate change responses, or lack thereof.

Financial investment by corporations and individuals has been central to building up climate denialism, vis-à-vis both political party official policy in particular countries and sentiments of the general public, both nationally and globally (e.g., see Meyer, 2017 on the rise of the radical right in the US and its ties to corporate fossil fuel interests). Elite financial networks are working with and through broader 'networks of communicative capitalism' (Dean, 2021), which appear to be increasingly shaping public and political action through forms of affective governance. In relation to climate change denialism, research on organized climate contrarianism (Coan et al., 2021) has established significant links in the funding flows and messaging on climate change between prominent denialist think-tanks such as the Heartland Institute; private anonymous donors; and contrarian blogs. Aided by the affective feedback loops of social media algorithms, hosted by corporations such as Facebook, online misinformation with well-funded distribution is playing a significant role in shifting public perceptions more broadly.

Algorithmically generated 'filter bubbles' curate what each person sees on social media platforms. They 'hypernudge' users toward micro-targeted content that maximizes the emotional influence on users in alignment with previously collected psycho-informatics (Williamson, 2017). While social media corporations use these 'economies of emotion' to better sell public viewers to advertisers, they have also been effectively mobilized, by the populist right, toward electoral victories as well as the general circulation of misinformation, including on climate change (Zembylas, 2021). As Jodi Dean (2021) explains, "The networks of communicative capitalism are affective because emotions circulate more rapidly than ideas" (p. x); while Megan Boler and Elizabeth Davis (2021), call this "the affective weaponization of communications technologies" (p. 1).

The expanded global digital environment has been central in growing political polarization, including the rise of right-wing populism and nationalism in many countries, globally (with a correlation with climate change denialism, e.g., Kulin et al., 2021). There is a rise, also, of related digital affiliations expanding across national borders. One example is QAnon, the online conspiracy theory movement which has captured significant adherence in the US and beyond. QAnon online adherents, self-named as 'digital soldiers,' along with a broader conspiracy theory movement, have been key in spreading online misinformation and 'feeling rules' about COVID-19 and vaccine safety, among other topics, including climate change (Cohen & Wild, 2021; Deaton, 2020; Newall, 2020; Vowles & Hultman, 2021). The far-right group, 'Proud Boys,' also linked to the attacks on Washington D.C.'s Capitol Hill, have, for example, used 'Telegram', an encrypted social media app based in Dubai, to promote a form of 'petro-masculinity' (Bell, 2021; Daggett, 2018). Described as a 'catastrophic convergence' of climate change, a global fossil fuel system past its best before date, and an 'increasingly fragile Western hypermasculinity', Cara Daggett (2018) proposes that both online extremist groups and mainstream politics in countries such as the US (e.g., Trump's 'Make America Great Again' motto) are grasping to hold on to a mid-twentieth-century fantasy "when white men ruled their households… with wages that could support housewives and children… predicated upon an ongoing supply of cheap fossil fuels" (pp. 31–32). Daggett (2018) goes on to suggest these are the 'psycho-affective dimensions' of the political economy of fossil fuels, requiring attention to "the collective desires of those whose identities are most tied to petrocultures", including their gender anxieties (p. 35; see also Pulé and Hultman, 2021, on masculinities and the (m)anthropocene). This nostalgia is also directly entwined with the growing wealth gaps and increased precarity in employment for a growing proportion of the population in many countries, including the US.

It is not only climate change denialism and 'petro-masculinities' which are circulating within and across national borders through the affective politics of digital platforms. Rising ecofascism is a different form of far-right populist movement which takes an active stance on climate and broader environmental action, interwoven with racist and white supremist beliefs and activities. As a re-emergence of earlier ecofascism in Nazi ideology which twinned environmental purity with ethnic genocide, recent ecofascism is promulgated through affective digital means. Examples range from El Paso and Christchurch shooters who shared their manifestos with ecofascism sentiments on the social media site 8Chan, to 'joyful', viral, fake news posts such as of dolphins returning to urban Venice promoting as nature in recovery from human impact due to the population lockdowns of COVID-19 (Allison, 2020; Owen, 2019). With mass migration and 'overpopulation of non-white populations in white spaces' seen as major contributors to climate change by ecofascists, the solution is framed as bringing the world back to the "natural order of things" (Allison, 2020, p. 43). With slogans of 'save trees not refugees,' and pine tree emojis as markers in Twitter bios, a potent affective mix of fear, entitlement, and hate has been circulating and building adherents in North

America, Europe, and elsewhere. Adler (quoted in Owen, 2019, np) suggests that "Climate change – and the prospect of 'scarce' resources that comes attached to it – is just fodder to a far-right that feeds on fear of the outside…The only reason that 'eco-fascism' might come as a surprise…is because the far-right…has clung so desperately to its climate denial that it's hard to imagine how they would marry their xenophobia with an acceptance of climate science". Like denialism and contrarian orientations to climate change, this digitally spread ecofascism also extends beyond individual actors to corporate media and broader far-right political movements (Forchtner, 2019).

There is a bleakness in the prognosis that these population segments of contrarianism and far-right polarization, and related digital social movements of 'petro-nostalgic' (Daggett, 2018) and ecofascist 'digital soldiers,' are growing. This growth is connected with the new forms of global mobilities enabled by communication technologies that, themselves, rely on fossil fuel infrastructures (Urry, 2011) and spread divisive climate politics through affective means of fear, hate, belonging, desire, and anxiety. However, many of the same and different digital venues – WhatsApp, Instagram, TikTok, et cetera – also offer platforms for pro-climate action movements that are not on the far right. These include movements such as the Extinction Rebellion, Idle No More and other global online Indigenous communities, the youth-led #FridaysforFuture or #ClimateStrike, as well as the circulation of pro-climate action sentiments more broadly.

Significantly, global youth populations are connecting into and virtually mobilizing forms of collective affect in relation to climate change. For example, the TikTok-created hashtag #ForClimate (launched as a campaign by TikTok in partnership with NGOs) has over 560 million views, with thousands of, largely, Gen Z content creators posting videos daily about their relationship to climate change (Hautea et al., 2021). Purporting to avoid a focus on 'doom and gloom' content, even though 'What gets the strongest emotional response is going to go viral,' some creators indicate they focus on fact-based content, such as through the collaborative TikTok account Eco_Tok, which has over 111 million followers (Pattee, 2021). In their recent study, Hautea et al. (2021) specifically examine how TikTok creators use the platform's affordances – particularly its modes of imitation and replication – to "harness waves of cascading social connection" (p. 1), in forms of affective contagion that create affective publics (Papacharissi, 2015). Samantha Hautea et al. (2021) analyze TikTok content on climate change, showing how a "networked atmosphere of concern" (p. 12), which promotes climate activism and/or an overwhelming sense of hopelessness, is circulating through "affective force and algorithmic serendipity" (p. 2). A search of ecofascism turns up a host of anti-ecofascist youth's TikTok videos with many thousands of views, with taglines such as '#ecofascism has no place in environmentalism [earth emoji]' (see, e.g., @thegarbagequeen).

The school strikes for climate initiated by Swedish youth Greta Thunberg in August 2018 have also spread globally through Twitter and social media platforms.

These #FridaysForFuture Twitter accounts cover a long list of countries and cities around the world, from Kenya to Dublin to Pakistan, with corresponding glob-ally coordinated dates for in-person strike marches. Both the online and face-to-face activism of youth are embedded within collective affective milieus. These include both shared worry and shared despair about the state of the planet, with increasing rates of youth mental health impacts (Burke, Sanson, & Van Hoorn, 2018). But they also include finding collective belonging, purpose and hope in a sense of contributing to the possibility of greater climate action (de Moor et al., 2021): "It's an *atmosphere* you can't beat. As soon as you meet other people who have the same concerns...there's a huge amount of solidarity" (Jones, quoted in Whitwell, 2021, emphasis added).

Considering the conceptualizations of affect introduced earlier, it is clear there are diverse ways in which collective affect on climate change is shared and spread, at least in part, through the 'affective publics' of social media platforms. The corporate platforms themselves play an active role in this with their designs to share and amplify affect though narrative forms and algorithmic structures. They funnel and shape climate change interactions through activities such as partnerships with NGOs (e.g., #ForClimate in the case of TikTok) or through targeted advertising and inadequate regulation of xenophobic and racist content (Siapera & Viejo-Otero, 2021). Their private, corporate nature, in some cases with elite networks wielding influence over platform content or functions, means they can be understood as techniques of digital governance over the affective lives of people across the globe, despite their feel as venues of a global public sphere. At least some of the time, they operate as 'apparatuses of power,' shaping sentiment, ideology, and politics (Anderson, 2014). At the same time, the virtual 'bodily encounters' between like-minded and diverse people can also be seen as contrib-uting to forms of collective affect and action that, in some cases, extend beyond the algorithmic ambitions of such platforms, such as in the role of social media in the global spread of the FridaysForFuture or school climate strike movements.

Climatic atmospheres

Changing tack to consider a different, but also related, global affective medium which is shaping individual and collective orientations to climate change, cli-matic weather (and related land) events are visceral bodily encounters that can influence global flows of collective affect on climate change. The sense of precar-ity catalyzed by experiencing climate change firsthand can contribute to shap-ing collective affect in relation to climate change. As Lauren Berlant (2011) put it in relation to increased precarity more broadly, "[t]he aesthetic and political point seems to be that the drama or adjustment to a pervasive atmosphere of unexpected precarity makes certain situations exemplary laboratories for sensing contemporary life in new idioms of affective realism" (p. 54). A 'cruel optimism' in continuing to hope for an already impossible future is a dominant response to precarity, as Berlant (2011) has illustrated. This is amply evident in the subtler forms of climate change denial displayed in continuing to plan for future generations, without reckoning with climate change's impacts on the possibility of that future or one's own part in contributing to its growing unlikelihood – what Norgaard (2011) calls 'implicatory denial.' However, it is one thing to keep climate change socially and psychologically at bay when it is a far away, global news item, and another when it shows up on one's doorstep or home territory via the changed weather or other climate impacts already affecting the future one might have expected or felt a responsibility to.

The effects of weather on individual and collectively experienced affect have been examined more generally, though often in terms of shorter-term mood or ambience changes (Adams-Hutcheson, 2019). However, global climate change, and its manifestations in the temperatures, sea levels, air quality, and other environmental and atmospheric conditions which cross national borders, are increasingly experienced in bodily and affective ways that go beyond a more temporary mood. Up-close encounters with more regular and widespread extreme weather events — forest or bush fires, their circulating smoke, flooding, hurricanes, drought, heat domes — in addition to more immediate mental health challenges, cause us to feel our increased environmental precarity, manifesting individually as emotions of fear, hopelessness, anger, anxiety, grief (Verlie, 2019). They cause us to understand climate change as a force of "unthinkable magnitude that create[s] unbearably intimate connections over vast gaps in time and space" (Ghosh, 2016, p. 62), as emissions in one place determine weather events and impacts for communities on the other side of the planet.

This includes climate change's effects on particular places, within which our social, affective, and economic lives are embedded (Tuck & McKenzie, 2015). For example, Gail Adams-Hutcheson (2019) examines the links between farmers' mental health and climatic conditions in Aotearoa New Zealand, such as during drought conditions and related effects on the land and cattle: "The troposphere… impacts on the everyday, it molds our most mundane practices and infiltrates time, space and context" (p. 1018). As discussed at the beginning of the chapter, more generally in relation to understanding affect, "[t]he materiality of climate change's atmospheres is experienced radically differently by different bodies in different places and different times" (Verlie, 2019, p. 6), including across cultural, geographic, economic, racialized, and gendered diversity. Many Indigenous communities have already significantly been affected by climate change, including in relation to "changing place attachment, disrupted cultural continuity, altered food systems, forced human mobility, and intangible loss and damages," with mental health outcomes such as strong emotions, suicide, depression, and anxiety as result of climate-related weather events (Middleton et al., 2020, p. 1). Studying both Inuit Indigenous communities and rural farmers, Ashlee Cunsolo and Neville Ellis (2018) discuss personal and collective ecological grief as a natural response in making sense of the changes "wrought upon their loved home environments" by climate change and the attendant 'loss of environmental futures' (p. 276).

In terms of how bodily experiences of weather events in particular places link into global climatic affective conditions, there are also points of intersection with digital considerations. Social media activity on climate change has been found to increase in response to climate-related extreme weather events (Berglez & Al-Saqaf, 2021), as local bodily experiences of climate change are conveyed in shared images and stories of flooding or fires that travel globally. The visibility, remixing, and memetic qualities of TikTok videos, for example, amplify local stories of climate change around the world (Hautea et al., 2021), such as in a video of flooding in Hawai'i with over 78,000 likes, with hashtags such as #climatecrisis and #floods. In introducing a special issue on reterritorializing social media, Alex Wilson et al. (2017) describe how social media is transforming how Indigenous people interact and connect with one another locally and globally, including in relation to climate change. They articulate this as a "cultural and political reterritorialization of social media spaces," in which "social media is being deployed to gather a global audience of allies" for Indigenous and climate justice, such as by the Sioux people of North Dakota in action against an oil pipeline planned for their traditional homelands (Wilson et al., 2017, p. 1). These and many other examples suggest some of the ways that local place-based encounters with climate change and its infrastructures can contribute to globally circulating collective affective understandings of our precarities and responsibilities in terms of climate change and climate action.

Imperatives of communication and education

In sketching out the global mobilities of affective biopolitics, this chapter aims to bring the global circulations of climate change into discussion with other recent global trends affecting education. These range from the global rise of populism following neoliberalism's heyday, related ideological and political polarizations, including as spurred on by corporate algorithmic governance, and increased disparities of wealth and racialization and associated economic and social precarities. Uneven global affective responses and orientations to climate change are bound up with these other circumstances and shape whether we can or will respond to climate change in time to enable continued human life on the planet (IPCC, 2018). It suggests the importance of effective communication and education concerned with climate change engaging with these interwoven affective factors, as well as showing how communication and education on climate change, of one type or another, is already abundant in virtual and place-based affinity communities.

There is growing recognition that curriculum and pedagogy concerned with climate change needs to go beyond science literacy education, to address the ideological and political barriers to broader social action on climate change (Henderson & Drewes, 2020) as well as their psychological effects (Armstrong, Krasny, & Schuldt, 2018). In their discussion of decolonial pedagogies concerned with climate change, Fikile Nxumalo and Marleen Villanueva (2020) suggest, for example, how 'learning to be affected by the weather' through walking can overcome barriers created in learning about the weather in a book or classroom. They share a range of other examples of affective learning encounters that work against colonizing 'sentiments that extend the settler state,' such as relating to nature as pure, separate, or awaiting discovery (p. 224). An increasing number of other resources discuss climate change and environmental learning in relation to testimony, reckoning, fabulation, care, digital media, and related affective encounters and effects that take on individual and collective psychosocial barriers to climate change action (e.g., Truman, 2021; Roussell et al., 2017; Verlie, 2019).

It is also key to consider how education and education policy are not immune to increased political polarization where "polarization adds an additional challenge to policymaking in already complex multi-level governance settings" (Jesuit & Williams, 2018, p. 2). Political polarization can stymie cross-party policy-making or result in policy that further contributes to that polarization, such as US state jurisdictions that prohibit teaching about climate change or Canadian provincial settings that use industry-supplied pro-fossil fuel curricular resources (Eaton & Day, 2020).

Education policy can be understood as an 'apparatus of power' that mobilizes collective affect to achieve certain learning or societal outcomes, such as socially dominant modes of behavior, aspirations to achieve certain ends, or colonial orientations to people and place. However, it can also provide openings for 'bodily encounters' that provide impetus to exceed dominant affective norms, such as in Williams (1961) 'emergent' structures of feeling. As Bessie Dernikos et al. (2020) write in *Mapping the Affective Turn in Education*, "Affect is happening all around us. It is precisely its emerging unpredictability that enables 'margins of maneuverability' (Massumi, 2015, p. 3) … [yet] simultaneously bears the risk of re-entrenching racism, classism, and other exclusions" (p. 19).

Collective affect is part of what shapes and circulates education policy, including on climate and related sustainability issues (McKenzie, 2017; Pitton & McKenzie, 2020). In prior research with administrators from school divisions and schools across Canada, a sense of environmental precarity was a factor in not simply wanting to include climate in education policy, but doing so in a way that tries to shield students from the anxiety and fear that can go with understanding the realities of climate change. This was evident in a local school division sustainability plan, for example, "which stressed the need for overcoming fatalism about the environment and avoiding the spread of despair among students," with a resulting focus on "connecting with nature" (Pitton & McKenzie, 2020, p. 10).

However, as the FridaysForFuture school climate strikes and climate TikTok activity suggest, many school students are not looking to be protected from knowledge of the realities of climate change. Rather, they are out of patience with their schools' and governments' affective orientations to climate change and associated lack of adequate response. Relatively few countries currently include climate change as a focus in primary and secondary curriculum and policy and, when there, typically it is in cursory ways (McKenzie, 2021). Perhaps more significantly, many students are not calling for stronger climate change curriculum for themselves but for emission reductions and just financing by government and public institutions. A more adequate response by education jurisdictions is the development of 'whole of institution' policy on climate: policy activity on emission reductions in relation to the buildings and technological infrastructures of schooling, through school–community partnerships, overall school governance priorities, as well as within curriculum and pedagogy (McKenzie & Kwauk, 2021; Selwyn, 2021).

This chapter has suggested how the globally circulating, affective biopolitics of digital media and climatic events are influencing children, youth, and adults across regions and ideologies. Collective affective conditions of fear, anxiety, despair, denial, and more are already incumbent upon much of the global population in relation to climate change. Not explicitly engaging with climate change in education and education policy becomes a matter of adding harm, and of being critically out of step with a most pressing global issue of the twenty-first century.

References

Adams-Hutcheson, G. (2019). Farming in the troposphere: Drawing together affective atmospheres and elemental geographies. *Social & Cultural Geography, 20* (7), 1004–1023.

Ahmed, S. (2004). Collective feelings: Or, on the impressions left by others. *Theory, Culture & Society, 2* (2), 25–42.

Allison, M. (2020), So long, and thanks for all the fish!: Urban dolphins as ecofascist fake news during COVID-19. *Journal of Environmental Media, 1*, 4.1–4.8. doi:10.1386/jem_00025_1

Anderson, B. (2009). Affective atmospheres. *Emotion, Space and Society, 2*, 77–81. doi:10.1016/j.emospa.2009.08.005

Anderson, B. (2012). Affective atmospheres. *Emotion, Space and Society, 2*, 77–81. doi:10.1016/j.emospa.2009.08.005

Anderson, B. (2014). *Encountering Affect: Capacities, Apparatuses, Conditions.* Ashgate.

Armstrong, A. K., Krasny, M. E., & Schuldt, J. P. (2018). *Communicating Climate Change: A Guide for Educators.* Cornell University Press.

Bell, S. (2021, February 3). Proud Boys added to Canada's list of terrorist groups. *Global News*, https://globalnews.ca/news/7616542/proud-boys-added-canada-list-terrorist-groups/. Accessed 01 December, 2021.

Berglez, P., & Al-Saqaf, W. (2021). Extreme weather and climate change: Social media results, 2008–2017, *Environmental Hazards, 20* (4), 382–399. doi:10.1080/17477891.2020.1829532

Berlant, L. G. (2011). *Cruel Optimism.* Duke University Press.

Bissell, D. (2010). Passenger mobilities: Affective atmospheres and the sociality of public transport. *Environment and Planning D, Society & Space, 28* (2), 270–289. doi:10.1068/d3909

Boler, M., & Davis, E. (2018). The affective politics of the 'post-truth' era: Feeling rules and networked subjectivity. *Emotion, Space and Society, 27*, 75–85.

Boler, M., & Davis, E. (2021). *Affective Politics of Digital Media: Propaganda by Other Means*. Routledge.

Burke, S. E. L., Sanson, A.V., & Van Hoorn, J. (2018). The psychological effects of climate change on children. *Current Psychiatry Reports, 20*(35). doi:10.1007/s11920-018-0896-9

Calliston, C. (2014). *How Climate Change Comes to Matter: The Communal Facts of Life*. Duke University Press.

Coan, T., Boussalis, C., Cook, J., & Nanko, M. O. (2021, March 9). Computer-assisted detection and classification of misinformation about climate change. doi:10.31235/osf.io/crxfm

Cohen, Z., & Wild,W. (2021, June 14). FBI warns lawmakers that QAnon 'digital soldiers' may become more violent. https://www.cnn.com/2021/06/14/politics/fbi-qanon-threat-assessment/index.html

Cunsolo, A., & Ellis, N. R. (2018). Ecological grief as a mental health response to climate change-related loss. *Nature Climate Change, 8*, 275–281. doi:10.1038/s41558-018-0092-2

Daggett, C. (2018). Petro-masculinity: Fossil fuels and authoritarian desire. *Millennium: Journal of International Studies, 47* (1), 25–44.

de Moor, J., De Vydt, M., Uba, K., & Wahlström, M. (2021). New kids on the block: Taking stock of the recent cycle of climate activism, *Social Movement Studies, 20* (5), 619–625. doi:10.1080/14742837.2020.1836617

Deaton, J. (2020, September 29). Climate change deniers are embracing QAnon to gain followers. *Teen Vogue*, https://www.teenvogue.com/story/climate-change-denial-qanon. Accessed 01 December, 2021.

Deaton, J. (2021, Faces as commons: The secondary visuality of communicative capitalism. In D. Della Ratta, G. Lovink, T. Numerico, & P. Sarram (Eds.), *The Aesthetics and Politics of the Online Self: A Savage Journey into the Heart of Digital Cultures*, (pp. 357–370). Springer International Publishing.

Dernikos, B., Lesko, N., McCall, D., & Niccolini, A. (2020). *The Affective Turn in Education: Theory, Research, and Pedagogies*. Routledge.

Eaton, E., & Day, N. A. (2020). Petro-pedagogy: Fossil fuel interests and the obstruction of climate justice in public education, *Environmental Education Research, 26* (4), 457–473. doi:10.1080/13504622.2019.1650164

Forchtner, B. (Ed.) (2019). *The Far Right and the Environment: Politics, Discourse and Communication*. Routledge.

Ghosh, A. (2016). *The Great Derangement Climate Change and the Unthinkable*: University of Chicago Press

Hautea, S., Parks, P., Takahashi, B., & Zeng, J. (2021). Showing they care (or don't): Affective publics and ambivalent climate activism on TikTok. *Social Media + Society*, 1014. doi:10.1177/20563051211012344

Henderson, J., & Drewes, A. (2020). *Teaching Climate Change in the United States*. Routledge.

Hochschild, A. R. (1983). *The Managed Heart: Commercialization of Human Feeling*, University of California Press.

Hoggett, P. (Ed.) (2019). *Climate Psychology: On Indifference to Disaster*. Palgrave Macmillan.

Intergovernmental Panel on Climate Change (2018). *Global warming of 1.5C: An IPCC special report*. Cambridge University Press

Jaquette Ray, S. (2020). *A Field Guide to Climate Anxiety: How to Keep Cool on a Warming Planet*. University of California Press.

Jesuit, D. K., & Williams, R. A. (2018). *Public Policy, Governance and Polarization*. Routledge.

Jupp, E., J. Pykett, & F. M. Smith (Eds.) (2016). *Emotional States: Sites and Spaces of Affective Governance*. Routledge.

Kahan, D. (2012). Ideology, motivated reasoning, and cognitive reflection: An experimental study. *Judgment and Decision Making 8*, 407–424.

Kulin, J., Sevä, I. J., & Dunlap, R. E. (2021). Nationalist ideology, rightwing populism, and public views about climate change. *Europe, Environmental Politics*. doi:10.1080/09644 016.2021.1898879

Lertzman, R. (2015). *Environmental Melancholia: Psychoanalytic Dimensions of Engagement*. Routledge.

Marks, E., Hickman, C., Panu, P., Clayton, S., Lewandowski, E. R., Mayall, E. E., Britt, W., Mellor, C., & van Susteren, L. (2021). Young people's voices on climate anxiety, government betrayal and moral injury: A global phenomenon. *The Lancet*, Preprint. doi:10.2139/ssrn.3918955

Massumi, B. (2015). *Politics of Affect*. John Wiley & Sons.

McKenzie, M. (2017). Affect theory and policy mobility: Challenges and possibilities for critical policy research. *Critical Studies in Education, 58* (2), 187–204. doi:10.1080/175 08487.2017.1308875

McKenzie, M. (2021). Climate change education and communication in global review: Tracking progress through national submissions to the UNFCCC Secretariat. *Environmental Education Research*. doi:10.1080/13504622.2021.1903838

McKenzie, M., & Kwauk, C. (2021). Intertwined states of emergency: Education in the time of Covid-19 and the climate crisis. *NORRAG*, Special Issue 06, 140–144. doi:10 .1080/14767724.2020.1821612

Meyer, J. (2017). *Dark Money: The Hidden History of the Billionaires Behind the Rise of the Radical Right*. Doubleday.

Middleton, J., Cunsolo, A., Jones-Bitton, A., Wright, C. J., & Harper, S. (2020). Indigenous mental health in a changing climate: A systemic scoping review of the global literature. *Environmental Research Letters, 15*. doi:10.1088/1748-9326/ab68a9

Moffat, B. (2020). *Populism: Key Concepts in Political Theory*. Polity Press.

Morganstein, J. C. (2019). *Climate Change and Mental Health Connections*. https://www. psychiatry.org/patients-families/climate-change-and-mental-health-connections

Newall, M. (2020, December 30). More than 1 in 3 Americans believe a 'deep state' is working to undermine Trump. Ipsos https://www.ipsos.com/en-us/news-polls/ npr-misinformation-123020

Norgaard, K. M. (2011). *Living in Denial: Climate Change, Emotions, and Everyday Life*. MIT Press.

Nxumalo, F., & Villanueva, M. (2020). (Re)storying water: Decolonial pedagogies of relational affect with young children. In B. Dernikos, N. Lesko, S. D. McCall, & A. Niccolini (Eds.), *Mapping the Affective Turn in Education: Theory, Research, and Pedagogy*. Routledge.

Owen, T. (2019 August, 6). Eco-fascism: The racist theory that inspired the El Paso and Christchurch shooters. *Vice, 6*. https://www.vice.com/en_us/article/59nmv5/eco-fascism-the-racist-theory-that-inspired-the-el-pasoand-christchurch-shooters-and-is-gaining-followers.

Papacharissi, Z. (2015). *Affective Publics: Sentiment, Technology, and Politics*. Oxford University Press.

Pattee, E. (2021 March, 11). Meet the climate change activists of TikTok: A crop of eco-creators is bent on educating their followers about the looming global disasters. Can their message translate into action? *Wired*. https://www.wired.com/story/ climate-change-tiktok-science-communication/

Pitton, V. O., & McKenzie, M. (2020). What moves us also moves policy: The role of affect in mobilizing education policy on sustainability. *Journal of Education Policy*. doi:10.108 0/02680939.2020.1852605

Pulé, P., & Hultman, M. (2021). *Men, Masculinities, and Earth: Contending with the (M) Anthropocene*. Palgrave Macmillan.

Roussell, D., Cutter-Mackenzie, A., & Foster, J. (2017). Children of an Earth to come: Speculative fiction, geophilosophy and climate change education research. *Educational Studies, 53*(6), 654–669. doi:10.1080/00131946.2017.1369086

Saad, L. (2021). Global warming attitudes frozen. *Gallup*. https://news.gallup.com/poll/343025/global-warming-attitudes-frozen-2016.aspx

Selwyn, N. (2021). Ed-tech within limits: Anticipating educational technology in times of environmental crisis. *E-Learning and Digital Media, 18* (5), 496–510. doi:10.1177/20427530211022951

Siapera, E., & Viejo-Otero, P. (2021). Governing hate: Facebook and digital racism. *Television & New Media, 22* (2), 112–130. doi:10.1177/1527476420982232

Sinatra, G., & Hofer, B. (2021). *Science Denial: Why It Happens and What to Do About It*. Oxford University Press.

Truman, S. (2021). *Feminist Speculations and the Practice of Research-Creation: Writing Pedagogies and Intertextual Affects*. Routledge.

Tuck, E., & McKenzie, M. (2015). Relational validity and the "where" of inquiry: Place and land in qualitative research. *Qualitative Inquiry, 21*(7), 633–638. doi:10.1177/1077800414563809

United Nations Development Program. (2021). *Climate vote*. www.undp.org/publications/peoples-climate-vote#modal-publication-download

United Nations Education, Scientific and Cultural Organization. (2021). *Learn For Our Planet. A Global Review of How Environmental Issues are Included in Education*. Author. https://unesdoc.unesco.org/ark:/48223/pf0000377362

United Nations Framework Convention on Climate Change. (1992). *United Nations General Assembly Decision*. https://unfccc.int/resource/docs/convkp/conveng.pdf

United Nations Framework Convention on Climate Change. (2015, December 12). *Paris Agreement*. T.I.A.S. No. 16-1104. https://unfccc.int/resource/docs/2015/cop21/eng/l09.pdf.

Urry, J. (2011). *Climate Change and Society*. Wiley.

Verlie, B. (2019). Bearing worlds: Learning to live-with climate change. *Environmental Education Research, 25* (5), 751–766, doi:10.1080/13504622.2019.1637823

Vowles, K., & Hultman, M. (2021). Scare-quoting climate: The rapid rise of climate denial in the Swedish far-right media ecosystem. *Nordic Journal of Media Studies, 3* (1). https://www.doi.org/10.2478/njms-2021-0005

Weintrobe, S. (2021). *Psychological Roots of the Climate Crisis: Neoliberal Exceptionalism and the Culture of Uncare*. Bloomsbury Press.

Wetherell, M. (2013). Feeling rules, atmospheres and affective practice: Some reflections on the analysis of emotional episodes. In Maxwell, C., & Aggleton, P. (Eds.), *Privilege, Agency and Affect: Understanding the Production and Effects of Action* (221–239). Palgrave Macmillan.

Whitwell, J. (2021 October, 3). What climate scientists can teach us about dealing with climate change doom. *BBC News*. https://www.bbc.com/news/science-environment-58756143

Williams, R. (1961). *The Long Revolution*. Penguin.

Williamson, B. (2017). Moulding student emotions through computational psychology: Affective learning technologies and algorithmic governance. *Educational Media International, 54* 4, 267–288. doi:10.1080/09523987.2017.1407080

Wilson, A., Carlson, B., & Sciascia, A. (2017). Reterritorialising social media: Indigenous people rise up. *Australasian Journal of Information Systems, 21*, 1–4. doi:10.3127/ajis. v21i0.1591

Zembylas, M. (2021). *Affect and the Rise of Right-Wing Populism.* Cambridge University Press.

12

RECONFIGURING EDUCATION REFORM IN NORDIC COUNTRIES UNDER EVER-CHANGING CONDITIONS OF GLOBALIZATION

Risto Rinne

Introduction[1]

It is evident that greater global interconnectedness and a nascent global educational community, mediated, translated and re-contextualized within national and local education structures, are creating a certain resemblance among educational policies across nations (e.g., Lingard, 2000). The waves of global policy reforms ('traveling policies') have a tendency to diffuse around the globe and reshape socially and politically different societies with dissimilar histories. It is clear that these transnational trends and tendencies do not simply shape the regional, national or local policies but, rather, collide and intertwine with 'embedded policies' to be found in 'local' spaces (national, provincial or local), where global policy agendas come up against existing practices and priorities (Ozga & Lingard 2007; Rinne, 2021; Simola, Varjo & Rinne, 2014, p. 224).

Globalization seems to be a one-way highway in the future of education politics. Globalization has been described as resulting in the rescaling of politics and policy (Lingard & Rawolle, 2011). It is walking hand in hand with the further complicated rise of a new mode of governance, at a distance, through data, indicators and numbers. It rests on the provision and translation of information about subjects, objects and processes and brings new limits and possibilities for agents (cf. Hansen & Flyverbom, 2014). New techniques and evaluation data are producing and re-shuffling the positions of nation states and local spaces.

> The term 'glocal' unites the concepts of global and local and underlines the situation where the position of the nation-state as the driver of education politics is questioned. The new architecture of governance relies on the ever-faster production, mobility and circulation of data (Ball, 2016; Clarke,

DOI: 10.4324/9781003207528-12

2012). The expanding practices of evaluation produce knowledge about education, which may also allow the nation-state to extend its capacity to govern across territory and into the classroom through standardization, commensuration, transparency and comparison.

(Rinne, 2019)

In addition to the intended aims, this is also having severe, unintended consequences on the education policies and behavior of educational agents. Simultaneously, states are increasingly incorporated into the global accountability regime that helps the 'national eye' to govern with the 'global eye' (Nóvoa & Yariv-Mashal, 2003). In this chapter, I analyse the future trends of glocalization of education politics in context and comparison with the history of Nordic educational politics.

I am discussing the rethinking of what globalization actually is today and how it has had an impact in reconfiguring education reforms in Nordic countries. First, I write about the changes and new understanding of globalization and then I focus on the changes and education reforms in Nordic countries. Finally, I draw conclusions regarding the impacts.

Globalization, international organizations and governance at a distance

The Organisation for Economic Co-operation and Development (OECD) has become one of the major agents of the internationalizing, globalizing and, thus, converging education policy and policy processes (Ozga & Lingard, 2007; Taylor et al., 1997). While the OECD is primarily concerned with economic policy, education has taken on increasing importance within its mandate. Founded in 1961, the OECD has taken on an enhanced role as a policy actor, as it seeks a niche in the post-Cold War, globalizing world in relation to other international organizations (IO) and supranational agencies (Henry et al., 2001; Rinne, Kallo, & Hokka, 2004). To this end, it has developed alliances with other IOs such as the United Nations Educational, Scientific and Cultural Organization (UNESCO), the European Union (EU) and the World Bank to actively promote its policy preferences (Grek, 2009, pp. 24–25).

Unlike the EU, the OECD does not have the legal instruments, nor the financial levers, to actively promote particular policy-making at the national level of its member nations. Compared to, for example, the World Bank, which has 'power' over nations through policy requirements and funding and loans, the OECD is weaker. Rankings such as the *Education at a Glance* reports, the International Adult Literacy Survey (IALS) and the *Indicators in Education* project with the World Bank have become massive and impressive. Through the Programme for International Student Assessment (PISA) and national and thematic policy reviews, the OECD's educational agenda has become significant in framing policy options in the constitution of a global policy space in education (Grek, 2009, p. 25).

IOs cannot be understood as 'mere epiphenomena' of impersonal policy machinery. They are also seen as purposive actors —"missionaries of our time" — who are "armed with a notion of progress, an idea of how to create a better life, and some understanding of the conversion process" (Barnett & Finnemore, 1999, p. 712). This raises the question of why and how the OECD has been transformed into one of the most powerful agents of transnational education governance. According to Sotiria Grek (2009, p. 25), this question has been substantially answered by Kerstin Martens who notes that a:

> ... comparative turn ... a scientific approach to political decision making, which has been the main driver of the success. Through OECD´s statistics, reports and studies, it has achieved a brand which most regard indisputable; OECD's policy recommendations are accepted as valid by politicians and scholars alike.
>
> *(Martens, 2007, p. 42)*

And there seems to be no need for questioning once the label of 'OECD' is attached to justify the authoritative character of the knowledge, facts and interpretations contained therein. The role of the OECD is as the leader of "the orchestration of global knowledge networks" (Grek, 2009, p. 25).

The OECD has "created a niche as a technically highly competent agency for the development of educational indicators and comparative educational performance measures" (Grek, 2009, p. 26). The data defined and collected by OECD on education are contributing to the creation of a global governable space of comparison and commensurability, including "the European Education Space" (ibid.; Nóvoa & Lawn, 2002). These developments reflect policy convergence around what Brown and his colleagues define as a new educational policy consensus:

> The new consensus is based on the idea that as the 'walled' economies in mid-century have given way to an increasingly global economy, the power of national government to control the outcome of economic competition has been weakened. [...] Indeed, the competitive advantage of nations is frequently redefined in terms of the quality of national education and training systems judged according to international standards.
>
> *(Brown et al., 1997, pp. 7–8)*

Policy instruments, like indicators and the whole audit and performance-monitoring nexus, have become a "significant element of the shift from government to the governance of national education systems through new institutional forms" (Grek, 2009, p. 27). The purpose is:

> [...] orienting relations between political society (via the administrative executive) and civil society (via its administered subjects) through

intermediaries in the form of devices that mix technical components (measuring, calculating the rule of law, procedure) and social components (representation, symbol).

(Lascoumes & Le Galès, 2007, p. 6)

The OECD has filled the niche of comparative evaluations in relation to education policy in terms of various kinds of indicators like *Education at a Glance* and PISA (Grek, 2009, p. 27).

Patrick Le Galès defines governance substantially as:

[…] a coordination process of actors, social groups and institutions that aims at reaching collectively defined and discussed objectives. Governance then concerns the whole range of institutions, networks, directives, regulations, norms, political and social uses as well as public and private actors which contribute to the stability of a society and a political regime, to its orientation, to its capacity to lead, to deliver services and to assume its legitimacy.

(Le Galès, 2004, p. 243)

The changes in governance due to the new steering tools, usually used by the expert community, have been widely noted. The ideas of 'steering at a distance' are helpful to understand that the principles of calculability and measurability, originating from economics, were increasingly transferred to fields previously regulated by old bureaucratic statutes and professional norms, usually located in the public sector. Rose (1999, p. 152) refers to the new governing technology based on accountability and assessment to which the public sector is subjected as "governance at a distance" (Rinne & Ozga, 2011, p. 67).

Education quality represents one key discursive justification for the diverse ongoing reforms in education. Using data as a tool of governance (Rose & Miller, 1992), quality assurance and evaluation (QAE) is a tool for attempting to reinforce central control at a distance while allocating more autonomy to the local actors. Simultaneously, the need for and reliance on new experts and data infrastructures is created (Lawn & Segerholm, 2011). Governing at a distance rests on the provision and translation of information about subjects, objects and processes to the centers of calculation and power (Hansen & Flyverbom, 2014; Piattoeva et al., 2018).

The OECD and the EU: two augurs of supranational educational policy?[2]

The OECD was founded originally as the Organisation for European Economic Co-operation (OEEC) in 1948 to support the reorganization, rebuilding and stability of Europe after World War II. With the help of this new system, the

US Marshall Plan aid was distributed and US influence increased in Europe. For political reasons, many European countries, Finland included, remained outside the organization at the start (Papadopoulos, 1994, pp. 21–22; Sarjala & Laukkanen, 2000, p. 9). Only when the situation in Europe was further normalized was the OECD proper, under that name, established in 1961, indeed still during the Cold War.[3]

The central idea behind the OECD was the promotion of economic growth. From the Washington conference (1961) onward, plans were made for massive expansion in education systems, particularly in secondary and higher education. A well-organized planning policy, for its part, required a workable statistical and data system on which to base the new planning. A separate organization within the OECD, the Centre for Educational Research and Innovation (CERI) was, therefore, founded in 1968. CERI's function was to produce information on education for comparative research (Papadopoulos, 1994, p. 59).

OECD member countries are the well-to-do elite of the world. The population of the OECD countries represents about one-sixth of the world's population but produces four-fifths of the world gross national product. In the OECD's own words, the only demands on members are commitment to a market economy and democracy, and respect for human rights (Henry et al., 2001, p. 8). The OECD has often been described as an analyzing body or think-tank. What the organization is *not* is a legal, political or monetary power. In other words, conclusions from its conferences do not directly oblige member countries to do anything. Member countries are supposed to learn from each other, mainly through peer pressure, and accustom themselves to self-criticism (ibid. pp. 45–46; cf. Rinne, Kallo & Hokka, 2004). According to some researchers (Henry et al., 2001, p. 3), the main objective of OECD educational policy is to produce human capital for the global market, reflecting its economic focus.

The OECD is seen as a globalizing organization whose role is central to the flow of educational ideas, innovation and provision, and the control of information relating to education. The activities of the OECD, in common with those of other supranational organizations, are often based on an ideology according to which the organizations offer orthodox solutions chiefly to the problems of rich countries (Dale, 1999, pp. 1–4; Dale & Robertson, 2002, p. 11; Jauhiainen et al. 2001, p. 10).

Control of nation states' policies under the EU, based as it is on action plans, directives, legislation and financing programs, is very different from that under the OECD. In the 1970s, for example, the first education directives issued by the EU concerned the education of the children of immigrants (EU, 1977). Later, in the 1980s and 1990s, even more determined efforts were made to guarantee the freedom of movement of the workforce and students, and to recognize respective educational qualifications. The Maastricht Treaty (1992) finally defined education as one of the central core areas of responsibility for the EU. This was followed by the consolidation of the EU's education program. The fashioning of a common educational space in Europe had begun, with its zones of lifelong learning and quality education (Nóvoa & Lawn, 2002, pp. 1–5). The central goal of the Maastricht Treaty was the creation of a European dimension in education. In the 1990s, the EU had advanced from policy talk to policy practice.

In the 2000s, the foothold of the EU in the national education policy of its Member States has only become firmer. The Lisbon Conference of the Council of Europe (2002) decided to move the EU toward a knowledge-based economy. Conference delegates recognized that the common interests of the EU area concerning education override national education interests, and approved the Education 2010 work program. The Lisbon strategy gave the EU the mandate to strengthen the European dimension in education over the educational policy of nation states, as a result of which a vision of the Europeanization of education was developed (Nóvoa & Lawn, 2002, pp. 1–5; Rinne 2019).

It can be seen, then, that, in contrast to the OECD, the EU controls, monitors and regulates the education policy of its Member States. Its power, as a uniform union of states, is visible and bureaucratic, and, in its approach to education, instrumental and efficient. Education is seen primarily as one part of economic growth and competitive ability. Like the OECD, the EU sits at the same tables as many supranational economic organizations, including the World Bank, the International Monetary Fund (IMF) or the World Trade Organization (WTO). The EU forms a kind of supranational, complementary shield of education policy, the layers of which have become even more tightly welded together in the past decade. Under this shield, nation states' education policies often have very little room to move. Nation states often have to settle for the role of follower or imitator when directives and other recommendations land on the national table, ready to be picked up (Rinne & Kallo, 2003). For instance, Finland, a nation of merely five million inhabitants in the north-east corner of Europe, may have little capacity for effectual comment, especially after the most recent enlargement of the EU into Central and Eastern Europe.

The steering mechanisms of the OECD and EU educational policy are summed up in Figure 12.1.

Increasingly, they also entice participation of talented and motivated subcontractors, consultancy firms, EU experts, organizations and masses of enthusiastic students from all the states of Europe and all over the world. The European Educational Space attracts, to itself, its own supranational professional Europeans in the field of education, forming a new class of supranational politicians cut off from their own regions.

Standardization

This world of ours is saturated with standards. They penetrate all spheres of human life. Not only ubiquitous, standards are also normative. They create ideals and norms and normalities but, also, the 'less-than-ideal' and the abnormalities.

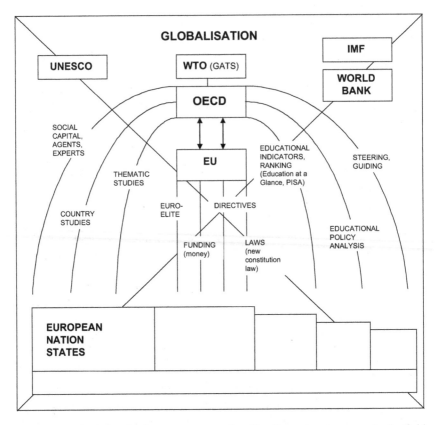

FIGURE 12.1 Relationship between supranational bodies and nation states in the field of educational policy. (Rinne, 2006)

"They produce social norms and encourage conformity to the ideal and dictate how things ought to be. They restrict decision-making possibilities, set parameters and narrow choice" (Gorur, 2013, p. 133). Standards also often incorporate standards of ethics, the breach of which may have legal and moral implications and sanctions. Standards, according to Radhika Gorur,

> [...] codify collective wisdom about what is acceptable in a given situation, and, explicitly or implicitly, what is not. This may create tension between individual autonomy and the codes of behavior set by anonymous, distant others, removed from the immediate context by space, time and perhaps understanding. Standardization is feared by some on the grounds that it promotes mechanistic behavior, devalues tacit and professional knowledge and attacks our very humanism by voiding idiosyncrasy, individuality, creativity, intuition and emotion.
>
> *(Gorur, 2013, pp. 132–133)*

To ensure conformity, standards are often institutionalized processes involving different kinds of certification and formalization. The more successfully the standards are mobilized and institutionalized, the less visible and noticeable they become. Many standards are thoroughly interwoven into the very fabric of our everyday lives, operating upon us in ways we scarcely recognize (Gorur, 2013).

Currently, there is a huge invasion of the politics of standardization in progress. Standardization builds uniformity in time and space by creating common standards and establishing political control, at a distance, on work and communities of practice. Standardization helps the State and public authorities compare and rank individuals and groups and create a common language shared by professionals, policy-makers and evaluators. Standards rely on a form of classification and measurement that defines limitations and exclusions in shaping the policy. They are based on scientific and expert knowledge, which give them legitimacy. "Their technicity prevents challenges and controversies, particularly when they involve a strong mobilization of expertise in time and space" (Normand, in press). Romauld Normand emphasizes that standardization is a strong policy instrument of power and coercion that effectively replaces traditional rules of authority, hierarchy and bureaucracy. Standards are grounded in the name of modernization and modernity and claimed to promote 'New Reason.'

Standards may be classified as "recipes for reality" (Gorur, 2013, p. 133). Standardization renders the test easily adaptable to different times and spaces and thus to expansion. For example, with the expectation of expanding into more than one hundred nations, PISA is entering the space of middle- and low-income nations with a modified version called PISA for Development (PISA-D). The pilot study is currently being conducted in Ecuador, Honduras, Paraguay, Senegal, Guatemala, Zambia, Cambodia and Panama. For these nations, where more students are expected to perform poorly, PISA is being modified through an expansion of the scale for results. The tests are still being standardized to allow students from PISA-D countries to be compared with their counterparts in PISA. To make these assessments comparable across such a diversity of contexts, a lot of important details have to be sacrificed (Gorur, 2016, p. 603).

By detaching children from around the world from their specific contexts,

> Standardising them and converting them into numbers, the OECD is able to create sophisticated calculations, identify problems, and suggest solutions and policy advice with extreme specificity. Performance can be disaggregated on the basis of gender, migration status, social capital, location and other dimensions. Specific areas for intervention can thus be isolated. With each round of the survey producing more information, trend data create patterns of growth and decline. This is the type of calculus that 'centres of calculation' can perform from afar, sitting in a distant office, with the numbers providing a synoptic overview of the entire phenomenon, if at the expense of detail.
>
> *(Gorur, 2011, 2016, p. 603)*

An enormous variety of things have now been converted into inscriptions on a completed form, coded according to pre-designated structures, and brought safely to the PISA offices. Citing Latour (1999, pp. 29, 39), Gorur writes that,

> The students and their learning – indeed, whole school systems, represented by these students, have all been 'detached, separated, preserved, classified, and tagged'. The world has now been transformed into 'two-dimensional, superposable, combinable inscriptions' that scientists are able to sit in the comfort of their offices and reassemble, reunite and redistribute them 'according to entirely new principles that depend on the researcher, on the discipline … and according to the institution that shelters them'.
>
> *(Gorur, 2016, p. 604, 2011, p. 88)*

The value of a 'synoptic view' is that it is available 'at a glance' and provides easily absorbed and easily represented information. PISA's league tables, on which 15-year-old children from distant and diverse parts of the world are "all gathered and organised into obedient rows and columns on a single spatio-temporal frame are a perfect example of such a synoptic view" (Gorur, 2011, p. 88).

PISA is bringing into being a kind of totally standardized school system with its calculations, policy guidance and recommendations. PISA does much more than merely provide a snapshot of how countries perform on PISA. Each round of PISA produces "not only the league tables with countries ranked according to performance, but also detailed analyses which correlate practices of schooling, funding patterns and policies with performance. It provides pointers to countries on how to improve their school systems" (Gorur, 2016, p. 614). In addition to PISA reports, the OECD produces thematic reports on particular topics and country reports focusing on particular countries. It advises how the countries can improve their systems, and offers consultancy to reform school systems and bring countries closer in line with OECD and PISA ideals (Gorur, 2016).

The interesting phenomenon, which Gorur (2016) calls 'Seeing like PISA,' is not just about the influence of PISA on national policies. Rather, it is about a particular set of approaches and understandings that are epitomized by PISA. 'Seeing like PISA' means standardization, the narrowing field of vision focused on literacy, numeracy and science outcomes, abstraction, and the generation of standardized templates and protocols to guide practices. As Gorur writes:

> If the cocktail of a narrow vision, widespread standardisation and abstraction, an exclusively fiscal view, a depleted curriculum, deprofessionalised teachers and market driven accountability systems which are currently in evidence continues unchecked, we can only speculate on the effects this will have not only on the economy, but also on the moral, intellectual and ethical fibre of society.
>
> *(Gorur, 2016, p. 612)*

German scientific forestry management practices serve as a way to understand the steps involved in making phenomena legible through a narrowing of vision, standardization and abstraction. The picture Peter Scott (1998) paints of the gradual transformation of forests, with all their diversity of flora and fauna, into standardized, monocultural forests standing in tidy rows and columns provides a compelling image. It may make us stop to

> [...] consider the possibility of the irreversible damage we may cause if 'seeing like PISA' goes unchecked. It is one thing to use such maps to aid governance, but quite another when we pave the way for commercial companies to proliferate 'schools-in-a-box', particularly to already vulnerable populations in the global south. If it is too soon to tell whether the effects of 'seeing like PISA' are dangerous or damaging, it is also too soon to have unmitigated faith in such an approach.
>
> *(Gorur, 2016, p. 613)*

Reconfiguring Nordic education reforms

Historically, in Nordic countries, the so-called social-democratic welfare model, with its core values and political, cultural and economic aims and ideologies, has been constructed. Some comparative researchers have claimed that one of the dimensions of this model has been the Nordic or social-democratic educational model, which has historically united the educational politics of Denmark, Finland, Iceland, Norway and Sweden, the five countries (e.g., Antikainen, 2006; Lundahl, 2016; NORDFORSK 2013–2018; Telhaug, Mediås & Aasen, 2004; Tjeldvoll, 1998a, 1998b). This situation has certainly changed in recent decades. The Nordic nations have made different kinds of educational political decisions, especially during the latest forty years of globalization under the mainstream of neoliberal educational politics. However, they have preserved some parts of their historical, common core.

Here, I take up the historical perspective to briefly describe the global turn toward neoliberal educational politics. I compare how the Nordic countries, especially Finland, have reacted and interpreted the global pressures of supranational organizations and reform movements in different dimensions. These dimensions or themes of global, neoliberal, educational politics involve, for example, new governance, New Public Management, steering at a distance, steering by numbers and privatization of education.

The state has traditionally played a prominent role in Nordic countries. With the help of large corps of state officials, central authorities have set out to seriously direct and control their citizens. There has been a very strong belief in the importance of education in building the nation. Since World War II, there has been a particularly heavy emphasis on the ideological 'social-democratic' concept of citizenship, and the ideal of the egalitarian *'citizen worker'* (cf. Hernes, 1988; Kivinen & Rinne, 1990b, 1992). The social-democratic regime has relied on corporatism, a strong public sector and symbiosis between social movements and political parties. Within this, state professionals, the social elite and its associated professional groups trained in public institutions of higher education and employed in the service of the state or the public sector, have been entrusted with a vital role (Kivinen & Rinne, 1990a, 1998).

A comparison of the Nordic countries with other European countries in the 1980s, before the great depression set in at the beginning of the 1990s, shows that the differences were striking. A clearly social-democratic welfare regime was the Nordic norm. In accordance with the Keynesian policy of 'full employment,' unemployment was kept low at 4 per cent, as against an average of 10 per cent in the EU countries. More Nordic women of working age (over 70 per cent) were employed outside the home than the 50 per cent in EU countries, and the level of public sector employment was higher, at more than 26 per cent in the Nordic countries compared with less than 18 per cent for the EU (Kosonen, 1992, 17; Rinne, 2004; Rinne & Kivinen, 2003).

It was not until the late 1980s and 1990s that the deeper discussion on types, models and regimes of welfare began. Gösta Esping-Andersen (1999) suggested that the different relations typically existing between welfare states, the labor market and families could be characterized in terms of three welfare regimes — the Liberal, the Social Democratic and the Conservative (which could also be called the Nordic regime, or the Nordic welfare model). He later elaborated on this classification but the Social Democratic regime has remained stable. Although Esping-Andersen's classification is socially and historically broader and he calls the model Nordic, it could also be interchanged with the Scandinavian model.

Scandinavia is often used by the Anglo-American world as an umbrella term which refers not specifically to the Scandinavian Peninsula (that comprises mainland Norway and Sweden, and north-western sections of Finland and Russia), but to the north-western region of Europe which includes Denmark, Finland, Iceland, Norway and Sweden (Erikson et al., 1987), and has a combined population of about 20 million people. Arild Tjeldvoll, in his introduction to *Education and Scandinavian Welfare State in 2000 – Equality, Policy and Reform* (Tjeldvoll, 1998a, xi–xii), claims, as does Esping-Andersen, that a typical characteristic of all five Scandinavian countries is the kind of welfare state model adopted therein. At the heart of this model, as he puts it, is a striving for social justice and the ideal of a democratic society that has been promoted historically through social and educational policies. Elsewhere, Tjeldvoll (1998b, 4–7) describes a particular '*Scandinavian education model*', the aim of which is to produce equal educational opportunities for all citizens. This educational system was, generally, strongly centralized nationally, in terms of the curriculum, examinations and governance, until the 1980s. Many other researchers, including Kjell Rubenson (2007) and Ari Antikainen (2008), have called this specific model the '*Nordic model of education*' and this term is adopted here.

For historical reasons, the Nordic education model was strongly influenced by a powerful nation state up until the late 1980s. The education systems in the Nordic countries were, in many ways, the inverted image of many systems elsewhere, such as in the US. The Nordic education model, adopted in Finland, has long been characterized by:

- Relatively small size and restricted markets.
- Strict centralization and the control of resources.
- Formal institutional uniformity with almost no hierarchy ostensibly recognized.
- Restricted competition, exercised with respect to state-controlled resources rather than markets, students or business.
- Low institutional initiative in that conditions of strict centralization have inhibited initiative taking, challenges to bureaucratic rule in the universities.
- The right to study in institutions of all education free of charge.
- A strong belief in fostering social equality by removing the obstacles preventing inequality of opportunities in all education.
- The education policy as a vital part of broader regional and social policies.

(Fägerlind & Strömqvist, 2004, p. 45; Rinne, 2004, p. 92)

The situation has, however, changed to take different directions in different Nordic countries. At present, for example, most of the Swedish free schools are owned by corporations which have a right to make profits from their education activities. In the three biggest Swedish cities, 25 per cent of all compulsory students and 40–55 per cent of upper secondary school students attend a free school. Within a decade, a veritable school market has emerged with attributes similar to those of a 'proper' market: aggressive marketing of a multitude of programs and schools, profit-making, chains of companies, increasing involvement of venture capitalists that buy and sell schools at a high pace, and so on. In contrast, Finland, Norway and Iceland still have little in the way of private education and do not allow private providers to extract profits (Lundahl, 2016; see Table 12.1).

In Finland, it was quite obvious that the radical municipal autonomy, spurred and deepened contingently by the recession of the 1990s, was one of the factors that buffered the implementation and technical development of an effective QAE system in

TABLE 12.1 'Private compulsory schools and profit-making possibilities year 2013'

	Sweden	Norway	Denmark	Finland	Iceland
Students in privately owned schools (%)	13	3	16	4	2
Profit-making allowed?	Yes	No	No	No	No

Source: National statistics of the five Nordic countries. (Denmark: https://www.dst.dk; Finland: https://www.stat.fi; Iceland: https://www.statice.is; Norway: https://www.ssb.no; Sweden: https://www.scb.seCiting Lundahl (2016)

Finnish comprehensive schooling. If the role of radical municipal autonomy has been prohibitive toward convergent tendencies, we may mention some other contingent factors that have supported the egalitarian path dependency. Those are revalorization of the comprehensive idea and the so-called 'Finnish PISA Miracle,' where comparative PISA results showed that Finland, surprisingly, topped the list of participant countries.

The consequences of the recession of the 1990s not only sped up the change, but also strengthened and revitalized the strong Nordic egalitarian ethos so far that even the comprehensive idea survived. For example, Sirkka Ahonen (2001, 2003) argues that the recession altered the political atmosphere in favor of market liberalism but the educational policy revised traditional, Nordic, welfare values and defended the public, common comprehensive school. Ahonen's argument is plausible when contextualized to national plans, at the time, to restructure the education system. The deep economic recession made the real worth of safety nets visible, even to the middle classes. In the late 1990s and 2000s, no political actors were willing to question the rhetoric of the equality in education discourse (Grek et al., 2009, 12; Kallo & Rinne, 2006; Patomäki, 2007; Simola et al., 2009). Respectively, no political actors we interviewed in the late 1990s and the early 2000s were willing to accept neoliberalism as an emblematic concept for Finnish policy-making (Rinne et al., 2003a).

It was totally unexpected for Finland to perform so well in the OECD PISA rankings. Quite controversially, this success stifled pressures for change in municipal and school autonomy. Finland had done pretty well, even in old, traditional, school performance assessments such as the International Association for the Evaluation of Educational Achievement (IEA) studies, but it never came up as a top performer. It was symptomatic but also ironic that just a few weeks before publication of the first PISA results in December 2001, the Education Committee of the Confederation of Finnish Industries and Employers (CIE) organized an Autumn Seminar during which the Finnish comprehensive school system was strongly criticized. The PISA success quashed pressures for change in municipal and school autonomy and buffered other (market-liberalist) innovations in the Finnish comprehensive schooling, under the adage 'if it ain't broke, don't fix it'. The success also saved the equality aims of the common comprehensive school from radical changes which were underway because of the political swing to the right in the Finnish Parliament.

Conclusions

It is quite obvious that global, international pressures from the OECD and EU have had strong influences on the formation of educational politics in Nordic countries. In almost every nation, the internationally comparative competition of the best results and forms of educational systems are established. These are, on a large scale, heavily grounded in the comparative statistics generated by the EU and OECD and in the educational advice given by these organizations.

The education systems of the five Nordic countries still display many common inclusive traits, enabled by continued, extensive, public funding of education. This funding provides free-of-charge education and related services at primary, secondary and tertiary levels; good, outside pre-school education and childcare; the integration of students in need of special support in ordinary classrooms; and so on. In addition, all the Nordic countries retain 9- or even 12-year, comprehensive, compulsory education with little tracking. In many respects, the academic and social divisions of Nordic students are small when international comparisons are made. So far, there remains a kind of Nordic education model that stresses social justice and equality, although individual counties have gone in different directions (Lundahl, 2016; Lundahl et al., 2018). Clearly, Sweden and Denmark have followed, at least in some respects, a more market-oriented direction than the other three Nordic nations.

Decentralization from the state to the local level and various neoliberal policy measures have been applied in all Nordic countries, changes which have undoubtedly undermined the foundations of the Nordic model. The Nordic countries also show evidence of increasing social and ethnic divisions, a disquieting trend that is most clearly visible in Denmark and Sweden (Lundahl, 2016).

It seems evident that an extremely strong contradiction has emerged between converging pursuit of international acceptance in the Western-advanced, neoliberal family, on the one hand, and a deeply-rooted path of adherence to traditional social democratic and agrarian egalitarianism, on the other. This has made Finnish QAE policy and overall educational policy remarkably complex. In the state educational rhetoric, neoliberalist reform discourse took a hegemonic position for only a short while but, even in those days, at the local level, there existed a silent consensus against its implementation based on antipathy and resistance against some fundamental neoliberal doctrines, particularly against ranking lists and wide parental school choice. Briefly, certain contingent factors strongly supported embedded egalitarianism and held traveling market liberalism at bay.

Bringing the concepts of path dependency and contingency together does assist, at least in part, in understanding the persistence and toughness of this poorly articulated, even silent, national consensus of refusal. A form of stubborn power has been shown where municipalities have restrained themselves from implementing studies that could be used to create school-based ranking lists and privatization of schooling. Here, we must remark that this treatment does not underestimate the importance of agency. Accepting a certain randomness in life does *not* lead to the abandonment of a certain amount of freedom for the actors, rather the contrary (see, e.g., Simola & Rinne, 2015).

Notes

1 This chapter is partly connected to my previous article: Rinne, R. (2020) The unintended consequences of governance of education at a distance through assessment standardisation. In Zajda, J. (ed.) *Globalisation, Ideology and Education Reforms – Emerging Paradigms. Globalisation. Comparative Education and Policy Research* Vol. 20. Amsterdam: Springer, 25–42 and my keynote speech at the NERA conference in Turku in 2020.

2 This section of the chapter is grounded heavily on my article: Rinne, R. (2006) Like a model pupil? globalisation, finnish educational policies and pressure from supranational organizations. In J. Kallo & R. Rinne (eds.) *Supranational Regimes and National Education Policies – Encountering Challenge. Research in educational sciences 24.* Turku: Finnish Educational Research Association, 183–216.

3 The founding members of the OECD were Austria, Belgium, Canada, Denmark, France, Germany, Greece, Iceland, Ireland, Italy, Luxemburg, the Netherlands, Norway, Portugal, Spain, Sweden, Switzerland, Turkey, the United Kingdom and the United States. Joining the organisation later were Japan (1964), Finland (1969), Australia (1971), New Zealand (1973), Mexico (1994), Czech Republic (1995), Hungary, Poland, Korea (1996), Slovakia (2000), Chile (2010), Estonia (2010), Israel (2010), Latvia (2016), Lithuania (2018), Colombia (2020) and Costa Rica (2021) (see Koivula, 2004).

References

Ahonen, S. (2001). The end of the common school: Change in the ethos and politics of education in Finland towards the end of the 1900s. In S. Ahonen, & J. Rantala (Eds.), *Nordic Lights: Education for Nation and Civic Society in the Nordic Countries, 1850–2000* (pp. 175–203). Finnish Literature Society.

Ahonen, S. (2003). *Yhteinen Koulu: Tasa-Arvoa Vai Tasapäisyyttä? Koulutuksellinen Tasa-Arvo Suomessa Snellmanista Tähän Päivään.* (The Common School) Vastapaino.

Antikainen, A. (2006). In search of the Nordic model in education. *Scandinavian Journal of Educational Research 50*(3), 229–243

Antikainen, A. (2008). Power, state and education: Restructuring the Nordic model. In J. Houtsonen, & A. Antikainen (Eds.), *Symbolic Power in Cultural Contexts: Uncovering Social Reality* (pp. 93–105). Sense Publishers.

Ball, S. J. (2016). Following policy: Networks, network ethnography and education policy mobilities. *Journal of Education Policy 31*(5), 549–566.

Barnett, M. N., & Finnemore, M. (1999). The politics, power and pathologies of international organisations. *International Organization 53*(4), 699–732.

Brown, P., Halsey, A. H., Lauder, H., & Stuart Wells, A. (1997). The transformation of education and society: An introduction. In A. Halsey, H. Lauder, P. Brown, & A. Stuart Wells (Eds.), *Education Culture Economy Society* (pp. 1–44). Oxford University Press.

Clarke, J. (2012). The work of governing. In K. Coulter, & W. R. Schumann (Eds.), *Governing Cultures: Anthropological Perspectives on Political Labor, Power and Government* (pp. 209–231). Palgrave Macmillan.

Dale, R. (1999). Specifying globalization effects on national education policy: Focus on mechanisms. *Journal of Education Policy 14*(1), 1–17.

Dale, R., & Robertson, S. L. (2002). The varying effects of regional organizations as subjects of globalization of education. *Comparative Education Review 46*(1), 10–36.

Erikson, R., Hansen, E. J., Ringen, S., & Uusitalo, H. (Eds.), (1987). *The Scandinavian Model – Welfare States and Welfare Research.* M. E. Sharpe, Inc.

Esping-Andersen, G. (1999). *Social Foundations of Postindustrial Economies.* Oxford University Press.

Fägerlind, I., & Strömqvist, G. (2004). Higher education reform in the global context – Whatever happened to the Nordic model? In I. Fägerlind, & G. Strömqvist (Eds.), *Reforming Higher Education in the Nordic Countries – Studies of Change in Denmark, Finland, Iceland, Norway and Sweden* (pp. 17–53). International Institute for Educational Planning.

Gorur, R. (2011). Policy as assemblage. *European Educational Research Journal 10*(4), 611–622.

Gorur, R. (2013). The invisible infrastructure of standards. *Critical Studies in Education 54*(2), 132–142.

Gorur, R. (2016). Seeing like PISA: A cautionary tale about the performativity of international assessments. *European Educational Research Journal 15*(5), 598–616.

Grek, S. (2009). Governing by numbers: The PISA 'effect' in Europe. *Journal of Education Policy 24*(1), 23–37.

Grek, S., Lawn, M., Lingard, B., Ozga, J., Rinne, R., Segerholm, C., & Simola, H. (2009). National policy brokering and the construction of the European Education Space in England, Sweden, Finland and Scotland. *Comparative Education 45*(1), 5–21.

Hansen, H. K., & Flyverbom, M. (2014). The politics of transparency and the Calibration of knowledge in the digital age. *Organization 22*(6), 872–889.

Henry, M., Lingard, B., Taylor, S., & Rizvi, F. (2001). *The OECD, Globalisation and Education Policy*. Pergamon.

Hernes, G. (1988). *Viva Academia*. Universitetsforlaget.

Jauhiainen, A., Rinne, R., & Tähtinen, J. (2001). Globaalin koulutuspolitiikan hyökyaalto. In A. Jauhiainen, R. Rinne, & J. Tähtinen (Eds.), *Koulutuspolitiikka Suomessa ja ylikansalliset mallit Kasvatusalan tutkimuksia 1*, (pp. 9–20) Suomen Kasvatustieteellinen Seura (Finnish Education Society).

Kallo, J., & Rinne, R. (Eds.) (2006). *Supranational Regimes and National Education Policies: Encountering Challenge*. Finnish Educational Research Association: Research In Educational Sciences.

Kivinen, O., & Rinne, R. (1990a). State Governance and Market Attraction: Models of higher education in the USA, Western Europe and Finland. In *European Regional Consultation on Management and Administration of Higher Education in a Market Economy* (pp. 1–13). UNESCO & Bulgarian Ministry of Science and Higher Education.

Kivinen, O., & Rinne, R. (1990b). The university, the state and the professional interest groups: A Finnish lesson in university development policy. *Higher Education Policy 3*(3), 15–18.

Kivinen, O., & Rinne, R. 1992. Higher education reforms and social change in Finland. *Education and Society 10*(2), 47–57.

Kivinen, O., & Rinne, R. (1998). From the mass to the elite: Structure, limits, and the future of Scandinavian educational systems. In A. Tjeldvoll (Ed.), *Education and the Scandinavian Welfare State in the Year 2000 – Equality, Policy, and Reform* (pp. 335–352). Garland Publishing, Taylor & Francis Group.

Koivula, J. (2004). *OECD ja Suomen* korkeakoulupolitiikka (OECD and Finland's higher education policy). OECD: n maatutkintojen yhteys Suomen korkeakoulupolitiikkaan kolmella vuosikymmenellä (OECD country degrees link with Finnish higher education policy in three decades). Pro gradu-tutkielma (Master's thesis). Turun yliopisto (University of Turku).

Kosonen, P. (1992). Johdanto. In P. Kosonen (Ed.), *European integraatio, työmarkkinat ja hyvinvointivaltio* (The European integration, labour market and the welfare state) (pp. 5–22) Gummerus.

Lascoumes, L., & Le Galès, P. (2007). Understanding public policy through its instrument: From the nature of instruments to the sociology of public policy instrumentation. *Governance 20*, 1–21.

Latour, B. (1999). *Pandora's Hope: Essays on the Reality of Science Studies* Harvard University Press.

Lawn, M., & Segerholm, C. (2011). Europe through experts and technologies. In J. Ozga, P. Dahler-Larsen, C. Segerholm, & H. Simola (Eds.), *Fabricating Quality in Education. Data and Governance in Europe* (pp. 32–46). Routledge.

Le Galès, P. (2004). Gouvernance. In L. Bousssaguet, S. Jacquot, & P. Ravinet (Eds.), *Dictionnaire des politiques publiques* (pp. 242–250). Presses de Sciences Po.

Lingard, B. 2000. It is and it isn't: Vernacular globalization, educational policy and restructuring. In N. Burbules, & C. Torres (Eds.), *Globalization and Education: Critical Perspective* (pp. 79–108). Routledge.

Lingard, B., & Rawolle, S. (2011). New scalar politics: Implications for education policy. *Comparative Education 47*, 367–377.

Lundahl, L. 2016. Equality, inclusion and marketization of Nordic education: Introductory notes. *Research in Comparative and International Education 11*(1), 3–12.

Lundahl, L., Arnesen, A., & Jónasson, J. 2018. Justice and marketization of education in three Nordic countries: Can existing large-scale datasets support comparisons? *Nordic Journal of Studies in Educational Policy 4*(3), 120–132

Martens, K. (2007). How to become an influential actor – The 'comparative turn' in OECD education policy. In K. Martens, A. Rusconi, & K. Lutz (Eds.), *Transformations of the State and Global Governance* (pp. 40–56). Routledge.

NORDFORSK. (2013-2018) JustEd – Nordic Centre of Excellence: Justice through Education in the Nordic Countries. http://www.justed.org/.

Normand, R. (in press). The Politics of metrics in education. A contribution to the history of the present. In *Handbook of Education Policies*. Springer.

Nóvoa, A., & Lawn, M. (2002). *Fabricating Europe: The Formation of an Education Space*. Kluwer Academic Boston.

Nóvoa, A., & Yariv-Mashal, T. (2003). Comparative research in education: A mode of governance or a historical journey? *Comparative Education 39*, 423–439.

Ozga, J., & Lingard, B. (2007). Globalisation, education policy and politics. In B. Lingard, & J. Ozga (Eds.), *The Routledge-Falmer Reader in Education Policy and Politics* (pp. 65–82). Routledge.

Papadopoulos, G. S. (1994). *Education 1960–1990. The OECD Perspective.* OECD.

Patomäki, H. 2007. *Uusliberalismi Suomessa. Lyhyt Historia ja Tulevaisuuden Vaihtoehdot. (New Liberalism in Finland).* WSOY.

Piattoeva, N., Gorodski Centeno, V., Suominen, O., & Rinne, R. (2018). Governance by data circulation? The production, availability, and use of national large-scale assessment data. In J. Kauko, R. Rinne, & T. Takala (Eds.), *Politics of Quality in Education: A Comparative Study on Brazil, China, and Russia* (pp. 115–136). Routledge.

Rinne, R. (2004). Searching for the Rainbow: Changing the course of Finnish higher education. In I. Fägerlind, & G. Strömqvist (Eds.), *Reforming Higher Education in the Nordic Countries – Studies of Change in Denmark, Finland, Iceland, Norway and Sweden* (pp. 89–135). International Institute for Educational Planning.

Rinne, R. (2006). Like a model pupil? Globalisation, Finnish educational policies and pressure from supranational organizations. In J. Kallo, & R. Rinne (Eds.), *Supranational Regimes and National Education Policies: Encountering Challenge; Research in Educational Sciences* Vol. 24 (pp. 183–216). Finnish Educational Research Association.

Rinne, R. (2020). The unintended consequences of governance of education at a distance through assessment standardisation. In J. Zajda (Ed.), *Globalisation, Ideology and Education Reforms: Emerging Paradigms. Globalisation. Comparative Education and Policy Research* Vol. 20. (pp. 25–42). Springer.

Rinne, R. (2021). The future of glocal education politics. In J. Zajda (Ed.), *Globalisation, Ideology and Education Reforms: Emerging Paradigms. Globalisation. Comparative Education and Policy Research* Vol. 22. (pp. 55–78). Springer.

Rinne, R., & Kallo, J. (2003). Knowledge broker: The role of the OECD in European education policies. *A paper presented at the 6th Conference of the European Sociological Association, in the Sociology of Education Research Network.* September 23–26, Murcia, Spain.

Rinne, R., Kallo, J., & Hokka, S. (2004). Too eager to comply? OECD education policies and the Finnish response. *European Educational Research Journal 3*(2), 454–485.

Rinne, R., & Kivinen, O. (2003). The Nordic welfare state model and European Union educational policies. In P. Rasmussen (Ed.), *Educational Policy and the Global Social Order* (pp. 23–42). Aalborg University, Centre for the Interdisciplinary Study of Learning.

Rinne, R., Kivirauma, J., & Simola, H. (2003a). Shoots of revisionist education policy or just slow readjustment? The Finnish case of educational reconstruction. *Journal of Education Policy 17*(6), 643–658.

Rinne, R., & Ozga, J. (2011). Europe and the global: The role of the OECD in education politics. In J. Ozga, P. Dahler-Larsen, C. Segerholm, & H. Simola (Eds.), *Fabricating Quality in Education. Data and Governance in Europe* (pp. 66–75). Routledge.

Rinne, R., Simola, H., & Kivirauma, J. (2003b). Abdication of the education state or just shifting responsibilities? The appearance of a new system of reason in constructing educational governance and social exclusion/inclusion in Finland. *Scandinavian Journal of Educational Research 46*(3), 237–246.

Rose, N. (1999). *Powers of Freedom: Reframing Political Thought.* Cambridge University Press.

Rose, N., & Miller, P. (1992). Political power beyond the state: Problematics of government. *British Journal of Sociology 43*(2), 173–205.

Rubenson, K. (2007). Participation in adult education: The Nordic welfare state model. In R. Rinne, A. Heikkinen, & P. Salo (Eds.), *Adult Education: Liberty, Fraternity, Equality? Nordic Views on Lifelong Learning* (pp. 47–66). Finnish Educational Research Association: Research in Educational Sciences Vol. 28. Painosalama Oy.

Sarjala, J., & Laukkanen, R. (2000). OECD: n näkökulma lähihistorian koulutuspoliittisessa keskustelussa (OECD perspective in the education policy debate in recent history). In R. Laukkanen, & M. Kyrö (Eds.), *Oppia OECD: n analyyseistä (Learning from OECD analyses)* (pp. 9–20) Opetushallitus.

Scott, J. C. (1998). *Seeing Like a State: How Certain Schemes to Improve the Human Condition Have Failed.* Yale University Press.

Simola, H., & Rinne, R. (2015). Kontingenssi ja koulutuspolitiikka (Contingencies and education policy). In T. H. Simola (Ed.), *Koulutusihmeen Paradoksit. Esseitä Suomalaisesta Koulutuspolitiikasta (Paradoxes of the Educational Miracle: Essays on Finnish Education Policy)* (pp. 355–380). Vastapaino.

Simola, H., Rinne, R., Varjo, J., Kauko, J., & Pitkänen, H. 2009. Quality Assurance and Evaluation (QAE) in Finnish compulsory schooling: A national model or just unintended effects of radical decentralisation? *Journal of Education Policy 24*(2), 163–178.

Simola, H., Varjo, J., & Rinne, R. (2014). Against the flow: Path dependence, convergence and contingency in understanding the Finnish QAE model. In H. Simola, I. Carlgren, S. Heikkinen, J. Kauko, O. Kivinen, J. Kivirauma, K. Klette, S. Myrdal, H. Pitkänen, R. Rinne, K. Schnack, J. Silvonen, & J. Varjo (Eds.), *The Finnish Education Mystery. Historical and Sociological Essays on Schooling in Finland* (pp. 224–251). Routledge.

Taylor, S., Rizvi, F., Lingard, B., & Henry, M. (1997). *Education Policy and the Politics of Change.* Routledge.

Telhaug, A. O. Mediås, O. A., & Aasen, P. (2004). From collectivism to individualism? education as nation building in a Scandinavian perspective. *Scandinavian Journal of Educational Research* 48(2), 141–158.

Tjeldvoll, A. (1998a). Introduction. In A. Tjeldvoll (Ed.), *Education and the Scandinavian Welfare State in the Year 2000: Equality, Policy, and Reform* (pp. xi–xviii). Garland Publishing, Taylor & Francis Group.

Tjeldvoll, A. (1998b). Quality of equality? Scandinavian education towards the year 2000. In A. Tjeldvoll (Ed.), *Education and the Scandinavian Welfare State in the Year 2000: Equality, Policy, and Reform* (pp. 3–23). Garland Publishing, Taylor & Francis Group.

13

THE RISE OF CHINA AND THE NEXT WAVE OF GLOBALIZATION

The Chinese Dream, the Belt and Road Initiative and the 'Asian century'

Michael A. Peters

Introduction

The concept of Asian globalization represents a tectonic shift in the development of modern world capitalism. The shift moves away from the Atlantic democracies and the dominance of Europe, Britain and America in the nineteenth and twentieth centuries, to an Asian form of globalization in the twenty-first century, driven by China's growth and dominance. This axial shift toward an Asian form of globalization also indicates the beginning of an Asian-centric world order where Asian countries, and, in particular, China, India and Japan, will be able to adjust the international rules for trade and globalization. The adjustment will occur through the new financial architecture of the New Development Bank, the Asian Infrastructure Bank and the Asian Development Bank. It will develop a set of new institutions and strategic partnerships that will modify existing world institutions and create new ones based on the emerging geography of world power. The Asia-Pacific will be dominated by a multipolar rebalancing of the interests and power of China, India and Japan, as well as the Association of Southeast Asian Nations (ASEAN) countries along with Australia, New Zealand and the Pacific Islands, in the integration of regional economic activity.

The shift is a reflection of demographic dynamics with an Asia population of some five billion people by 2050. It is also evidenced in the development of new pan-Asian cultures, cuisines and religions. China has taken a major role in realizing this axial shift. The old Silk Road was an early example of Chinese globalization which provides the inspiration for the Belt and Road Initiative (BRI), and comprehensive regional free trade agreements, like the Trans-Pacific Partnership Agreement (TPP) and the Regional Comprehensive Economic Partnership (RCEP), that promote free trade and liberalize investment with economies of the Asia-Pacific.

DOI: 10.4324/9781003207528-13

This chapter provides a brief history of the rise of China and examines the Silk Road as the first globalization and birth of trade-based merchant capitalism, while Europe was only emerging from feudalism. The second section theorizes the BRI as a distinctive form of development known as 'socialism with Chinese characteristics' based on 'Chinese infrastructuralism.' This is part of the essence of the Chinese Dream. The Chinese Dream is very different from the American Dream in that the social market system is obliged to eliminate poverty and check the power of the largest corporations. By contrast, in the American neoliberal system, capital takes flight, eliminates jobs and pays no tax. The BRI has been seen as the Chinese model for infrastructural development – a distinctive feature of Chinese globalization – underwritten by an alternate set of financial institutions and development banks that focus trade facilitation along six regional corridors, leading to the integration of a Chinese, regional Asian, economic system structured by the comprehensive trade agreements (Comprehensive and Progressive Agreement for Trans-Pacific Partnership or CPTPP, RCEP) that are shaping and integrating Asian globalization.

The Silk Road and the Birth of Merchant Capitalism

While some historians believe that globalization started in 1491 with Christopher Columbus, others have emphasized early developments in pre-Columbian Mesoamerica. Yale historian Valeria Hansen (2020) maintains that globalization began decisively in the year 1000, nearly 500 years before Columbus set sail for the Americas, when the Vikings sailed to North America. For the first time, artisans produced goods for distant markets over which they had no control. Slaves were a common commodity and were sourced in twenty different locations in Afro-Asia to be transported to the Islamic World. There were similar encounters by Muslim traders who traveled to West Africa in the year 1000. Hansen (2020) indicates that, if globalization has a systematic starting point, it was in China in the Sung Dynasty when, in places like Fujian province, dragon kilns fired 10,000–30,000 pieces of pottery in a single firing. Archaeologists have discovered Chinese ceramics in the coastal ports of East Africa.

Recent scholarship on the Silk Road indicates that, five hundred years before Columbus or Marco Polo, it was an ancient network for the birth of merchant capitalism and, truly, the basis of systematic trade. The Silk Road existed for over one thousand years as a set of networked links between the East and West. It was the beginning of the establishment of a market in central and western Asia (dela Vaissiere, 2014). As a series of routes within a large network of strategically located trading and military posts, markets and thoroughfares, The silk road was an extensive trading network that connected China, Persia and the Middle East to Europe.

The early sea routes predated the Silk Road and later were incorporated into these trading networks. The ancient Silk Road is more than an historical relic that serves as a modern metaphor for 'Chinese infrastructuralism' of the Belt and Road Initiative. It also represents the very early beginnings of capitalism as a form of merchant capitalism or mercantilism that predated the development of capitalism in Europe. Etienne de la Vaissiere (2014) provides evidence of the expeditions of the first merchants from the Indo-Iranian borderlands (Gandhara and Bactria) to northern China in the fifth century BCE. These were experienced traders, gaining their experience from selling precious stones along the Indus. In the second century, Zhang Qian organized the first Chinese envoy to western central Asia. De la Vaissiere (2014, pp. 102–103) concludes: "the creation of the Silk Road can be regarded as the combination of the old Middle Eastern trade with the Han expansionist policy. The systems coalesced."

The Silk Road, as a network of trade routes, was further facilitated by religious and, therefore, cultural and artistic exchanges. These included the development of Buddhism in China, sometimes known as Han Buddhism, dating from the first century BCE with established monastic settlements like the Mogao Caves, now a heritage site. Buddhism significantly shaped Chinese culture, assisted through the familiar concepts of Daoism. With the influence of Buddhism came art, politics, literature, and philosophy that helped create a material culture that strengthened the links between the civilizations of China, Korea, Japan, India, Iran, Europe and Arabia. It contributed to the development of the Sinitic group of languages during the Shang Dynasty, some three thousand years ago, as the basis of language for the ethnic Han Chinese and, thus, also to Classical Chinese literature. The Chinese language and script spread to northern Vietnam and later to East Asia, becoming the language of government and administration in Japan, Korea and Vietnam, even though these countries later developed their own writing systems. The early and wide adoption of the Chinese language in East Asia dates from the second century and its early use facilitated trade, law and administration. It created a Sinitic-language group with ten dialects that enabled intercultural communication. Standard Chinese is now spoken or understood in East Asia and throughout much of South-East Asia. With some 1.3 billion native speakers, it is by far the most spoken language in the world.

The historical narrative of the Silk Road provides a different interpretation of globalization from the received view, which is that globalization was characterized by the development of maritime European powers in the fifteenth and sixteenth centuries during the so-called Age of Empire. Chinese merchant capitalism, which emerged with the Silk Road during the Han dynasty, continued for centuries, expanding international trade with India, Arabia and Europe. Confucianism provided a set of philosophical tenets that rejected the unequal development of wealth and promoted state control over elements of the trade system in relation to money, agricultural markets, and the credit system. Not only did it represent a Chinese Buddhist/Confucian early form of merchant capitalism but it also provides a source of historical understanding for the development of the BRI based on three layers:

(i)   The exchange of goods – silk and paper products, precious stones, jewelry, clothing, gunpowder, animals and animal skins, paper and paper products, and all the necessities that are required for long-distance travel, including food, guides, and so on;

(ii) The growth of 'services' as a set of networks of relationships among and between those traveling the ancient Silk Road – kith and kin, professionals, the military, administrators, scribes and scholars, 'foreigners' – who established various kinds of networks – postal stations, military posts, tribal affiliations, and, of course, what we call 'technology transfer' of the processes of paper, silk and glass making;

(iii) The 'webs of knowledge' – these ideational elements are the most important but the least obvious and the most difficult to document – routines, knowledge of routes, language skills, intercultural exchange rituals shared when people eat together or communication, calculations, religious practices, art, sculpture and design, meditation techniques, and knowledge of 'who' (the networks of contacts)

(Peters, 2019a, p. 3)

These are the three different layers that make up the distinctive ethos of Chinese *infrastructuralism* that characterizes the BRI, linking it to the concept of the Chinese Dream, socialism with Chinese characteristics, and firmly distinguishing it from both the historical proto-globalization of the European colonial period and neoliberal globalization (Peters, 2020a). Infrastructuralism is also the means to promote greater interconnectivity and regionalization. As a development philosophy, it is wedded to the speed, mobility and exchange that integrates trading activities and encourages a hard/soft dimension in the creation of digital knowledge exchange networks. These networks are linked to platforms as an major alternative in the political economy of an emerging world knowledge system tied and harnessed by the new strategic technologies of Artificial Intelligence (AI), machine learning (ML), deep learning (DL), quantum computing (QC), genomic science (GS) (Peters, 2019b).

The Chinese Dream/The American Dream

The Chinese Dream is comprised of the major intersecting narratives of contemporary China — Liberal, Confucian and Marxist — and charts the period from 'the century of national humiliation' to China as an economic and diplomatic world power. Under *Xi Jinping Thought on Socialism with Chinese Characteristics*, China is committed to the value of openness in trade. This at a time when, under President Trump, America closed its doors to immigrants and turned its back on globalization in a series of embargoes and trade sanctions, based on a far-right form of populism expressed in the slogans 'America First' and 'Make America Great Again' (MAGA) (Peters & Chiang, 2017). It is useful to compare these two competing forms of globalization.

MAGA is a different narrative of the American Dream achieved through the liberal internationalism of the Obama years. It is based on a mixed or blended discourse derived from the principle of 'America First': withdrawal from international agreements in trade and climate change; a resentful attitude to traditional allies; and a strong alignment with far-right ideas. It was formulated to appeal to deindustrialized voting constituencies in the Rust Belt that suffered from neoliberal globalization when capital and jobs moved to the East. Trump came to power on the basis of a strong, populist reaction against globalization. Globalization was held to have robbed the US of manufacturing jobs as US multinationals, including the soon-to-be trillion-dollar Big Tech companies, located themselves offshore so that they did not have to pay any tax. The workers who lost their jobs were among a large groundswell of the disaffected who had, over a generation, seen their incomes diminish and witnessed growing income inequalities in housing, health and education. Trump capitalized on this anti-globalization narrative, directing anger and generating racist paranoia against China. The tide of neoliberal globalization turned with the election of Donald Trump. Trump tried to attract American companies back home, offering tax breaks and subsidies while also engaging, in the offensive, with trade and technology wars with China. This was a significant anti-globalization policy discourse that also restricted trade practices and was further magnified with the arrival of the COVID-19 virus that Trump called the 'China virus' (Peters & Chiang, 2017).

Trump's narrative of the American Dream was directed against all outsiders — Mexicans, undocumented folk, the black community, women, Muslims — and functioned by casting aspersions and tapping into existing prejudices and deep-seated racist disaffection. Trump stated in his inaugural address: "Rusted out factories are scattered like tombstones across the landscape of our nation. The wealth of our middle class has been ripped from our homes and redistributed all across the world."[1] But if the narrative was essentially directed inward, it also signified 'America closed' as against 'America open' — an attitude which is refracted in the hasty recoil from global moral leadership and from being 'leader of the free world.'

The turn to national populism was the symbolic end of neoliberal globalization and Trump made the most of generating an anti-China rhetoric to displace Obama's liberal internationalism. Obama had consistently made reference to the American Dream — both during his campaigning for the Presidency and after — often focusing on his own remarkable story as being emblematic of the possible. He also carefully used the intellectual resources of the American Dream to unify Americans and to provide the vision for the society he wants others to dream of. Obama's question was: in a time of decline, was the American Dream still serviceable? Could it be restored and is it possible for its core ideals to be refashioned (Peters, 2012, 2021)? MAGA is a different narrative of the American Dream from Obama's liberal internationalism. Populism and white supremacist nationalism are not compatible with neoliberal globalization. Under President Biden, human rights and freedom of expression have become the new spearhead of US foreign policy. At the same time, the US focuses on the creation of new plan for a double, US$2 trillion, state-led, infrastructure investment in emulation of China's Belt and Road Initiative. Biden has focused on building alliances and defense pacts such as the Quadrilateral Security Dialogue (a strategic dialogue between the United States, India, Japan and Australia) and AUKUS (the Australia, UK, US alliance), to contain China in the Asia-Pacific. All the while, commentators anxiously await the next flip-flop in American foreign policy with Trump waiting in the wings for the next election in 2024.

By contrast, Xi Jinping developed the concept of the Chinese Dream first in 2012 in a concept that bears little resemblance to the American version, at least on first comparison, although it might be said to share some features with the openness and free trade of versions of liberal internationalism. *Xi Jinping Thought on Socialism with Chinese Characteristics for a New Era* was added to the Communist Party of China's (CPC) Constitution, setting the tone and direction for the 15-year period following the establishment of 'Xiaokang,' originally a Confucian term meaning 'moderately prosperous society.' It was used first by Hu Jintao (General Secretary, 2002–2012) to refer to economic policies designed to create a more equal distribution of wealth within China (Peters, 2011, 2017). Xi has emerged as the strongest leader of CPC since Mao.

The original CPC Constitution was adopted at the Second Congress of the Party in 1922, and Mao Zedong Thought was established as CPC's guiding ideology at the 7th Congress in 1945. Deng Xiaoping's theory of building socialism 'with Chinese characteristics' was written into the Constitution in 1992 at the 14th Congress and adopted as CPC's guiding theory at the 15th Congress in 1997. The Constitution is an evolving doctrine. The original force of Mao's Thought after the Cultural Revolution gave away to greater political pragmatism following Deng's 'opening up' reforms. Deng Xiaoping recognized the forces integrating world markets and sought to develop a Chinese program of 'post-socialism' or 'market socialism,' sometimes also referred to as 'state capitalism,' that became the basis for Chinese globalization. It is very clear that the CPC understand the Constitution must reflect the dynamism of historical change and that the guiding ideology must provide a 'road map' that takes account of the evolution of human economy, culture, society and environment.

Xi, elected as leader for his lifetime, has also centralized power to an unprecedented extent in modern times. He created the Central National Security Commission which coordinates the police, army and national security agencies as well as the Central Military Commission. Xi's *The Governance of China* (2014) helps to clarify the principles of governance of the CPC, China's development path and the new concept of the Chinese Dream (中国梦), which he first introduced into Chinese politics in 2012. Xi's book was published in response to rising international interest and to enhance the rest of the world's understanding of the Chinese government's philosophy and its domestic and foreign policies. Above all, it was intended to provide a statement about China's peaceful development in order to alleviate Western fears about China's rise to superpower status and the attendant implications for global stability and the international order. *The Governance of China* contains a firm commitment to 'opening up' internationally, with an emphasis on competitive globalization, market-based interest and exchange rates, and greater market access with the protection of foreign investors' interests and rights (Peters, 2017).

The significance of education for the future and the principles that lie behind the BRI as the new Silk Road and its importance for the Chinese Dream can be understood by focusing on a set of interrelated, overlapping characteristics of Chinese globalization:

1. *Socialist market economy with Chinese characteristics* as the path of Chinese modernity and for China becoming a fully modern, socialist nation by 2049 based on neo-Confucian cultural and legal values, and Chinese Marxism. This path implies necessary developmental stages in human progress that expresses a fundamental teleology and dialectical struggle (*yinyang* thought) based on a vision of social justice *datong shehui* (*Great Unity*) and *Li Ji* (*The Book of Rites*).

2. *Xi Jinping Thought on Socialism with Chinese Characteristics for a New Era*, incorporated into the Constitution of the CCP to lead China out of the 'long night' to establish, to develop, and to consolidate the socialist system with an unwavering commitment to historical materialism. Xi Thought mentions the adoption of new science-based ideas for 'innovative, coordinated, green, open and shared development,' respect for the Rule of Law, strengthening party discipline and national security, and the well-being of the Chinese people (Peters, 2017).

3. *The BRI* is an open, global, free trade regime with over seventy participating countries. It is new, Chinese, economic globalization, inspired by the old Silk Road and directed toward a multipolar world, open regional cooperation, and greater recognition of cultural diversity.

4. *'Chinese infrastructuralism'* is a new Chinese development model incorporating 'hard' and 'soft' infrastructure, including: (i) roads, rail and ports, with an accent on transport hubs; (ii) digital and mobile networks, including financial, insurance and legal networks and services; (iii) education and research SPACE networks; (iii) strategic communications (mobile, satellite and fiber), telecommunications, Chinese internet; (iv) people-to-people (education and cultural exchanges).

5. *Greater interconnectivity* highlights a parallel digital technological system with increased speed and compression to develop the digital Silk Road, led by Big Tech giants such as Baidu, Ten Cent, WeChat, Alibaba.

6. *China is an emerging techno-state* based on decades-old state investment in strategic digital technologies AI, 5G/6G, ML, DL, QC, and GS to lead the new development philosophy.

7. *The notion of 'the civilizational state'* along with civilizational dialogue and learning, and 'the future of humanity' as representing China's world diplomacy.

8. *Eurasia as a geopolitical civilizational* concept led by historic Sino-Russian rapprochement and greater Eurasian regional integration, including the China–Pakistan–Afghanistan–Iran corridor.
9. *A communicational and media model of AI education* with a three-level content, code, infrastructure with discrimination among data, information, knowledge and wisdom.
10. *The analysis of the three main philosophical narratives* (Marxist, Confucian, Liberal) that comprise the Chinese Dream, and future Dreams (the Green Dream, the World Diplomacy Dream, the Space Dream, Science Dream, and the Dream of the Bioinformational Becoming).

These elements, taken together, form an attempt to build a philosophical approach to the Chinese Dream through the analysis of narrative and the employment of narratology to highlight the BRI and the future significance of education as an emerging cultural and economic evolutionary development. This vision blends economic strategy with civilizational history, recognizing the crucial importance of past events and the significance of language, culture and education in contributing a very distinctive approach to a form of CCP state-led globalization. This is a remarkable achievement for a party of 100 million that celebrated its centennial anniversary on July 1, 2021. Symbolically standing at the Gate of Heavenly Peace under a portrait of Mao, President Xi Jinping took the opportunity to say "We have never bullied, oppressed or subjugated the people of any country and we never will."[2] In saying this, Xi indicated that China will not accept bullying from former imperial countries who preach to China and try to export their own liberal values. These were strong words that had military backing, especially regarding Taiwan as a break-away province that will be reunited with China, by force if necessary. There is little doubt that the CCP is the strongest political party the world has ever seen, a party committed to socialism with Chinese characteristics and a form of Chinese globalization as the distinctive pathway to Chinese modernity.

China's trajectory and its grand strategy comes at a time when liberal internationalism has been failing, especially under the US President Donald Trump. Trump recoiled from international institutions such as UN and WHO and reneged on traditional alliances with Europe and NATO while fueling a white supremacist ideology that led to the political insurrection on the Capitol. Liberal internationalism has been failing for some time, perhaps since the Global Financial Crisis (GFC). The Chinese believe they are on the right side of history, having witnessed the Soviet breakup following by the GFC. Neoliberalism is seen as decoupled from US politics and, therefore, has little accountability: it has stripped out jobs and caused huge inequalities. The CCP, by contrast, is still in charge of China's massive state-owned enterprises (SOEs) and private companies put an emphasis on alleviating poverty and providing regional infrastructure to the regional areas.

The Belt and Road Initiative

China's Belt and Road Initiative refers to the Silk Road Economic Belt and the 21st-Century Maritime Silk Road. It is a new development model and modernization strategy launched by the Chinese government to promote "peace and cooperation, openness and inclusiveness, mutual learning and mutual benefit" among the more than 65 countries that comprise the land and sea routes linking Eurasia. As the National Development and Reform Commission explain, in their 2015 news release:

> The initiative to jointly build the Belt and Road, embracing the trend toward a multipolar world, economic globalization, cultural diversity and greater IT application, is designed to uphold the global free trade regime and the open world economy in the spirit of open regional cooperation.[3]

This massive infrastructure project is designed to develop the seamless flow of capital, goods, services and cultural exchanges between Asia and the rest of the world, by promoting further market integration in the region and by forging new ties among the nations and cultures that comprise the new Silk Road. The original intent focused on fostering development opportunities in opportunities in five areas with a planned completion date of 2049.

The five major areas of the original plan included: (1) coordinating development policies; (2) forging infrastructure and facilities networks; (3) strengthening investment and trade relations; (4) enhancing financial cooperation; and (5) deepening social and cultural exchanges. The last of these has become increasingly important, especially the development of higher education as the component that not only emphasizes 'social and cultural exchanges' but also highlights the 'knowledge economy' future-oriented digital infrastructure and interconnectivity. The initiative was first announced in 2013 as a global trade and investment strategy. The first BRI Summit was held in Beijing on May 14–15, 2017 with representatives from 130 countries and 70 world organizations as a platform for international cooperation. This represented 'Globalization 5.0' after the Old Silk Road and Deng's opening-up reforms of the 1990s that led to the Chinese economic miracle and China joining the World Trade Organization in 2001. Since then, the Chinese economy has supported growth rates unequaled in the development of any other country (Peters, 2020b; Peters & Zhu, 2021).

What started as the world's most massive infrastructure project has developed around a new series of goals that now understand that culture and education, in the broadest sense, including vocationally oriented education and training, is a necessary part of the 'soft infrastructure' that needs to accompany the base in engineering and transport. The initiative envisages the building of six major economic cooperation corridors and several key maritime pivot points across Eurasia. On land, the plan is to build a new Eurasian land bridge and develop the economic corridors of: (1) China–Mongolia–Russia; (2) China–Central Asia–West Asia; (3) the China–Indochina peninsula; (4) China–Pakistan; and (5) Bangladesh–China–India–Myanmar. On the seas, the initiative will focus on jointly building smooth, secure and efficient transport routes connecting major seaports along the Belt and Road. With the US withdrawal from the 'forever' war in Afghanistan, it is clear that now there is a strong corridor linking China, Pakistan, Afghanistan and Iran.

The total trade volume between China and its BRI-participating countries was more than US\$6 trillion in the 2013–2018 period, during which more than 244,000 jobs were created for the locals. China's direct foreign investment in those countries has exceeded US\$80 billion. China's import from and export to BRI-participating countries totalled US\$300 billion in the first quarter of 2019, up 7.8 per cent year-on-year and occupying 28.6 per cent of the country's total foreign trade volume in the period. The Asian Infrastructure Investment Bank (AIIB) is set up to forge closer partnerships with key regional and international development institutions, such as the Asian Development Bank (ADB) and the World Bank. In operation since 2016 with an authorized capital of US\$100 billion, the AIIB was founded by China to fund infrastructure investment in Asia and beyond.

Russia, Kazakhstan and Mongolia are major partners in the Belt and Road Initiative. China and Russia signed the great Eurasia partnership in 2017 coordinating both BRI and EEU, Russia's Eurasia Economic Union (Armenia, Belarus, Kazakhstan, Kyrgyzstan, and Russia). Russia is keen to develop rail container transportation, the Trans-Siberian Railway, and other infrastructure projects to boost cross-border trade. These will include spending several billion dollars on the development of port infrastructure, the development of track facilities on the approaches to ports, and the development of terminal network with the prospect of Russia–China cargo transport growing to 10 per cent. Russia and Mongolia have advantageous geographical locations and abundant oil and gas resources, and cooperation with their production capacity is of great strategic significance for China's development. Kazakhstan is the most important investment target country, and China became the largest trading partner of Kyrgyzstan and Turkmenistan in 2016. The key industries in this area focus on mining, construction and manufacturing but the demand for high-tech and the financial industry is growing.

It is essential to note that the BRI has grown and evolved since 2013 into an expansive, grand strategy of China's state-led investment model, even though there have been some problems with SOEs and state-owned banks dominating the investment and financing of projects (He, 2019). BRI is no longer only a form of infrastructure construction of transport hubs and networks. It is also not just foreign investment with greater uptake on cross-border trade, international finance, internet, education, media, tourism and other fields. The Asian Infrastructure Investment Bank (AIIB), the first ever multilateral development bank in the twenty first century initiated by China, is working with the BRICS New Development Bank, the World Bank and other world financial institutions to develop cooperation between China and more than 70 other countries to support the Belt and Road Initiative. Deloitte China, looking forward, recommends: (i) Strengthening bilateral and multilateral cooperation mechanisms; (ii) the promotion and realization of 'new globalization': (ii) the introduction of diversified shareholders and partners; (iv) cross-border mergers and acquisitions to replace greenfield investment as the main investment method; and (v) regulatory agencies' compliance review of foreign investment to be further strengthened.[4]

Chinese BRI investment in Africa has been growing. In 2021, Botswana became the 46th African nation signatory to BRI that has become reoriented to sustainability. China's total investment in the region since 2000 has involved 1,141 loan commitments involving some US$153 billion, encompassing utilities, port construction, agriculture, fishing and telecommunications.[5] Latin America is the second-largest recipient of Chinese investment at 12 per cent FDI, after Asia at 66 per cent, where investments are in dams, railway development and China's investment of billions is powering the tech boom, especially mobiles.[6] While there have been criticisms of neocolonial debt burdens, especially with small island states like Tonga, it is also increasing clear that 'soft infrastructure' in telecommunications and education provide a passport for a new raft of knowledge-based goods and services, including the new platforms for industries and start-ups based on AI, intelligent manufacturing systems, robotics, healthcare technologies, autonomous vehicles and clean energy. China is making investments in long-term markets for new platform financial services, venture capital, insurance and legal services as well as education (AI education), human capital development, talent recruitment, and the creative industries.

China, Trade and the Asian Century

The McKinsey Global Institute's (2019) discussion paper 'The future of Asia: Asian flows and networks are defining the next phase of globalization', led by Oliver Tonby, begins: "Asia is the world's largest regional economy, and its power is expected to grow as its constituent economies integrate more deeply with one another in trade, innovation, and culture and people flows. Asia will fuel and shape the next phase of globalization in what can justifiably be called the Asian Century."[7] In terms of accelerating economic trends, it still may be an exaggeration to talk of the 'Asia century,' although it is evident that Asia is becoming more Asian as intraregional flows expand. Moving within the region are 60 percent of goods traded by Asian economies, 59 percent of foreign direct investment, 74 percent of Asian air travellers, and 71 percent of Asian investment in start-ups.[8]

As the intraregional flows and economic integration increases, so too does the political integrity of the region, rivalling both the EU and US. But how will traditional security arrangements sit with new economic realities and how far will the regional identity be tolerant of Australia and New Zealand as core members? The world is becoming less Westernized and more Asianized. In this process of Asia-fication, China's influence undoubtedly will grow stronger. Although the

China compass emphasizes integration along the six major corridors of the BRI, and one focus will be on Eurasia, Central Asia and the bridge to the Near East, others will reach out to Southeast Asia and also focus on the blue economy — Oceania and the Pacific, with its massive marine resources and deep-sea minerals.

In 2020, 15 countries, including members of the ASEAN and five regional partners (China, Japan, South Korea, Australia and New Zealand), signed the RCEP, the largest free trade agreement in history, projected to add $186 billion to the world economy. Both India and the US withdrew from the agreement. It clearly provides huge access to the most dynamic regional market in the world, offering one set of trade rules across the Asia-Pacific region. Together with the CPTPP, which concluded in 2018, it represents a consolidation of the largest trade bloc in the world, dominated by East Asian members and by China who has a history of bilateral trade with ASEAN countries and other member countries of the twin trade agreements. These agreements will not only aid member countries and assist free trade but almost certainly will also bolster the BRI. RCEP, with a population of 2.3 billion or roughly 30 per cent of the world's population and around $38,813 billion or 30 per cent of global GDP, delivers not only a single set of trade rules but also reductions of tariffs and trade barriers, promoting opportunities for export economies and regional value chains with greater transparency and certainty around investment.

These agreements, along with Asia-Pacific Economic Cooperation (APEC), are game-changers for Chinese globalization. They facilitate extensive regional trade integration in the Asia-Pacific along with cultural and educational exchanges that rivals the trans-Atlantic democracies and represents a fundamental shift in the economic center of gravity. This will have implications for American superpower hegemony and, more broadly, the waning of liberalism and the development of Asia financial institutions that will compete with the Bretton Woods institutional architecture set up after World War II. The likelihood is that the Asian Century will become a reality before 2050 and that Chinese globalization will entice both the EU and Britain to seek associate membership status of these trading relationships, signalling the rise of China as a world economic and diplomatic superpower and, perhaps, also, if the transition can be managed, a world no longer tied to a reflection of past European colonial powers and American hegemony (Peters et al., 2021).

These trends are reflected in international higher education. Today, the Asian student diaspora is leading international education demand with China, the market leader for the last two decades, as the largest source market for over 1 million international students. China is followed by India (0.5 million), the fastest-growing source market growing at 8.5 per cent p.a., and Bangladesh, Vietnam and Indonesia. This growth in the Asian market is a result of "demographic trends, rising affordability and household incomes, poor quality of local education provision, improved accessibility of international education, premium salaries commanded by foreign graduates, and a greater desire to emigrate to Anglophone countries" (Laard & Sharma, 2021), although there has been significant geopolitical disruption, particularly in China–Australia relations that look set to disrupt the AUS $40 billion (2019) market over the next few years.[9] The key destination markets are still those of the Anglophone countries — the UK, the US, Australia, Canada and New Zealand — although China is fast becoming a regional hub for Asian and BRI students.

COVID-19 has disrupted the global economy, but China is coping better than most Western democratic states and consolidating its position as the new magnet economy within a complex of trading relationships in the Asia-Pacific. This consolidation comes at a time when the US is divided against itself following the politics of insurrection with Trump waiting in the wings. Accordingly, both the US and the United Kingdom have slipped in the rankings of world democracies with the US now regarded as a 'flawed democracy.' In these conditions, in the next decade, China will only strengthen its position and help to facilitate, through trade agreements, the emergence of the Asian Century.

The discourse of the 'Asian Century', now an accepted term used by world leaders, major development banks and the news media, explains how Asian flows and networks are defining the next, distinctively Asian, phase of globalization characterized as the 'Asian Century'. The discourse of Asian Century is best depicted as an increasingly integrated, regional, trading bloc based on trade facilitation through new trade agreements that are organized in four major hubs: South Asia led by India; East Asia led by the 'tiger economies' (China/Japan/Korea); Central Asia led by a new Sino-Russian accord; and South-East Asia developed through ASEAN countries. Broadly conceived, this view of the 'Asian Century' constitutes four hubs within the regional trading system, coordinated through the Trans-Pacific Partnership Agreement (TPP), a free trade agreement signed in 2016 that aims to liberalize trade and investment between 12 Pacific Rim countries. Existing trade flows between China and ASEAN countries are very strong with total ASEAN trade already greater than the 50 per cent with China.

The capacity of the Chinese market to consume high-quality goods is a reflection of the growing middle class which, now numbering some 300 million, is more than the US and the EU combined. With another 300 million consumers joining the middle class in the next 10 years, the combined purchasing power will make China the basis of the most dynamic market the world has ever seen and a multiple generator for Asia as a whole. The growth of the Indian economy and its rapidly growing middle class means that the Asian Century will last at least fifty years.

The Asian Century is a result of huge, but uneven demographic growth in the late twentieth and early twenty-first centuries (although population dynamics are beginning to slow for China) and an estimated Asia population of five billion people by 2050. It is also evidenced in the development of newly confident, Asian cultures (Bollywood, Asian cuisines, martial arts, tourism, social media) and rapidly spreading religions, especially rejuvenated Buddhism. It is clear that

China has taken a major role in realizing the Asian Century through the BRI and comprehensive regional free trade agreements, like the RCEP, which deepens trade connections with 15 economies of the Asia-Pacific, excluding, at present, both India and the US.

China's emergence as a global power has established the next wave of globalization, which is one of the main forces responsible for developing an Asian Century based on trade and regional economic integration. It is clear that international education will continue to create a global market that institutes regional hubs in Asia, with greater emphasis on regional networks and cooperation, as the capacity of the BRI to progressively reshape higher education develops. We might, indeed, theorize that the BRI represents a new stage of globalization with the ability to build interconnectivity with Eurasia and work collaboratively with universities of 130 countries to establish new partnerships with Asian countries, Russia and the EU. Increasingly, foreign students along the Belt and Road are competing to enrol in China's universities. Drawn by Chinese scholarships, students from nations along the route of China's massive infrastructure plan are pouring into China, reshaping Asian regional education, reconfiguring international education and redrawing the pattern of global higher education.

Notes

1 https://www.cnbc.com/2017/01/20/transcript-of-president-trumps-inauguration-speech.html
2 http://www.news.cn/english/special/2021-07/01/c_1310037372.htm
3 http://en.ndrc.gov.cn/newsrelease/201503/t20150330_669367.html
4 https://www2.deloitte.com/cn/zh/pages/international-business-support/articles/russia-kazakhstan-mongolia-belt-and-road-investment-seminar.html
5 https://cms.law/en/int/publication/belt-and-road-initiative/bri-view-from-africa
6 https://www.bloomberg.com/news/articles/2019-01-08/guess-who-s-behind-latin-america-s-tech-boom-china-of-course
7 https://www.mckinsey.com/featured-insights/asia-pacific/the-future-of-asia-asian-flows-and-networks-are-defining-the-next-phase-of-globalization
8 https://www.mckinsey.com/featured-insights/future-of-asia/topics/trade-and-network-flows-in-asia
9 https://monitor.icef.com/2021/05/australia-large-scale-return-of-international-students-not-expected-until-2022/

References

Hansen, V. (2020). *The Year 1000. When Explorers Connected the World—and Globalization Began.* Simon & Schuster.
Laard, S. & Sharma, A. (2021). *Global student mobility trends: 2021 and beyond.* https://www.lek.com/insights/global-student-mobility-trends-2021-and-beyond
McKinsey Global Institute (2019). *The Future of Asia: Asian Flows and Networks are Defining the Next Phase of Globalization.* https://www.mckinsey.com/featured-insights/

asia-pacific/the-future-of-asia-asian-flows-and-networks-are-defining-the-next-phase-of-globalization

Peters, M.A. (2012). *Obama and the End of the American Dream*. Brill.

Peters, M.A. (2017). The Chinese Dream: Xi Jinping Thought on socialism with Chinese characteristics for a new era, *Educational Philosophy and Theory*, *(14)*, 1299–1304, doi:10.1080/00131857.2017.1407578

Peters, M.A. (2019a). The ancient Silk Road and the birth of merchant capitalism, *Educational Philosophy and Theory*. doi:10.1080/00131857.2019.1691481

Peters, M.A. (2019b). The Chinese Dream, Belt and Road Initiative and the future of education: A philosophical postscript, *Educational Philosophy and Theory*. doi:10.1080/00131857.2019.1696272

Peters, M.A. (2020a). *The Chinese Dream: Education the Future*. Routledge.

Peters, M.A. (2020b). China's belt and road initiative: Reshaping global higher education, *Educational Philosophy and Theory*, *52*(6), 586–592, doi:10.1080/00131857.2019.1615174

Peters, M.A., Means, A.J., Ericson, D.P., Tukdeo, S., Bradley, J., Jackson, L., Mu, M., Luke, T.W., & Misiaszek, G.W. (2021). The China-threat discourse, trade, and the future of Asia: A symposium, *Educational Philosophy and Theory*. doi:10.1080/00131857.2021.1897573

Peters, M.A. (2021). The Chinese Dream, the Wuhan Nightmare, and Covid-19 Conspiracy Theory. In R.C. Hauer & M. Sardoc (Eds.), *The Routledge Handbook on the American Dream*, pp. 250–262. Routledge.

Peters, M.A., & Chiang, Tien-Hui (2017). America closed, China open, *Educational Philosophy and Theory*, *49*(9), 843–847. doi:10.1080/00131857.2017.1288347

Peters, M.A., & X. Zhu (2021). Education and the Belt and Road Initiative (BRI) Beijing *International Review of Education*. https://brill.com/view/journals/bire/3/1/article-p1_1.xml.

dela Vaissiere, E. (2014). Trans-Asian trade, or the Silk Road deconstructed. In L. Neal & J.G. Williamson (Eds.), *The Cambridge History of Capitalism Volume I: The Rise of Capitalism: From Ancient Origins to 184* pp. 101–124. Cambridge University Press.

Xi, J. (2014). *The Governance of China*. Foreign Languages Press.

14

THE COMPLEXITIES AND PARADOXES OF DECOLONIZATION IN EDUCATION

Sharon Stein, Vanessa Andreotti, Cash Ahenakew, and Dallas Hunt

Decolonization has become a buzzword across many academic disciplines. As Moosavi (2020), notes, "one can find calls to decolonise everything from sexualities to cameras, from dieting to counseling, from disability to peacebuilding" (p. 333). However, this growing interest in decolonization has not necessarily been accompanied by deep and sincere commitments to address the historical, systemic, and ongoing impacts of colonial harm. This is as true in education as it is in other disciplines and fields of practice. While it is increasingly clear to many educators that they can no longer simply ignore the issue of colonization, this does not mean that there is consensus around the importance of enacting decolonial transformation and redress nor consensus around what form that transformation and redress should take. Furthermore, there are many circular ways in which colonial patterns are reproduced, even within efforts that are framed as 'decolonizing'. In these cases, we see decolonization commitments in theory but the continuity of colonial business as usual in practice. These colonial circularities have to do, in part, with enduring investments in the promises, securities, comforts, and enjoyments that the colonial system offers those it is designed to benefit. For instance, some scholars who previously indicated no interest in questions of colonization have embraced frameworks of decolonization as a means to access funding opportunities, maintain relevance, or deny their implication in colonial harm (McFarling, 2020; Mendoza, 2021). This can be understood as an attempt to transcend complicity in colonization while maintaining one's colonial privileges (Jefferess, 2012; Tuck & Yang, 2012).

However, the reproduction of colonial circularities in efforts framed under the umbrella of decolonization is also rooted in the complexities and paradoxes involved in any effort to truly enact education otherwise. In particular, it is difficult, for educators and students alike, to navigate possibilities for decolonial

DOI: 10.4324/9781003207528-14

change given the many layers of colonial harm that operate in any context, the depth of our own colonial socialization, and the generalized lack of capacity to discern the most generative intervention that one can make within our hyper-complex and hyper-polarized institutional contexts. In this chapter, we consider some of the colonial circularities that tend to emerge in decolonization efforts. We also outline some of the different approaches to decolonizing education in practice. We do not do this to prescribe a universal pathway toward decolonization and how it should be thought of and practiced in relation to globalization. Rather, we invite educators to deepen their capacity to approach globalization in ways that are oriented by more self-reflexive and responsible engagements with education's complicity in ongoing social and ecological harm.

We begin the chapter by outlining the analysis of colonialism that orients our work. Then, to illustrate the range of different approaches to decolonization within and across particular contexts, we briefly consider how decolonization is engaged within South Africa and Canada, keeping at the fore the distinctions and overlaps between approaches that are articulated both within and across these contexts. Having offered this contextualization, we then review four primary approaches to decolonization in education that are commonly found across these contexts. We conclude by reflecting on the implications of decolonization on the globalization of education.

Coloniality in 'VUCA' times

The starting point for our analysis of current conversations about decolonization in education is the current time/space nexus of globalization that is characterized by 'VUCA', which stands for volatility, uncertainty, complexity and ambiguity (Bennett & Lemoine, 2014; Stein, 2021; Truant, Corazza, & Scagnelli, 2017). Our analysis is also informed by different decolonial critiques that emphasize that our current modern global system was both created and continues to be sustained through exploitation, expropriation, dispossession, destitution, militarization, genocides, and ecocides. Throughout this chapter, we often use the term 'coloniality', following Quijano (2007) and other scholars in the Latin American, modernity/coloniality, research group. While many people use the term 'colonialism' to describe the occupation and administration of lands and the domination of the original peoples of those lands by external political powers or groups, 'coloniality' can be used to describe the ongoing reproduction of colonial modes of knowing, being, and relating, even in places where formal structures of power and governance have been officially decolonized. Coloniality organizes and orders bodies, time, knowledge, relationships, labor, resources, and space in ways that seek to maximize economic efficiency and profits, for the benefit of particular groups of people (Quijano, 2007).

Based on decolonial critiques that highlight the costs of modernity for humans, non-humans and the planet, and the impact of modernity on the thinking, desires, imagination, and organization of those who are socialized within it, we employ the term 'modernity/coloniality' throughout this chapter as a pedagogical strategy to remind us that the modern global system cannot exist without historical and systemic ongoing social and ecological violence. In other words, we adopt the premise that coloniality is not just the collateral damage of our current modern global system but, more fundamentally, the underlying condition of possibility for this system and its persistence. In this sense, it is not only that many people are *excluded* from the promises of modern comforts, securities, and enjoyments but rather that these promises are maintained by a system that was created and is sustained *at the expense* of other people and the planet itself. Many of these analyses also highlight that trying to simply fix coloniality with more modernity (e.g., by including more people within modern institutions) not only outsources the violence that sustains those institutions but accelerates ecological destruction.

It is important to note that even those who agree on these critiques of the root causes of colonization do not necessarily agree on a single way forward for social and global change. Colonialism, coloniality, decolonization and decoloniality are all interpreted differently in different geopolitical contexts, and there are also many competing interpretations within the same context. The impossibility of achieving consensus around these issues is heightened within the realities of a VUCA world. By the end of this chapter, our intention is to provide some useful considerations for those who seek to engage in the long-term work of decolonizing education around the globe, without seeking to either direct or determine what decolonization should look like in any given context.

Interpretations of decolonization in different geopolitical contexts

One of the interventions commonly offered by decolonial critiques is to challenge and provincialize the supposed universalism of Western ways of knowing, being, and relating. However, some decolonial critiques go further to suggest that the very idea of universalism itself is a colonial imposition that seeks totalizing, decontextualized, and apolitical knowledges and practices. Conversely, some decolonial critiques position themselves as universal in ways that seek to impose hegemonic approaches to social and global change. For instance, there is a risk of imposing decolonial theories and practices that were generated in the Global North onto sites of struggle in the Global South where they may not be applicable, at least not without significant adaptation (Kelley, 2017). Others point out the risks of conflating the struggles of different communities within the Global South itself, thereby erasing uneven relations between these communities. For instance, when we conflate the marginalization of European-descended people in Latin American with the marginalization of Indigenous peoples there, we consequently erase the former's complicity in the dispossession and destitution of the latter (Cusicanqui, 2012). Others point out that exclusively focusing on European forms of colonization erases the ways that non-European countries have also enacted colonial projects which, paradoxically, recenters Europe in efforts otherwise intended to provincialize it (Mendoza, 2021). Conversely, efforts to critique non-European colonialism can also be weaponized as a means to deflect attention away from the need to challenge globally-dominant, European, colonial projects (Stein et al., 2020). This is only a small sampling of the complexities that arise when thinking about colonization on a global scale. Moosavi (2020) suggests that the complexities and risks arising in decolonizing work require 'a heightened reflexivity' among those who are committed to decolonization – including many of us who benefit from, and are deeply implicated in, enduring structures of colonial violence, such as the university.

Taking the call for self-reflexivity among decolonial scholars seriously, and in an effort to avoid the imposition of a 'new' decolonial universal as a replacement for an old colonial universal, we offer, in this section, a brief review of debates about decolonization taking place in South Africa and Canada. Differences in decolonization efforts around the globe have to do not only with the distinct colonial histories that characterize any given context but also with the different analyses and strategies that are used to challenge and interrupt coloniality (in the context of education and beyond). As well, we highlight that, just as decolonization efforts look different across these geographic locations, there is significant disagreement about what constitutes decolonization *within* these locations.

South Africa

To many outside the South African context, there is an assumption that the formal end of Apartheid in 1994 meant the end of colonialism as well. However, others consider decolonization to be 'unfinished business' (Madlingozi, 2018), and argue that the organization of social, political, and economic relations in South Africa continues to be characterized by ongoing coloniality. Some argue this is because the end of Apartheid did not result in the significant redistribution of power, land, or resources. Today, White people continue to control much of South Africa's wealth and disproportionately occupy positions of social and political power (Madlingozi, 2018). Others point to the limitations of the country's Truth and Reconciliation Commission (e.g., Al-Kassim, 2008) which, nonetheless, inspired similar reconciliation efforts elsewhere, including in Canada.

Decolonization efforts in South Africa gained global attention in 2015 when the student #Fallist movements emerged, including #RhodesMustFall and #FeesMustFall. As is the case in many other colonial contexts, K-12 schooling and higher education were key sites of socialization for different social groups in the colonial society of South Africa both before and during Apartheid. This socialization was rooted in an anti-Black hierarchy of humanity in which White people were considered to be the apex of humanity, and Black Africans were considered the nadir. Apartheid institutionalized the racial segregation of schools, including universities. Since the formal end of Apartheid, various programs and policies have set out to address enduring inequalities in access to, resourcing of, and quality of higher education. Yet still, today, historically Black universities remain significantly under-resourced compared to historically White universities (Xaba, 2017). Given the racist and colonial histories that shaped South African higher education, and the enduring social, economic, and epistemological inequities that continue to characterize these institutions, Xaba (2017) suggests it should come as no surprise that universities became a site of decolonial struggle in 2015. She argues universities are a "microcosm of a broader colonial [South Africa]" (p. 100). Diversity within the #Fallist movements themselves is arguably also a microcosm of heterogeneity in South Africa.

The #Fallist movements were united by calls for free education, critiques of the outsourcing of university laborers that negatively impacted low-income Black workers, and the imperative to challenge the supposed supremacy of European knowledge (Tshabalala, 2019; Xaba, 2017). However, Xaba (2017) argues that students at historically Black universities made different demands than those at historically White universities. She notes, "[a]t historically White universities racism, exclusionary language policies and colonial symbolism form part of the national call for free education. At historically Black universities, however, other issues that form part of protest include the basic functioning of universities, better resources such as accommodation and access to technology, and the return of student activists who were excluded for ongoing protests years before [#FeesMustFall]" (p. 98).

Many other differences also emerged among the #Fallist movements. For instance, feminist and queer activists highlighted the need to confront not only state/state-sanctioned racism and coloniality but also patriarchy, misogyny, and homophobia within the university and within student activism and wider social movements themselves. Meanwhile, responses to the student protests from within South African society varied, with some people critiquing the militarized responses and offering solidarity to the students. However, especially when some students responded to the violence of police and private security, protestors were characterized as violent themselves (Xaba, 2017).

Canada

As Coulthard (2014) notes, since the onset of colonialism, Canada has sought to "marginalize Indigenous people and communities with the ultimate goal being our elimination, if not physically, then as cultural, political, and legal peoples distinguishable from the rest of Canadian society" (p. 4). In response, Indigenous people have resisted their attempted elimination by various means. Current widespread interest in the decolonization of education within Canada can be traced to the persistent efforts by Indigenous communities to seek more culturally relevant and self-determined forms of education, as well as to the contemporary context of reconciliation. From 2008 to 2015, the Truth and Reconciliation

Commission (TRC) of Canada examined the legacy of the Indian residential school system (IRSS) which, for over one hundred years, removed more than 150,000 Indigenous children from their families, against their will, and forced them to attend schools away from their communities (TRC, 2015). The schools sought to break young Indigenous peoples' connection to their lands and assimilate them into mainstream white society.

Since the establishment of the TRC, and especially following the release of its final report and 94 Calls to Action in 2015, 'reconciliation' has entered mainstream public discourse. Within Canadian colleges and universities, this has prompted renewed commitments to 'Indigenize,' and in some cases 'decolonize,' their institutions. These commitments have often taken a form of Indigenization described by Adam Gaudry & Danielle Lorenz (2018) as 'Indigenous inclusion,' which is heavily focused on recruiting more Indigenous staff, faculty, and students. However, there is also a growing critique that this approach to educational transformation is largely tokenistic and deflects deeper individual and institutional responsibilities for redress and reparations (Daigle, 2019), with some declaring 'Reconciliation is dead.' These critical perspectives argue that Indigenous peoples are being asked to 'reconcile' themselves to ongoing colonization, as there is little indication of a fundamental shift in colonial relations (Flowers, 2015).

Calls for reconciliation and decolonization have been met with a wide range of responses among both Indigenous and non-Indigenous peoples. This includes those who outright resist the premise that the Canadian government and institutions are, in any way, accountable for colonialism to those who believe that any commitment to decolonization that does not entail the return of lands to Indigenous peoples is insufficient and disingenuous. The latter view is articulated most clearly and famously by Eve Tuck and K. Wayne Yang (2012). They problematize the growing popularization of the term decolonization in educational theory and practice. They argue it has largely become a metaphor that "kills the very possibility of decolonization" (p. 3), i.e., the rematriation (return) of land.

Students and others in Canadian universities continue to push for deeper institutional change. A recent example comes from what was formerly known as Ryerson University. For decades, members of the university community drew critical attention to the role of the school's namesake, Egerton Ryerson, in the development of the IRSS. In 2017, the former student union president and the Vice-President of Equity made a list of demands, including that the university remove the statue of Ryerson on campus and change the university's name. The university did not accede to these demands but implemented other changes, including offering an Indigenous language course, holding an annual Pow Wow, and creating and funding a research program around reconciliation. In 2018, the university released a report about its response to the TRC but it did not remove the Ryerson statue. In 2020, petitions and open letters demanded the removal of the statue. Later that year, the university president created a task force to address Egerton Ryerson's legacy. Students and faculty expressed their support to change the university's name, including in an open letter from Indigenous students that pledged to replace 'Ryerson University' in email signatures and other documents with 'X University.' The task force released its final report in August 2021, and the university's board of governors approved the report and its 22 recommendations, including to rename the university.

Decolonization across contexts

In both South Africa and Canada, resistance to European colonization has been ongoing since its onset. As with colonization itself, decolonization efforts have taken many different forms across time and local geographies. Broadly speaking, these efforts have historically been centered within communities of struggle, rather than at academic or educational institutions. Contemporary decolonization efforts in both countries have entailed many exchanges between community-based efforts and academic conversations but there nonetheless exists a university–community divide.

Recent calls for decolonization in education in the two countries have somewhat different but resonant catalysts. In South Africa, these calls have largely come out of the frustrations of a new generation of young people with the unfulfilled promises of a post-Apartheid 'rainbow nation' meant to be premised on equity and opportunity rather than racialization. Meanwhile, in Canada, calls for decolonization have been amplified by the context of a national call for reconciliation. At the same time, decolonization has also been articulated as a more radical alternative to (mainstream) reconciliation. Both contexts have further nuances and complexities that we are unable to fully address here. In both cases, though, current conversations about decolonization are informed by different degrees of frustration with the officially sanctioned narratives of change and reconciliation that (often indirectly) claim colonization is over while largely leaving the enduring structures of coloniality in place.

Growing interest in decolonization in both contexts does not necessarily mean that decolonization is widely endorsed but, rather, that it has become a topic generally impossible for educational institutions and those who work within them to continue to ignore (Moosavi, 2020). Yet, even among those who agree that decolonization is necessary and must go beyond tokenistic forms of change, there are a wide range of perspectives about precisely what the root causes of coloniality are, and what needs to be done in order to interrupt it and remake relationships. The heterogeneity, hyper-complexity, and polarization that characterize conversations about decolonization in these and other countries can be overwhelming and immobilizing, especially for those who are new to these discussions.

In order to support deepened capacity for generative engagement with these complexities, in the next section we present a social cartography of different interpretations of decolonization in education, before finally considering how these conversations relate to globalization and education.

Multiple interpretations of decolonization in education

Our social cartography of four commonly articulated interpretations of decolonization in education emphasizes their distinct horizons of hope and change. The map we offer does not attempt to cover all available possibilities. Instead, it seeks to identify key tensions, complexities, and paradoxes of decolonization, and to invite deepened engagements with the orienting assumptions, current challenges, and future possibilities that are offered by each approach. Undoubtedly, there are other possible interpretations and other ways of grouping and describing the approaches we review. These other cartographies are not mutually exclusive to our own, which is meant to serve as a pedagogical invitation people can engage in ways relevant to their context, rather than serve as a universal representation of reality that can dictate practice. Thus, our cartography does not prescribe a particular educational future: it invites those who engage it to pluralize possible decolonial futures of education in more accountable ways.

This map is informed by our previous collaborative efforts to map interpretations of decolonization in higher education (Andreotti, Stein, Ahenakew & Hunt, 2015; Stein, Andreotti, Hunt, & Ahenakew, 2021), and our work in educational institutions across North and South America, as well as our community research collaborations with Indigenous communities in these contexts. Finally, we note that these interpretations are not mutually exclusive and can be relevant across different contexts. In this way, rather than being narrowly and exclusively wedded to one interpretation, the same person might strategically draw on different interpretations to mobilize contextually-relevant change.

Horizon 1: Decolonization as equity, diversity, and inclusion

Perhaps the most common practice of decolonization in education is that which seeks to integrate decolonization into existing practices of 'EDI' – equity, diversity, and inclusion. This interpretation assumes that the primary harm of colonization is exclusion from the benefits and promises offered by mainstream, modern educational institutions. Thus, the primary focus of decolonization as EDI is to increase Indigenous peoples' inclusion into these institutions. More critical EDI approaches emphasize that access alone is insufficient. These advocate for additional measures such as the creation of courses focused on Indigenous knowledges, increased funding for Indigenous research, formalized agreements and collaborations with local Indigenous communities, and dedicated spaces and resources to serve and ensure the success of Indigenous students. Thus, this interpretation of decolonization seeks to radically reform and transform institutions through representation, recognition, and redistribution.

Those who point to the limits of this approach to decolonization argue that it requires Indigenous peoples to adapt to existing institutions, rather than the other way around (Ahenakew, 2016; Gaudry & Lorenz, 2018). This not only imposes colonial institutional norms of achievement and success onto Indigenous peoples, but also punishes those who push back against these norms and advocate for different or deeper forms of institutional change (Jimmy et al., 2019). Some point out that decolonization-as-inclusion is often framed as a conditional 'concession' to Indigenous peoples (Ahenakew & Naepi, 2016), rather than as an important but insufficient form of redress for systemic and historical colonial harm. Others note that simply adding 'decolonization' to existing EDI efforts, placing EDI under an umbrella of decolonization, or adding Indigenous peoples to the list of marginalized communities, tends to flatten the specificity of different experiences of systemic marginalization. Among other things, this reproduces the false notion that racialized non-Indigenous people cannot be complicit in settler colonization because they are subject to other forms of marginalization (Tuck & Yang, 2012).

Change efforts organized around the interpretation of decolonization as EDI can lead to important, immediate changes and opportunities within existing educational institutions. They can also serve as initial openings for conversations about more substantive engagements with decolonization. However, on their own, they are unlikely to prompt deeper examination of the ways that universities and schools are systemically complicit in colonial harm or deeper commitments to enact institutional redress for that harm. Those who critique the limits of decolonization as EDI ask: equity as defined by who, on whose terms, and for whose benefit? Inclusion into what, in whose name, and to what ends?

Beyond these basic questions, the remaining three interpretations of decolonization we review in this chapter all suggest that existing educational institutions may be 'beyond reform' – that is, they are so deeply structured by colonialism and coloniality that they might not be able to be decolonized. This challenges the notion that decolonial efforts should invest their hope in transforming existing institutions. These interpretations are all rooted in an analysis that the violence of coloniality is not a product of the exclusion of Indigenous and other marginalized communities from modernity's promises but that coloniality is the constitutive underside of modernity. In other words, the promises made by modern institutions (including the promise of EDI) are always granted at the expense of the well-being of Indigenous peoples, other marginalized communities, and the planet itself. Thus, each of the remaining interpretations of decolonization emphasize the importance of disinvesting from harmful modern promises and reorienting one's horizons of hope away from the continuity of existing institutions. However, they approach this disinvestment differently and reorient themselves in different directions.

Horizon 2: Decolonization as alternatives with guarantees

Those who approach decolonization in education as a means to create alternatives with guarantees may work within existing institutions and/or develop educational communities or practices outside of formal institutions altogether. Having concluded that existing institutions are not recuperable, at least in the long term, this approach to decolonization is oriented by a horizon of hope that seeks to either: seize power and resources within existing institutions, so as to remake them in ways that would be essentially unrecognizable; or create alternative institutions or communities that can take the place of existing institutions. In both cases, a guiding assumption is that an exceptional and innocent group — often those who are deemed to have the most radical critique and/or those with the most lived experiences of marginalization — should lead decolonization efforts by creating alternative forms of education that are superior to what is offered by existing institutions. While the specific securities and certainties offered by existing institutions are dismissed in this interpretation of decolonization, other forms of security and certainty are sought through 'alternatives with guarantees'.

One example of an educational initiative rooted in the 'alternatives with guarantees' interpretation of decolonization is Swaraj University, which Jain (2013) describes as "India's first gift culture university dedicated to regenerating the local economy, local culture and local ecology" (pp. 89–90). Swaraj is part of the global 'deschooling' movement which emphasizes the reclamation of education from its institutionalized, and especially Westernized, forms. Swaraj is also part of the Ecoversities Alliance, which seeks to reimagine higher education by asking: "What might the university look like if it were at the service of our diverse ecologies, cultures, economies, spiritualities, and life within our planetary home?" Jain (2016) has articulated a 'Declaration of Decolonizing Education' to help orient this work. The Declaration leads with the statement, "I can no longer accept a narrative of education, which teaches me that my village grandmother was illiterate, primitive, backward, stupid, uneducated, underdeveloped, uncivilized and not capable of managing their own affairs" (Jain, 2016). Another example of decolonization as 'alternatives with guarantees' is Abolitionist University Studies, which is more aligned with decolonization efforts to 'take over' and repurpose existing educational institutions than create entirely new ones. This group of scholars and activists seek to "negotiate these two paths at once: reckoning with universities' complicity with a carceral, racial-capitalist society while creating an alternative, abolition university" (Boggs, Mitchell, Meyerhoff, & Schwartz-Weinstein, 2019, p. 2).

The creation of educational alternatives by those invested in this horizon of hope can be extremely generative in terms of possible avenues for questioning and rethinking inherited educational paradigms. At the same time, there is a risk of reproducing colonial circularities in the desire for an assurance that one's efforts to imagine and practice education otherwise will lead to something different, and 'better.' In particular, there is an assumption that these efforts will interrupt colonial patterns of knowing, being, and relating. In turn, this assumption is rooted in an understanding that, if we consciously choose to interrupt colonial patterns, we will not recreate them. Yet, in practice, it is often the case that colonial patterns are unintentionally and unconsciously reproduced because of how deeply engrained they are within us. However, when we are deeply invested in the idea that our alternative educational efforts will be the solution to our educational problems and will result in universally relevant models, this can lead us to look past inevitable limitations or failures (Amsler, 2019).

A different way of engaging with alternatives might be to view them as inherently partial, contextually-relevant, limited but also indispensable experiments that can result in deep learning – including learning from mistakes and failures (Gesturing Towards Decolonial Futures, 2021). Rather than seek out or try to create a fixed model of alternatives, we might view efforts in this area as an important element of a much longer (and, likely, never ending) process of trying to decolonize education.

Horizon 3: Decolonization as hacking

The approach of decolonization as 'hacking' emphasizes the importance of redistributing resources from existing colonial institutions toward different ends than they were initially designed, especially toward decolonial projects that do not presume the continuity of those institutions. A hacking approach emphasizes that existing institutions likely cannot be decolonized, at least not in any significant way, but that one can mobilize the resources of those institutions toward alternatives that can thrive either within the small decolonial 'cracks' of an institution, and/or outside the institution altogether.

Both hacking and hospicing (described below) interpretations of decolonization are rooted in 'disinvestment' from existing educational institutions (Agathangelou et al., 2015). Compared to divestment, disinvestment does not entail entirely removing oneself from an ethically compromised context. Thus, those seeking political 'purity' in their approach to decolonization or organizational change (Shotwell, 2016) might find this approach limiting in the fact that it often operates and engages in strategic compromises within existing institutions. Disinvestment entails at once acknowledging and acting responsibly in relation to: the depth of the extent to which existing institutions are constructed by and through colonial relations; the extent of our individual complicity in those colonial relations; a commitment to rearrange one's desires away from the continuity of the institution and toward the possibility of learning from its mistakes; and experimentations with formations of education that are not premised on the continuity of colonial violence and ecological destruction.

In the process of disinvestment, there are no guarantees that we will ever fully unlearn or unravel our deeply-embedded colonial investments. Nor are there guarantees that the new possibilities we make space for will not reproduce the same mistakes or create new ones. This can be frustrating for those seeking alternatives with guarantees. A hacking approach to decolonization often operates within existing institutions in the short term, pushing the boundaries of what is possible without pushing too far, too fast, with a long-term, decolonial horizon in mind but without assuming that one can ever operate outside of complicity. Those engaged in hacking approaches may ask themselves, in whatever institutional contexts they find themselves: What is the next, most responsible, small thing I can do to reduce harm and/or enable more responsible futures? Yet, they also continually ask themselves: What have I had to compromise in order to 'hack' the institution? Was it a responsible compromise? And how can I be more accountable for the compromises that I make?

While hacking is often done on a small scale (as described above), there are also examples of it operating on a larger scale. One such example is the Dechinta Centre for Research and Learning. Dechinta is a land-based, Indigenous-centered, educational initiative with a deep focus on Indigenous self-determination (Simpson & Coulthard, 2014). Dechinta prioritizes the educational needs of Indigenous communities in northern Canada and emphasizes the knowledges held by Indigenous elders. At the same time that it offers an educational alternative, Dechinta is not entirely disentangled from mainstream institutions or independent from economic and political constraints. It engages with these limitations in strategic ways that enable its commitment to supporting epistemological educational alternatives. For instance, it partners with mainstream universities to offer accredited courses. This approach is not entirely disentangled from colonial institutions, but it seeks to mobilize their resources to experiment with educational possibilities that do not presume the continuity of those institutions.

Horizon 4: Decolonization as hospicing

Much like decolonization as hacking, decolonization as hospicing is oriented by the notion that existing institutions – like the modern/colonial system itself – are inherently violent and unsustainable. Thus, our horizons of hope must look beyond the continuity of those institutions and toward alternative futures. The metaphor of hospicing is chosen to contrast with other approaches that also presume the end of the system and its institutions, especially decolonization as alternatives with guarantees which seeks to actively dismantle and replace the system and its institutions. The hospicing interpretation of decolonization is guided by an underlying assumption that the modern/colonial system and its institutions are inherently unsustainable and already past several tipping points toward their decline (Andreotti et al., 2015). Distinct from divestment and replacement, hospicing is focused on offering dignified palliative care: gradual and careful disinvestment from harmful desires and practices, deep learning from the decline, failures and mistakes of modernity/coloniality, and clearing space for something new to arise in its place. The latter can be thought of as 'midwifing' new possibilities that may be wiser than what preceded it. The metaphor of midwifing better captures this process than 'birthing,' since it is assumed from this approach to decolonization that the process by which systems decline and emerge is not something that can be wholly or even primarily determined by human will and agency alone.

Much like the EDI and hacking interpretations of decolonization, a hospicing interpretation is concerned to reduce the harm enacted by existing institutions and not just within but also outside their walls. Much like the hacking approach, a hospicing interpretation asks how institutional resources can be redistributed and redirected toward imagining educational alternatives that are viable, but likely unimaginable from within existing institutions. Finally, like the alternatives with guarantees interpretation of decolonization, a hospicing approach is invested in the possibility of educational futures outside existing institutions. However, in contrast to the alternatives with guarantees approach, hospicing views the fostering and regeneration of alternatives as a continuous process of experimentation that will inevitably entail mistakes and missteps, alongside successes. This is not viewed as a problem but, rather, as an opportunity for the continuation of deeper learning and unlearning.

An example of hospicing is the educational project 'The University of the Forest' of the Huni Kui Federation of Acre, in the Amazon region of Brazil. The Huni Kui are one of the Indigenous groups of the Amazon that consider themselves guardians of the rainforest. Their project not only displaces anthropocentric notions of knowledge production, but also conceptualizes the role of education as preparing people to recognize how humanity's fantasies of separation and superiority are jeopardizing human survival on the planet. The University of the Forest offers stories, from the perspectives of trees, rivers, and non-human animals, that highlight how human greed and arrogance – which are reflected in mining and deforestation for cattle, soy and corn – are causing the Amazon to reach a tipping point where it will turn from a carbon sink to a carbon source and exponentially accelerate climate change. The project invites learners to face their complicity in systemic harm and unsustainability and to see the contradictions and harms inflicted by a single story of progress, development, prosperity, and civilization.

Implications for discussions about globalization in education

Decolonial critiques, and various interpretations of decolonization, are extremely relevant for rethinking the relationship between globalization and education, as some decolonial scholars have suggested European colonization can be understood as the original form of globalization (Mignolo, 2021). In this understanding of globalization, the West sought to impose a single, 'global' way of thinking across the planet as a means to assert its universal value and relevance, and to justify its economic and political domination of the rest of the world toward its own ends. Similarly, Gayatri Spivak (1990) has described colonialism as the West's attempt to 'world the world,' or remake the world in its own image and to its own benefit. In turn, contemporary forms of globalization are understood as a continuation of European colonialism and imperialism that largely still benefit the West, as well as those outside the West who have embraced the West's modern/colonial 'global design.'

Yet the complexities that characterize contemporary forms of globalization mean that the implications of decolonization are not always clear. Given that the imposition of a modern/colonial global system has been ongoing for over five centuries, virtually no one is left unaffected by it – including those who both reject and embrace it. Many people fall somewhere in between this reject/ embrace continuum because many people both benefit from *and* are marginalized by this system. Although complicity in modern/colonial violences is very unevenly distributed, few of us are entirely outside implication in harm. This means that it is no easy or straightforward task to navigate and discern between different layers of complexity and complicity in order to determine contextually-relevant and socially and ecologically accountable decolonization interventions.

There is no universal formula or strategy for interrupting and redressing colonial harm that will work across all geopolitical contexts or that can address the many legacies and layers of harm all at once. Furthermore, decolonial critiques are just one of many important ways of critically examining the educational implications of globalization. It is important to also note that just as the globalization of education can feed the intensification of harmful colonial patterns, it can generate new opportunities for critical collaborative engagements and ethical solidarities. Indeed, previous generations of decolonial thinkers who recognized these opportunities in their own time offer examples for us to think with and learn from. However, as with decolonization efforts more generally, all possibilities for imagining and enacting a decolonial approach to globalization are partial and precarious, and should be approached with caution and consideration of the possible reproduction of colonial dynamics.

In this chapter, we have sought to provide some guideposts for navigating calls for the decolonization of education in a contemporary global context characterized by volatility, uncertainty, complexity, and ambiguity. We also offered an overview of some of the most salient interpretations of decolonization in practice. Of course, it is up to individual scholars and practitioners to determine how they will respond to growing calls for decolonization, and how they will relate these calls to the dynamics of globalization. However, it is clear these calls are not going away any time soon. They are rooted in critical responses to long-standing patterns of social and ecological violence whose impacts on educational policy and practice are ongoing and, in some contexts, intensifying.

If, as predicted by many, the institutions and wider global system initially instituted by and continually reproduced through processes of Western colonization continue to experience unprecedented social and ecological challenges, there may be growing interest in decolonial critiques and alternative futures that could be made possible through decolonization practices. This work should be approached with attention to and consideration of: the socio-historical context that brought us to current crises; the complexities, contradictions, and complicities that characterize any educational change effort (whether rooted in decolonial critiques or not); and the reality that, while our education contexts are separated by many tangible barriers and differences, we are all facing – in extremely uneven ways – the sedimented impacts of colonialism's initial 'global design.' How we respond to these impacts will depend on many factors, including where we find ourselves in relation to the dominant global imaginary, and where we invest our horizons of hope. But the decolonial critiques we have drawn on in this chapter invite us to respond by asking difficult, uncomfortable questions about how we are complicit in creating the problems of the present, and how we might responsibly respond.

References

Agathangelou, A. M., Olwan, D. M., Spira, T. L., & Turcotte, H. M. (2015). Sexual divestments from empire: Women's Studies, institutional feelings, and the "odious" machine. *Feminist Formations, 27*(3), 139–167.

Ahenakew, C. (2016). Grafting Indigenous ways of knowing onto non-Indigenous ways of being: The (underestimated) challenges of a decolonial imagination. *International Review of Qualitative Research, 9*(3), 323–340.

Ahenakew, C., & Naepi, S. (2016). The difficult task of turning walls into tables. In A. Macfarlane, S. Macfarlane, & M. Webber (Eds.), *Sociocultural realities: Exploring new horizons* (pp. 181–194), Canterbury Press.

Al-Kassim, D. (2008). Archiving. resistance: Women's testimony at the threshold of the state. *Cultural Dynamics, 20*(2), 167–192.

Amsler, S. (2019). Gesturing towards radical futurity in education for alternative futures. *Sustainability Science, 14*(4), 925–930.

Andreotti, V. D. O., Stein, S., Ahenakew, C., & Hunt, D. (2015). Mapping interpretations of decolonization in the context of higher education. *Decolonization: Indigeneity, Education & Society, 4*(1), 21–40.

Bennett, N., & Lemoine, L. (2014). What VUCA really means for you. *Harvard Business Review, 92*(1/2), 27.

Boggs, A., Meyerhoff, E., Mitchell, N., & Schwartz-Weinstein, Z. (2019). Abolitionist university studies: An invitation. https://abolitionjournal.org/abolitionist-university-studies-an-invitation/. Accessed December 10, 2021.

Coulthard, C. (2014). *Red Skin, White Masks.* University of Minnesota Press.

Cusicanqui, S. R. (2012). Ch'ixinakax utxiwa: A reflection on the practices and discourses of decolonization. *South Atlantic Quarterly, 111*(1), 95–109.

Daigle, M. (2019). The spectacle of reconciliation: On (the) unsettling responsibilities to Indigenous peoples in the academy. *Environment and Planning D: Society and Space, 37*(4), 703–721.

Flowers, R. (2015). Refusal to forgive: Indigenous women's love and rage. *Decolonization: Indigeneity, Education & Society, 4*(2), 32–49.

Gaudry, A., & Lorenz, L. (2018). Indigenization as inclusion, reconciliation, and decolonization: Navigating different visions for Indigenizing the Canadian academy. *AlterNative, 14*(3), 218–227.

Gesturing Towards Decolonial Futures (GTDF) (2021). The gifts of failure. https://decolonialfutures.net/portfolio/the-gifts-of-failure/

Jain, M. (2013). McEducation for all: Whose agenda does global education really serve? *Critical Literacy: Theories and Practices, 7*(1), 84–90.

Jain, M. (2016). Declaration of decolonizing education. https://medium.com/the-emperor-has-no-clothes/declaration-of-decolonizing-education-37ddc32a4cde. Accessed December 10, 2021.

Jefferess, D. (2012). The "Me to We" social enterprise: Global education as lifestyle brand. *Critical Literacy: Theories and Practices, 6*(1), 18–30.

Jimmy, E., Andreotti, V., & Stein, S. (2019). *Towards braiding.* Musagetes Foundation.

Kelley, R. D. (2017). The rest of us: Rethinking settler and native. *American Quarterly, 69*(2), 267–276.

Madlingozi, T. (2018). The proposed amendment to the South African constitution: Finishing the unfinished business of decolonisation? *Critical Legal Thinking.* https://criticallegalthinking.com/2018/04/06/the-proposed-amendment-to-the-south-african-constitution/ Accessed December 10, 2021.

McFarling, L. U. (2020). 'Health equity tourists': How white scholars are colonizing research on health disparities. *STAT.* https://www.statnews.com/2021/09/23/health-equity-tourists-white-scholars-colonizing-health-disparities-research/ Accessed December 10, 2021.

Mendoza, B. (2021). Decolonial theories in comparison. In S-M Shih & L-C Tsai (Eds.), *Indigenous Knowledge in Taiwan and Beyond* (pp. 249–271). Springer.

Mignolo, W. D. (2021). Coloniality and globalization: A decolonial take. *Globalizations, 18*(5), 720–737.

Moosavi, L. (2020). The decolonial bandwagon and the dangers of intellectual decolonisation. *International Review of Sociology, 30*(2), 332–354.

Quijano, A. (2007). Coloniality and modernity/rationality. *Cultural Studies, 21*(2–3), 168–178.

Shotwell, A. (2016). *Against Purity: Living Ethically in Compromised Times.* University of Minnesota Press.

Simpson, L., & Coulthard, G. (2014). Dechinta Bush University, Indigenous land-based education and embodied resurgence. *Decolonization, Indigeneity, Society & Education.* https://decolonization.wordpress.com/2014/11/26/leanne-simpson-and-glen-coulthard-on-dechinta-bush-university-indigenous-land-based-education-and-embodied-resurgence

Spivak, G. (1990). *The Post-Colonial Critic: Interviews, Strategies, Dialogues* (S. Harasym, Ed.). Routledge.

Stein, S. (2021). Reimagining global citizenship for a volatile, uncertain, complex, and ambiguous (VUCA) world. *Globalisation, Societies and Education, 19*(4), 482–495.

Stein, S., Andreotti, V., de Souza, L. M., Ahenakew, C., & Suša, R. (2020). Who decides? In whose name? For whose benefit? Decoloniality and its discontents. *On Education: Journal for Research and Debate, 3*(7), 1–6.

Stein, S., Andreotti, V., Hunt, D., & Ahenakew, C. (2021). Complexities and challenges of decolonizing higher education: Lessons from Canada. In S. H. Kumalo (Ed.), *Decolonisation as Democratisation: Global Insights into the South Africa Experience.* UKZN Press

Truant, E., Corazza, L., & Scagnelli, S. D. (2017). Sustainability and risk disclosure: An exploratory study on sustainability reports. *Sustainability, 9*(4), 1–20.

Truth and Reconciliation Commission of Canada (2015). *Honouring the truth, reconciling for the future: Summary report of the final report of Truth and Reconciliation Commission of Canada.* http://www.trc.ca/websites/trcinstitution/File/2015/Findings/Exec_Summary_2015_05_31_web_o.pdf. Accessed December 10, 2021.

Tshabalala, M. M. (2019). Contrasting decolonisation debates in South Africa and the UK. *London School of Economics.* https://blogs.lse.ac.uk/africaatlse/2019/08/12/decolonisation-debates-south-africa-uk-must-fall/. Accessed December 10, 2021.

Tuck, E., & Yang, K. W. (2012). Decolonization is not a metaphor. *Decolonization: Indigeneity, Education, and Society, 1*(1), 1–40.

Xaba, W. (2017). Challenging Fanon: A Black radical feminist perspective on violence and the Fees Must Fall movement. *Agenda, 31*(3–4), 96–104.

15

EDUCATION AND THE POLITICS OF ANTI-GLOBALIZATION

Fazal Rizvi

Introduction

During the course of the 1990s and 2000s, much of the opposition to globalization came from scholars and activists on the broadly defined political left. This opposition was largely focused on the social consequences of the globalization of the capitalist economy. It was most evident in the street protests in Seattle in 1999 against the World Trade Organization's (WTO) attempts to re-write the rules of global trade, which, it was believed, largely favored the interests of the multinational corporations but not ordinary people. The protestors included environmentalists, labor unions, indigenous groups, international NGOs, and students. They insisted that the new WTO rules would undermine workers' rights and would inevitably lead to greater inequalities both within and across nations. These rules would also be exploitative of the environment and would damage the prospects of any democratic control that local communities had over their own affairs. A few years later, the Occupy Movement, an international, progressive, socio-political coalition, represented a more determined and better organized effort to oppose globalization, pointing to the role that global capital was playing in perpetuating social and economic inequality. The prospects of 'real democracy', the movement's spokespeople insisted, were undermined by the predatory practices of global capitalism. The anti-globalization sentiments of the Occupy Movement were thus "situated within the struggle for sustainability taking place amid looming resources shortages, climate change, economic instability, and ecological breakdown" (Evans, 2012, p. 1).

Around the turn of the century, anti-globalization activism was also supported by a large number of scholarly critiques. In his widely-read book, *Globalization*, first published in 2000, Jan Scholte showed, for example, how globalization

DOI: 10.4324/9781003207528-15

produced various forms of (in)security, not only military but also ecological, economic, cultural and psychological; (in)equality and (in)justice, both within and across nations; and what he called (un)democracy. Around the same time, both Saskia Sassen (1998) and Joseph Stiglitz (2002) published books with the same title, *Globalization and its Discontents*, to suggest that the current global systems were unsustainable, and that sooner or later they would create conditions of considerable political volatility. In their highly influential book *Empire*, Michael Hardt and Antoni Negri (2000) argued that globalization represented a new form of imperialism that was no longer centered on nation states but constituted by a coalition of G8 nations led by the United States, along with international organizations, which promoted the market economy and the weakest form of liberal democracy. A few years later, the Canadian journalist Naomi Klein published a book, *No Logo* (2004), which showed how, under the emerging operations of the global economy, multinational corporations were able to relocate production to places where labor was the cheapest and where workers could be easily exploited.

Each of these critiques demonstrated how globalization constituted a new form of capitalism, even more exploitative and manipulative than its earlier practices. However, much of the opposition to economic globalization from the left was largely contained and controlled through the use of various political strategies that included the claim that 'there was no alternative.' It was argued (by Bhagwati, 2004, for example) that economic globalization had virtually eradicated extreme global poverty and that it had enabled many countries to grow at a rapid rate. Besides, the arguments continued, its core ideas had even been accepted by socialist states, such as China and Vietnam. Over the past decade, however, much of the activist energy against globalization has come from the political right, articulated in populist forms. As Walden Bello (2019) has noted, the populist right has, in effect, stolen the left's working-class base by opposing some of the core ideological proposals associated with globalization. In this chapter, I want to examine this political transference, focusing in particular on the ways in which the political right has embraced various aspects of the left's anti-globalization sentiments, though in the service of an aggressive nationalism, leaving the core ideas of global capitalism unaffected. I want to identify the major differences in the ideological character of the opposition to globalization by the left and the right, and to argue that anti-globalization sentiments have now become a major site of political struggle over the ways in which the prospects of our futures might be conceptualized in most aspects of our social life, including education.

Globalization and its discontents

From the very beginning of the triumphalist discourses of globalization in the early 1990s, as expressed for example by Francis Fukuyama's 'end of history thesis' (1991), concerns about each of its economic, political and cultural aspects were widely articulated. Economically, it was argued that globalization only benefited a very small minority of people, while a much larger majority had their lives disrupted, perhaps even destroyed. Economic globalization had led to unsustainable and unacceptable levels of inequality. Politically, it was maintained that the New World Order that globalization had spawned had left global power in the hands of a transnational elite, squeezing out the democratic voices of citizens to shape their own communities. This had caused a 'democratic deficit.' And, culturally, globalization had unsettled deeply-held values and traditions that people cherished, especially as a result of the growing levels of mobility across national boundaries, not only of people but also of ideas and ideologies.

Over the past three decades, it has become abundantly clear that the gains of globalization of economic activities are unequally distributed, both within and across nations. Big business has done very well. The corporate elites have been able to keep wages down, allowing their incomes and stock market values to rise rapidly. The rules governing the global economy have been imposed on national governments while multinational corporations have been able to mount a powerful ideological campaign to dominate decision-making processes. Social safety measures have been watered down, with the ideological discourses of austerity and the need to balance the budget serving to silence the voices of opposition. The balance of power has clearly shifted, most notably with the decline in the power of trade unions to demand fairer distribution of productivity gains.

While in some countries, such as China and Korea, the global economy has created new opportunities, these have often been limited to the economic elite. They have exacerbated various forms of social stratification that had already existed with respect to class, gender, race, age and the urban–rural divide. Even in those countries that have allegedly benefited from globalization, gaps in people's life chances have widened markedly. In the global cities in China, for example, many more people are now able to enjoy the cosmopolitan lifestyles of advanced economies but, in rural areas, the benefits of globalization are scarce. In India, corporatization and globalization of agriculture have led to suicides among farmers (Sainath, 2004). In many African countries, globalization has come in thne form of structural adjustment schemes that have transformed their economies and institutions but this, too, has only benefited a few who are now able to join the transnational elite class. Per capita incomes have continued to fall in the poorest countries. In 2010, for example, almost three billion people lived on under $2 a day, while more than 800 million continued to suffer from malnutrition (Pieterse, 2018, p. 88).

In Europe and the United States, discontents associated with globalization are no less severe. Their industrial cities, in particular, have had to carry much of the burden of global economic transformation, leading workers to believe that their jobs and wealth have been unfairly exported to Asia. The combined forces of automation of work and globalization of production have reduced the availability of employment that was once plentiful. Unemployment rates have soared in the so-called 'rust-belt' communities, forcing people to move to places where the new service jobs supposedly are. People have had to retrain for these new jobs, but the privatized training systems have demanded an investment that many cannot afford. At the same time, welfare provisions have been cut, as governments are either not able to afford them or, more frequently, have an ideological objection to them. It is assumed that state subsidies and programs frequently encourage inefficiencies and make people dependent on handouts. There has thus been a relentless ideological campaign that has celebrated the logic of the markets, suggesting that individuals themselves should be responsible for their welfare.

While most people's capacities to enjoy the various benefits of globalization, such as the availability of a vast array of consumer goods, have declined, they are constantly subjected to lifestyle choices that are often beyond their grasp. Mass advertising campaigns are designed to elicit desire for goods and services that only a few can afford. Clearly, a gap has grown between those who can afford the cosmopolitan tastes and those who are left to fantasize about them. As Zygmunt Bauman (1999) pointed out in his widely-read paper, 'Tourists and Vagabonds,' globalization has thus given rise to new forms of social differentiations around consumptive desires — between those who can realize them and those who are left outside the gate wishing they could, often with envy or anger. This qualitative account of social inequalities parallels Thomas Piketty's (2013) quantitative account of the growing levels of wealth and income inequality under the conditions of globalization. What both of these analyses reveal is that economic inequalities are produced both materially and culturally and have significant political outcomes.

Yet the political left has been unable to persuade the people it is the new character of global capitalism that has caused job losses, not only in developing countries but also in the developed world. For instance, in the United States, five million manufacturing jobs were lost between 2000 and 2015. Academic critiques of global capitalism have been powerful and compelling but, it must be admitted, these critiques have not been very successful in mobilizing the people politically. Activists' initiatives such as the World Social Forum and the Occupy Movement fizzled out before they had a chance to become politically effective. Their impact was contained by either the power of large corporations and the global media, or the parties of the so-called left which embraced ideas such as the Third Way, which did very little to check the forces of globalization and were, in fact, complicit in the march of global capitalism.

Paradoxically, it has been the political right that has managed to benefit politically from the left's anti-globalization sentiments, linking their opposition to a strident form of nationalism. For example, while the idea that not everybody is playing by the same rules with respect to global trade was first advanced by the left, it is the right that has been able to convert it into an anti-China refrain. Donald Trump, for example, continues to insist that the West has opened its markets to Chinese exports yet China has not properly reciprocated, thereby hurting working-class communities in the United States. This arguably compelling mode of thinking has become a common refrain among populist politicians, not only

in the United States but also elsewhere. Nationalist explanation for economic demise and distress have become commonplace. In this manner, Bello (2019, p. 127) argues, "The Right eats the Left's lunch."

Even before Trump came on the political stage, Guy Standing (2011) had elaborated the nature of this incipient politics of anti-globalization. He referred to the emergence of a class of people badly affected by the processes of globalization as the 'precariat.' The emerging precariat class, Standing argues, is a heterogeneous group — an agglomeration of several different social groups that include young, poorly educated people as well as those who have fallen out of the old-style, industrial, working class. However, the precariat are not only suffering from job insecurity, Standing notes, but also extremely concerned about their identity. They feel that recent public policies have diminished the cultural privileges they once enjoyed and that they have lost democratic control over their destinies they assume they once had. Standing warned that this group was politically dangerous — not only because it was internally divided but also because its members were susceptible to the siren calls of political extremism. Politically expedient politicians have, of course, never been reluctant to stoke fears by creating a cultural chasm within marginalized communities. Thus, in recent years, we have witnessed the more extensive vilification of migrants, refugees, indigenous peoples and other vulnerable groups.

The rise of right-wing populism

It is the right-wing, populist leaders and parties around the world who have, over the past decade in particular, been able to better mobilize the concerns and fears of the precariat. They have been able in ways the left never could, to convince the precariat that the loss of their political voice and economic fortunes is largely due to globalization. The right has even been able to persuade many within the working class that it is the cultural dimensions of globalization that have undermined their economic prospects by destroying their nationally-based institutions and traditions (Urbinati, 2015). They have pointed to the damage done by globalized markets, globalized communication systems and global agencies such as the European Union and the United Nations, which have extended into aspects of life best handled at local or national levels. Globalization has not only produced unacceptable levels of economic and social inequalities but has also caused cultural dislocation and insecurities. They portray the globalized world order as inherently unfavorable to the interests of ordinary people, and they demand conditions in which international trade serves national interests rather than the interests of the global elite (Müller, 2016).

While many of these concerns are also expressed by the left, what is distinctive about the claims of the populist right is that they are located within a politics of ethno-nationalism, a form of nationalism through which various political issues are linked to the national affirmation of a particular ethnic group (de la Torres, 2019). The right's critique of globalization is expressed in the terms of a loss of a set of ethnic traditions that were once nationally prescribed. It harkens back to a presumed golden era when social cohesion was presumably achieved through a set of shared values unaffected by external forces. The right-wing populist leaders and parties are thus able to mobilize political prejudices of an ethnic group that predated the contemporary manifestations of globalization. They do this not only by mounting a rhetoric critical of global migration but also by holding the cultural others as responsible for many of their social afflictions and economic vulnerabilities. As Lowndes (2019, p. 198) points out, this populist rage is marshaled around "a language of permanent loss." So, for example, while Trump's campaign slogan 'Make America Great Again' implies a positive agenda, much more emphasis is placed on defeat. Trump is less a champion of the working people than a figure who confirms their anger and anxieties about their declining social status.

In Europe, the major source of populist discontentment is migration and refugees, which focuses on the ease with which people are supposedly able to move across national borders. The Brexit campaign, for example, portrayed migration as a major threat to the job prospects of working people and the kind of good life they imagined they once had. It was argued that EU's globalization agenda had undermined the UK's cultural and religious traditions, and was forcing it to accept the foreign values of diversity and cultural exchange. Elsewhere in Europe, fear of cultural heterogeneity has also been widely stoked by leaders such as Hungary's Victor Orban and Poland's Andrzej Duda (Applebaum, 2020), even if the number of immigrants and refugees in their communities is relatively small (Appadurai, 2006). Throughout Europe, resentment lies at the heart of the distress about the cultural 'others' who, it is felt, have been undeservedly given a set of rights and privileges by supranational organizations such as the European Union and, therefore, represent unfair competition for local populations (Cohen, 2019).

Of course, many of these fears are unfounded. But that is the point. The success of the populist right has, instead, been in capturing and articulating these fears into a political narrative to which a large proportion of the electorate can relate at a visceral level. In this way, the global rise of the populist right represents a story of political mobilization, successfully converted into a highly effective movement. Populist movements are, of course, as old as politics itself. They can be both right wing and left wing in nature but only some reach a critical mass of power while others remain on the sidelines. As Benjamin Moffit (2016, p. 3) has argued, "today's populism is not one entity but a political style that is performed, embodied, and enacted across political and cultural contexts." It involves various political strategies to mobilize people around a loosely connected set of ideas. It is constituted not by a coherent set of ideas but by a discursive assemblage that is grounded in affect and emotions, and is often based on a sharp differentiation between 'our' feelings and those of 'theirs.' A loose and shared characterization of the enemy is necessary for populism to get its political purchase. A state of victimhood is often assumed, which requires the construction of an exploitative elite who is in control and needs to be fought against (Mudd & Kaltwasser, 2017).

Thus, the contemporary, right-wing, populist rhetoric has a number of discrete threads that are lumped together in an ideologically expedient fashion without any serious attempt to ensure coherence across its various claims (Geiselberger, 2017). While many of these threads have mimicked the complaints of the left, such as those about the global rules of trade and how they have disadvantaged the poor, the right has been more focused on the loss of national prestige and privileges. Its main concern is with the ways in which national authority and power have shifted to global institutions. It is assumed that these transformations have adversely affected local industries and workers because developing countries have been able to take advantage of the new global rules, and because leaders in the advanced countries have displayed ineptitude in negotiating better deals. Global corporations and managers are the direct beneficiaries of the political weaknesses displayed at the national level, resulting in growing levels of economic inequality and social anguish.

The populist right has thus linked issues of economic anxieties to cultural concerns. The global economy, it is asserted, has enabled unfettered flows of not only capital but, more alarmingly, people across national boundaries. A discourse of 'losing control over our borders' has become a rallying cry, intensifying prejudices directed at immigrants and refugees. In the United States, for example, it is widely assumed that jobs are lost to the cultural 'others' either within the nation or elsewhere and that these jobs can only 'come back' if the global flows of people are more rigorously controlled or, better still, stopped altogether. At the same time, a powerful narrative of national security has emerged in which the Chinese and Muslims are assumed to be the major culprits, taking advantage of global flows. Despite their small numbers, minorities are moreover assumed to have the potential to dilute local cultural and religious traditions. It is claimed that Western values are undermined by a globally homogenizing culture, on the one hand, and the unjustifiable tolerance of foreign cultural practices, on the other. This thinking is encapsulated in the ideologies of diversity and multiculturalism that globalization has supposedly promoted.

The persistence of neoliberal rationality

In this way, the populist right has tied issues of economic decline to cultural concerns. It has been remarkably successful in synthesizing its diffuse and contradictory ideas under a broad ideological umbrella that suggests the main sources of material discontent lie, mostly, in the cultural shifts driven by globalization. The narrative of the populist right has thus managed to satisfy a diverse range of political prejudices, from overtly xenophobic sentiments to economic nationalism. What this politics has not done, however, is to name the contradictions of global capitalism which has, arguably, had a greater impact on the economic distress of the marginalized. Instead, the injustices of globalization are assumed to be inherent in the global flows of people and cultural practices, the excesses of global institutions and the cosmopolitan tastes of the transnational elite, rather than in the policy approaches to the shifting geography. Moreover, failures of national leaders are assumed to lie in not getting a more favorable deal in international trade rather than in the contradictions inherent in the capitalist logic of the markets. In this way, the populist right does not deny the importance of international trade but prefers to view it through a narrow, nationalist prism.

This line of thinking clearly masks the fact that global interconnectivity may, in fact, not be the problem afflicting societies but the neoliberal terms in which it is defined and managed. This understanding of globalization remains tied to the key tenets of neoliberalism and, in particular, its assumptions regarding the ways in which societies and their institutions are best organized and governed. It continues to stress the importance of free markets, with a distinct preference for the ideas of the deregulation of industries and capital flows, radical reduction in welfare state provisions, and the importance of privatizing public goods and services. It assumes that human beings are largely motivated by their economic self-interest, always seeking to strengthen their competitive advantage within the free markets. There is, thus, a strong libertarian streak in contemporary, right-wing, populist attitudes, with an emphasis on minimal state intervention in the free market and the unimpeded private lives of citizens.

These attitudes are located in a system of thought, a distinctive mode of reason that Wendy Brown (2015, p. 33) refers to as a form of rationality that advocates "the economisation of subjects." She argues that this 'neoliberal rationality' imagines that economics can "remake other fields of existence in and through its own terms and metrics." In this logic, human beings are configured as human capital across all spheres of life. This line of thinking is consistent with the analysis that Lingard and I provided in 2010, in our book *Globalizing Education Policy* (Rizvi & Lingard, 2010), of a 'neoliberal imaginary' through which people try to make sense of their identity and social relations. As an imaginary, we argued, neoliberalism implies the ways in which we need both to interpret the world and to imagine the ways it should be. Or, as Brown (2015, p. 36) puts it, "within neoliberal rationality, human capital is both our 'is' and our 'ought'—what we are said to be, what we should be, and what the rationality makes us into through its norms and construction of environments."

What right-wing populism refuses to acknowledge, however, is that it might be the policies and practices associated with this form of rationality that has produced the social outcomes that have entrenched economic inequalities. When everything, everywhere, is defined in terms of capital investment and appreciation, the idea of public good loses its significance, as the philosopher Michael Sandel (2013) has noted. Everyone, including the government, is no longer identified with the people but is increasingly viewed as merely another economic actor, among many others. As economic actors, corporations feel obliged to work for their shareholders rather than the community at large. They demand greater tax breaks so that they can compete in the market more effectively. It is unsurprising, therefore, that they do not favor increases in the wages of their workers: such egalitarian measures invariably cut into the profits that the corporations are expected to make for their shareholders.

If this is so, then social inequalities and discontent are an outcome of the unequal distribution of wealth rather than global processes as such. As Jack Ma, the Chinese owner of Ali Baba, one of the world's largest companies, pointed out in 2015 at the World Economic Forum in Davos, Western countries such as the United States have benefited greatly from the globalization of trade in industries such as telecommunications, tourism and retail services. However, they have not used their profits wisely, preferring to spend their economic gains on military misadventures and in giving tax cuts to the rich, instead of looking after the dislocated and disadvantaged members of its community. The problem, Ma insisted, is not globalization of trade as such but the failure to pursue policies that are more redistributive than they are punitive and uncaring. Jack Ma's analysis thus points to a complicated relationship between globalization and neoliberalism.

It needs to be noted, moreover, that the neoliberal imaginary of globalization is a product of Anglo-American political preferences. It is an outcome of the post-war efforts of the United States to remake the world in its own image, in support of its own economic, strategic and political interests. Indeed, it is the United States, far more than any other country, that has played the most decisive role in determining the content of the policies and procedures that have accompanied economic globalization. Even today, it retains a dominant say in multilateral organizations such as the World Bank, the Organisation for Economic Co-operation and Development (OECD) and International Monetary Fund (IMF). It has played a powerful role in shaping the rules the WTO now enforces. Similarly, the United Kingdom cannot claim to be a bystander in the forging of the Schengen Agreement that encouraged the mobility of people within EU countries, considering its earlier conviction that the global mobility of people and capital was fundamental to its economic growth, productivity and prosperity.

If these arguments are valid then populist politics is, indeed, a ruse masking the contradictions of neoliberal rationality as well as its impact on the life chances of the marginalized. Holding immigrants and refugees responsible for unemployment and deteriorating labor conditions and fueling the fires of Islamophobia has clearly been successful in mobilizing political discontent in the United States and Europe, as well as in countries such as India. However, such political strategies hide the fundamental fact that neither economic productivity nor social cohesion is possible without addressing the structural contradictions associated with global capitalism. Yet, while this may be true, 'playing the culture card' continues to pay considerable political dividends to populist leaders and parties. Unsurprisingly, therefore, many of them, from Trump to Orban, have 'doubled down' on the populist uses of the politics of cultural discontent while remaining committed to neoliberal rationality which is oblivious to the issues of economic and social inequalities.

Populism and educational policy

This tension is fundamentally embedded within public policies, including those that relate to education, pursued by recent right-wing populist governments. This can be illustrated by examining the approach to educational policy taken by the Trump administration. The Trump administration portrayed itself as the champion of the American working class but tenaciously pursued the basic assumptions of neoliberal rationality. It cut taxes in ways that shamelessly favored the rich. It talked about balancing the budget by cutting back on expenditure on social programs. It sought to stimulate the economy by an extensive program of deregulation and privatization. Trump also appointed a cabinet that was wedded to the interests of the 'big end of town,' to an ideologically rigid form of capitalism. Some members of the Trump cabinet were hostile to the goals of the agencies they were asked to oversee, as well as to any form of unionization. The idea of a minimum wage was repeatedly ruled out. In short, the Trump administration displayed a strong commitment to neoliberal rationality applied not only to the operations of the state but also to the renegotiation of treaties and its engagement with international organizations.

In education, the Trump government's commitment to neoliberal rationality could not have been clearer with the appointment of Betsy DeVos as his Secretary of Education. This was one of the mostly ideologically driven appointments in recent history — DeVos had no experience in running a public school system or a state university or in shaping state-wide education policy. Her signature issue, school vouchers, was based on her deep commitment to a free-market ideology. Repeatedly in her speeches, DeVos argued (for example, 2019): "Let the education dollars follow each child, instead of forcing the child to follow the dollars. People deserve choices and options." As a former chairwoman of the Republican Party in Michigan, and as a major donor to Trump, she supported policies and programs of vouchers, privatization, deregulation and charter schools, at the expense of public education.

DeVos argued that charter schools would inevitably improve the quality of educational provision and outcomes, and would provide greater access to educational opportunities throughout poorer communities. Neither of these claims was supported by evidence, however. A review of research on publicly-funded private schools in the United States indicated no clear advantage or improvement in academic achievement among students attending private schools. According to Christopher Lubienski and Sarah Lubienski (2014), the evidence about charter school effectiveness was equally mixed. More disturbing was the finding that private schools were more economically and racially segregated than the public schools, and that they underrepresented students with special needs. Furthermore, poorly-funded private schools were less likely to provide access to new technologies, science laboratories and secure environments. In the end, they exacerbated cultural divisions, perpetuating social conflict, without doing anything to minimize levels of economic inequalities and despair.

In his book, *The End of Public Schools*, David Hursh (2016) showed how privatization policies also undermine democracy. Public schools have traditionally aimed to create effective 'learning communities' by developing trusting and caring relationships. Yet Hursh showed how, in schools where students were viewed as customers and parents as shareholders, this democratic function of education was necessarily compromised as students were prepared for a world of individualized competition. In the end, the idea of privatization grounded in neoliberal rationality projects a different view of society; one that encourages individuals to compete for scarce resources and in which the market defines modes of social relationships. While the ideas of democracy and equality are not abandoned entirely, they are rearticulated in market terms. The concept of democracy becomes largely representative rather than participatory, symbolic rather than substantive, while equality is redefined in terms of entitlement, suggesting that individuals deserve what they have earned, rather than what they might need or what might contribute to the collective good.

In higher education, DeVos' policy preferences also favored large financial corporations that provided student loans. She refused to entertain any policy options that might have reduced the financial burden that many students in the United States carry. She insisted on a curriculum that met the needs of the employers. At the same time, she did not hesitate to blame the universities for the cultural tensions that had long existed in the United States. The Trump administration never missed an opportunity to criticize identity politics on campuses, even as it perfected the art of supporting white privilege and promoting its distinctively singular and essentialist view of American citizenship as Christian. It also reduced the federal government's support for Title 1, Title 6 and Title 9 programs focusing on public schools, international studies and equality of opportunity, respectively. It even sought to penalize those local and state authorities that provided help to immigrants and refugees.

Re-imagining globalization

It is hard to see how such a contradictory approach to education, based on the assumptions of neoliberal rationality, on the one hand, and ethno-nationalist values, on the other, can bring any great benefits to the members of marginalized groups now attracted to populism. Nor is it clear how the populist preference to 'go it alone' and 'put the nation first' is likely, in the long run, to be productive. Indeed, such an isolationist philosophy can be counter-productive in a world in which the facts of global interconnectivity and interdependence can no longer be ignored. While educational policy-making in the United States has seldom been keen to draw on ideas from elsewhere, it has readily promoted its own vision of education throughout the world, through development aid programs and its active steering of such international agencies as the OECD. Despite its nationalist agenda and anti-multilateralism under Trump, the United States did not entirely abandon its desire to influence its allies and international agencies, especially when it involved protecting its own national interests.

The isolationist tendencies within the Brexit movement in the United Kingdom, similarly, recognized the damage that delinking from the European Union would do to the prestige of its higher education institutions (HEIs). Even Brexit's most ardent supporters could not fail to acknowledge that the support British HEIs receive for academic and student mobility and exchange programs from the European Union would evaporate, as indeed would funding for programs of collaborative research. Britain would also lose an important forum in which educational ideas are explored and debated, and where programs of educational reform are compared and benchmarked. The financial benefits Britain derives from international students in its universities might also decline.

The question arises, then, as to whether it is possible for populist governments to remain committed to neoliberal assumptions but abandon globalization and, instead, embrace various ideologies of ethno-nationalism and isolationism. Certainly, it is possible for such governments to promote a more vigorous nationalist regime and close their borders to refugees and immigrants who do not serve their immediate interests. It is also possible to impose some further restrictions on the global flows of goods and services, and perhaps also capital. In education, it is possible to imagine that the traditional commitment to multiculturalism, human rights education and internationalization could be abandoned, instead promoting an education that stresses the importance of religious and patriotic nationalist values.

Yet it is hard to imagine educational institutions — anywhere — turning entirely to an era in which nation systems once again separate themselves from global forces and opportunities. There are some aspects of global interconnectivity that now appear ontologically fixed. Developments in information and communications technologies have, for example, rendered inevitable the global flows of ideas, images and ideologies. They have intensified transnational connectedness and an awareness of such intensification. They have dis-embedded social relations from their local contexts of interactions, leading to accelerated change through time-space compression. Most communities have already become transformed through the global flows of people. Cultural diversity, exchange and hybridity have become facts of life that cannot simply be wished away. Economies are increasingly services-oriented, with such industries as tourism, education and retail predicated, fundamentally, on transcultural exchange. At the same time, there is now a deep awareness, especially among the young, that many of the serious problems facing humanity, such as the environment and pandemics, are global, requiring collective action.

These ontological realities make it difficult to imagine a world without global interconnectivity and exchange. Many aspects of globalization are here to stay, as has become clearer within the context of COVID-19 and growing awareness about climate change. The issue now is how globalization might be redefined and what might be the terms of our global interdependence. This is a moral question as much as it is political. As I have noted, over the past few decades, the terms of global economic, political and cultural exchange have been framed in neoliberal terms. Globalization has not only been about the material structure of power but it is also constituted, by a particular way of interpreting and representing the world, a common sense. An awareness of the contradictions of current populist politics has the potential to unmask the common sense generated by neoliberal rationality, showing the benefits of globalization to be unevenly distributed, disempowering some communities and minimizing the potential of global cooperation. What is needed is the development of a new common sense.

The development of such a common sense needs to begin with the premise that it is impossible to abandon globalization and the ontological realities it represents. Nonetheless, it is possible to interrogate the ways in which its hegemonic understanding has been framed, as a way of better understanding its effects and discontents. The challenge before us is to explore ways of rescuing globalization from the clutches of neoliberalism and imagining a conception which is neither wedded to neoliberalism's deeply ideological structures nor falls back into a dangerous nativism. For the danger with the kind of ethno-nationalism that populists advocate is that it is likely to produce a cultural politics that is based on a permanent state of fear, resentment and conflict while, at the same time, being unable to deliver the economic and social benefits it promises.

An alternative to neoliberal globalization must begin with the realization of a paradox. As David Held (2013, p. 34) points out, "the collective issues we must grapple with are of growing cross-border extensity and intensity, yet the means of addressing these are local and national." We must recognize that the world is increasingly multipolar, where some states are strong in almost all respects while others are not. The stronger states, such as the United States and the United Kingdom, are now tempted to go it alone, and put themselves first, but the problem with the neoliberal logic of competition is that, in an increasingly interdependent world, this harms not only the weaker states but also the weaker sections within the stronger states. This suggests that, while nation states retain their importance and will invariably pursue their own interests, national pursuits should be accompanied by an ethical outlook of care toward members of one's own communities and also care of others. This demands a new rationality, a new way of defining and enacting global exchange.

References

Appadurai, A. (2006). *Fear of Small Numbers*. Duke University Press.
Applebaum, A. (2020). *Twilight of Democracy: The Lure of Authoritarianism*. Doubleday.
Bauman, Z. (1999). Tourists and vagabonds: Being a consumer in a consumer society. In *Globalization: The Human Consequences*. Polity Press.
Bello, W. (2019. *Counter Revolution: The Global Rise of the Far Right*. Practical Action Press.
Bhagwati, J. (2004). In Defence of Globalization. Oxford University Press.
Brown, W. (2015). *Undoing the Demos: Neoliberal Stealth Revolution*. Zone Books.

Cohen, J. (2019). Populism and the politics of resentment. *Jus Cogen: A Critical Journal of The Philosophy of Law and Politics*, *1*(1), 5–39.

de la Torres, C. (2019) (ed.) Routledge Handbook of Global Populism. Routledge

DeVos, B. (2019). *Prepared Remarks by Secretary DeVos at the Manhattan Institute's 19th annual Alexander Hamilton Award Dinner*. U.S. Department of Education, May 1 JULY 2020. https://www.ed.gov/news/speeches/prepared-remarks-secretary-devos-manhattan-institutes-19th-annual-alexander-hamilton-award-dinner. Accessed July 2020.

Evans, T. L. (2012). *Occupy Education: Living and Learning Sustainability*. Peter Lang.

Fukuyama, F. (1991). *The End of History and the Last Man*. Free Press.

Geiselberger, H. (Ed.) 2017. *The Great Regression*. Polity Press.

Hardt, M. & A. Negri (2000). *Empire*. Harvard University Press.

Held, D. (2013). Cosmopolitanism in a multipolar world. In R. Braidotti, P. Hanafin, & B. Blaagaard (Eds.) *After Cosmopolitanism*. Routledge.

Hursh, D. (2016). *The End of Public Schools: The Corporate Reform Agenda to Privatize Education*. Routledge.

Klein, N. (2004) *No Logo*. Picador

Lowndes, J. (2019) 'Populism and Race in the United States from George Wallace to Donald Trump, in de la Torres, C. (2019) (ed.) Routledge Handbook of Global Populism. Routledge. pp. 190–200.

Lubienski, C., & Lubienski, S. (2014). *The Public School Advantage: Why Public Schools Outperform Private Schools*. University of Chicago Press.

Moffit, B. (2016). *The Global Rise of Populism: Performance, Political Style and Representation*. Stanford University Press.

Mudd, C., & Kaltwasser, C. R. (2017). *Populism: A Very Short Introduction*. Oxford University Press.

Muller, J.-W. (2016). *What Is Populism?* Penguin

Pieterse, J. N. (2018). *Multilateral Globalization: Emerging Economies and Development*. Routledge.

Piketty, T. (2013). *Capital in the Twenty First Century*. Belknap Press.

Rizvi, F., & Lingard, B. (2010). *Globalizing Education Policy*. Routledge.

Sainath, P. (2004) *Everybody Loves a Good Drought: Stories from India's Poorest Districts*. Penguin.

Sandel, M. (2013) *What Money Can't Buy: The Moral Limits of the Markets*. Farrar, Straus and Giroux.

Sassen, S. (1998). *Globalization and its Discontents*. New Press.

Standing, G. (2011). *Precariat: The New Dangerous Class*. Bloomsbury.

Stiglitz, J. (2002). *Globalization and Its Discontents*. Norton and Co.

Urbinati, N. (2015). A revolt against intermediary bodies. *Constellations*, *22*(4), 477–486.

INDEX

Page numbers in **bold** indicate tables. Page numbers in *italic* indicate figures.